MAKING
COMMUNICATIVE
LANGUAGE TEACHING
HAPPEN

THE McGRAW-HILL FOREIGN LANGUAGE PROFESSIONAL SERIES

Directions for Language Learning and Teaching

General Editors: James F. Lee and Bill VanPatten

Volume 1: *Making Communicative Language Teaching Happen*
by James F. Lee and Bill VanPatten

Directions for Language Learning and Teaching provides a forum for ideas connecting theory and research to teaching practice. Each volume in the series explores issues related to how languages are learned, how they are taught, and how both learning and teaching can be enhanced. The series also addresses teacher education and preparation at both the undergraduate and graduate levels. Each volume serves as both a resource for teachers seeking ideas for classroom materials and a reference work for scholars interested in current issues in language learning and teaching.

James F. Lee and Bill VanPatten
General Editors
University of Illinois at Urbana–Champaign

MAKING
COMMUNICATIVE
LANGUAGE TEACHING
HAPPEN

JAMES F. LEE   **BILL VANPATTEN**

UNIVERSITY OF ILLINOIS AT URBANA-CHAMPAIGN

McGraw-Hill, Inc.

New York   St. Louis   San Francisco   Auckland   Bogotá   Caracas
Lisbon   London   Madrid   Mexico City   Milan   Montreal
New Delhi   San Juan   Singapore   Sydney   Tokyo   Toronto

GENERAL EDITORS: JAMES F. LEE AND BILL VANPATTEN

Making Communicative Language Teaching Happen

Copyright © 1995 by McGraw-Hill, Inc. All rights reserved. Printed in the United States of America. Except as permitted under the United States Copyright Act of 1976, no part of this publication may be reproduced or distributed in any form or by any means, or stored in a data base or retrieval system, without the prior written permission of the publisher.

This book is printed on acid-free paper.

3 4 5 6 7 8 9 0 **DOC/DOC** 9 0 9 8 7 6

ISBN 0-07-037693-X

This book was set in Palatino by Clarinda Typesetting.
The editors were Thalia Dorwick, Richard Wallis, and Richard Mason.
The production supervisor was Louis Swaim.
The text designer was Elizabeth Williamson.
The cover designer was Deborah Chusid.
The book was printed and bound by R. R. Donnelley.

Library of Congress Cataloging-in-Publication Data

Lee, James F.
    Directions for language learning and teaching / James F. Lee, Bill VanPatten.
        p.cm. — (The McGraw-Hill foreign language professional series)
    Contents: v. 1. Making communicative language teaching happen.
    ISBN 0-07-037693-X (v. 1)
    1. Language and languages—Study and teaching.   2. Communicative competence.   I. VanPatten, Bill.   II. Title.   III. Series.
P53.L437   1995
418'.007—dc20   94-38416
                                                            CIP

DEDICATION

To Lucy and Ginger, two beautiful branches on the Lee-VanPatten family tree.

To Tracy D. Terrell, whose death left a tremendous void in the profession. Tracy was a role model both personally and professionally. His research in Spanish linguistics is standard reading, and his contributions to language instruction shaped the direction of communicative language teaching throughout the 1980s. From the start of our careers, Tracy encouraged us to explore and develop our ideas, to publish, to research, to make changes, and to challenge tradition.

To Ivan A. Schulman, under whose tenure as head of our department second language acquisition became recognized as a legitimate field of scholarly endeavor. We hope that other applied linguists and second language acquisitionists working in foreign language departments find the support, challenge, freedom, friendship, and mentoring that we found in Ivan.

ABOUT THE AUTHORS

James F. Lee is Associate Professor of Spanish at the University of Illinois at Urbana–Champaign, where he served as Director of Basic Language Instruction in the Department of Spanish, Italian, and Portuguese from 1986 to 1993. He is currently the Director of Lesbian, Gay, and Bisexual Concerns and Associate Ombuds Officer at the University. He received his Ph.D. in Hispanic Linguistics from the University of Texas at Austin in 1984. His research field is second language reading comprehension, and he has published many articles and chapters in this area. He has published articles and a monograph on language program direction and TA training, co-edited several research volumes, designed and developed the *Spanish Placement Examination* for American College Testing, and co-authored several McGraw-Hill textbooks.

Bill VanPatten is Associate Professor of Spanish at the University of Illinois at Urbana–Champaign, where he is Director of Graduate Studies in the Department of Spanish, Italian, and Portuguese and the Advisor for the undergraduate program in Spanish teacher education. He received his Ph.D. in Hispanic Linguistics from the University of Texas at Austin in 1983. His areas of research are input and input processing in second language acquisition, the impact of instruction on second language acquisition, and the acquisition of Spanish syntax and morphology. He teaches a wide range of courses from beginning Spanish to doctoral seminars on language acquisition. He has published numerous articles and chapters in books and is the co-author of several McGraw-Hill Spanish textbooks. He is also the designer of *Destinos,* a television course for PBS.

CONTENTS

PREFACE   ix

I PRELIMINARY CONSIDERATIONS IN COMMUNICATIVE LANGUAGE TEACHING   1

CHAPTER 1   On Roles and Tasks   3
CHAPTER 2   Research Insights   21
CHAPTER 3   Comprehensible Input   37
CHAPTER 4   Listening Comprehension   59

II GRAMMAR IN COMMUNICATIVE LANGUAGE TEACHING   87

CHAPTER 5   Grammar Instruction as Structured Input   89
CHAPTER 6   Structured Output: A Focus on Form in Language Production   116
CHAPTER 7   Suggestions for Testing Grammar   133

III SPOKEN LANGUAGE   145

CHAPTER 8   Spoken Language and Information-Exchange Tasks   147
CHAPTER 9   Suggestions for Evaluating Spoken Language   169

IV READING AND WRITING   187

CHAPTER 10   Comprehending Written Language   189
CHAPTER 11   Writing and Composing in a Second Language   214
CHAPTER 12   Issues in Testing Reading and Evaluating Writing   227

V A LOOK FORWARD   243

CHAPTER 13   Building Toward a Proficiency Goal   245
EPILOGUE   269
BIBLIOGRAPHY   275
INDEX   284

PREFACE

What Is This Book About?

What does it mean to communicate in a language? Can communication take place in the language classroom? What roles should instructors and students assume in order to make classrooms communication rich? What kinds of tasks are appropriate for developing communicative abilities in second language learners? What is an appropriate role for grammar instruction in communicative classes? For reading and writing? *Making Communicative Language Teaching Happen* is a book in which we examine these and other questions. Starting from the perspective that communication is not simply oral expression—that communication is the *expression, interpretation* and *negotiation* of meaning—we intend *Making Communicative Language Teaching Happen* to be a guide to help instructors develop communicative classroom environments that blend listening, speaking, reading and writing. What you will find in this book are explorations of various topics that lead to concrete suggestions for implementing communicative language teaching. Among the topics are:

- a new classroom dynamic in which the instructor and language learner take on new roles and responsibilities
- the important role of comprehensible, meaning-bearing input in second language acquisition and suggestions for making classrooms input rich
- an approach to grammar instruction based on structured-input and structured-output activities that help learners connect meaning to grammatical forms
- an examination of classroom oral communication and suggestions for redirecting oral communication toward information-exchange tasks
- contemporary approaches to teaching reading and writing
- suggestions on how to build toward proficiency goals
- three separate chapters on testing that explain a variety of testing principles and make recommendations for adapting classroom activities to use on tests.

Who Is This Book For?

We wrote *Making Communicative Language Teaching Happen* for a variety of readers. First, we wrote it for graduate teaching assistants and undergraduate teacher education majors who might benefit from a directed exploration, reflection, and application of particular topics related to communicative language teaching. We also wrote *Making Communicative Language Teaching Happen* for practicing teachers who need a resource manual for developing tasks and materials for their classrooms. For them, as well as for instructors-in-training, there are some two hundred activities and test sections throughout the book.

What Is Different About This Book?

There are a number of books about communicative language teaching available today. What makes *Making Communicative Language Teaching Happen* different? First and foremost is the unique pedagogical framework for the book. From **Pause to consider . . .** to **Exploring the Topics Further** to the **Activities** and the **Material Portfolio Assignments** in the accompanying Workbook, we have attempted to provide a rich, flexible, and active learning experience for those who use this book in a course on language teaching. This book is also different because it is not the product of a particular theory, method, or school of thought. Instead, it culls from the second language research as well as our own experiences as researchers, language program directors, teacher educators, and materials developers. Many ideas and suggestions contained in *Making Communicative Language Teaching Happen* represent our attempts to shape practice out of research and theory on second language acquisition.

How Is This Book Organized?

I. Preliminary Considerations in Communicative Language Teaching

Through a survey of selected research on second language acquisition, we examine roles and tasks and establish the important role that input plays in language acquisition. We then suggest ways to provide comprehensible, meaning-bearing input in classrooms and examine the nature of listening comprehension.

II. Grammar Instruction

We reorient the debate on grammar teaching from *whether or not* to teach grammar to *how* to teach grammar. Recognizing the strategies learners use while processing input, we propose grammar instruction that centers on providing learners with structured-input and structured-output practice. We also suggest ways to test grammar consistent with the way it is taught.

III. Spoken Language

We examine the nature of oral communication and suggest ways in which classroom communication can be more like communication in nonclassroom settings. We demonstrate how classroom communication can be reoriented through the use of information-exchange tasks. We also suggest ways to test oral communicative language ability by adapting classroom practices to testing situations.

IV. Reading and Writing

We explore how reading and writing have traditionally been taught in language classes, and we propose alternative frameworks for teaching second language literacy. The instructional framework for reading that we propose encourages readers to read the second language as a second language and not to translate it into their first language. The approach to writing that we advocate encourages language learners to engage in the thought processes characteristic of good writers.

V. A Look Forward

In the last chapter we explore how to build toward a proficiency goal within a class period, across a chapter, and across a unit of material. We propose ways in which instructors can set and meet specific goals and subgoals in their teaching by using information-exchange tasks.

Special Features

Because we have used *Making Communicative Language Teaching Happen* with our own students, we have created a pedagogical framework to enhance the content of the chapters. Each chapter of the book contains three features that reinforce and expand upon the main points.

- **Pause to consider** . . . boxes throughout each chapter
- lists of **Key Terms, Concepts, and Issues** at the end of the chapter
- suggested readings at the end of the chapter in **Exploring the Topics Further**
- a special Workbook containing **Activities, Mini-Research Projects,** and **Materials Portfolio Assignments**

Pause to consider . . . boxes are strategically placed where relevant issues present themselves. When you encounter these boxes, you are invited to stop and think about a particular issue. Here is a small sampling of the various topics addressed:

- classroom management
- error correction
- lesson planning
- testing and evaluation procedures
- how language works
- the components of communicative language ability

The list of **Key Terms, Concepts, and Issues** provides you with a quick review of the content of the chapter. By reviewing the significance of each term and the context(s) in which the term was used, you will be assured of having understood the main ideas.

Making Communicative Language Teaching Happen is an overview of topics and issues related to language teaching. Because no overview can provide an in-depth treatment of all topics relevant to language teaching, we suggest other resources to enhance what you have learned. The suggested readings in **Exploring the Topics Further** provide you with other sources of information and other perspectives.

Ideally, you will read the chapter to *gain* knowledge. You will **Pause to consider** . . . to *reflect* on your knowledge, use the **Key Terms, Concepts and Issues** to *check* on your knowledge, and then *extend* your knowledge through **Exploring the Topics Further.**

Another special feature of this book is its accompanying Workbook. This separate volume is intended for use with *Making Communicative Language Teaching Happen* when the latter serves as the main text in a course on language teaching. The Workbook contains **Activities** for further exploration of the chapter content, **Mini-Research Projects** for investigating language learning and teaching, and **Materials Portfolio Assignments** so that students can apply what they have learned in a practical and professional way. Like the main text, the Workbook has been field-tested with our and our colleagues' students. Due to the very positive responses we have received on the various activities and projects in it, we strongly suggest the use of the Workbook as a learning tool in both graduate teaching-assistant training and undergraduate teacher-education courses.

Acknowledgments

We are very grateful to a large number of people who have helped us along the way with this book. We begin by acknowledging our own students whose reading, (mis)understanding, and questions have helped shape this book from the first draft we created in the Fall of 1992 to the subsequent drafts from which we have taught. We are grateful to a number of colleagues who read parts or all of the manuscript and commented on it.

Terry L. Ballman, University of Northern Colorado
Jane E. Berne, University of North Dakota
Frank B. Brooks, Florida State University
Paul Chandler, University of Hawaii
Jerome L. Packard, University of Illinois
Gail L. Riley, Syracuse University
Lourdes Torres, University of Kentucky
Cira Torruella, University of Illinois
Darlene Wolf, University of Alabama
Dolly J. Young, University of Tennessee

We are indebted to our friends and colleagues who used the manuscript in their courses. They and their students gave us valuable feedback that helped us as we revised and finalized the manuscript.

Donna Deans Binkowski, Kansas State University
William R. Glass, Pennsylvania State University
Carol Klee, University of Minnesota

We would like to thank Kim Potowski for her help in preparing the bibliography.

We would like to acknowledge the following people who reviewed the first draft of manuscript. Their comments were very helpful.

H. Jay Siskin, University of Oregon
Susan Bacon, University of Cincinatti
Richard Kern, University of California, Berkeley

We owe many thanks to Thalia Dorwick, our publisher, who over the years has supported this and other efforts. We thank Robert DiDonato for his input in early stages of the project. We also extend our thanks to Richard Wallis who edited and prepared the manuscript for production, and to Richard Mason, who helped with many aspects of editorial production.

And thanks to Lucy, Ginger, Tracy and Ivan; they get their due on the dedication page.

J.F.L., B.VP., Champaign, IL., October, 1994

PART I

Preliminary Considerations in Communicative Language Teaching

The focus of this book is a particular approach to communicative language teaching—what it is, why it can be justified, and how to implement it in the classroom. We shall see in this opening unit that the learner is at the center of communicative language teaching. In effect, language learners must learn how to communicate in a new context: to interpret, express, and negotiate meaning in the new language.

We question in Chapter 1 a traditional classroom dynamic, the Atlas Complex, in which the instructor transmits knowledge to a passive, minimally engaged audience. We propose instead new relationships between instructors and learners to achieve the goals of communicative language teaching. Chapter 2 is a survey of some of the results of second language acquisition research that provide a critical focal point for rethinking traditional approaches to instruction. In Chapter 3, we begin with the fundamental building block of language acquisition—comprehensible, meaning-bearing input—and explore ways to provide it in a communicative classroom. In Chapter 4, we explore various aspects of listening comprehension, an important area of concern for teaching a second language.

CHAPTER 1

On Roles and Tasks

At-las *(ăt'ləs)* n. Greek mythology. *1. a
Titan condemned to support the heavens
upon his shoulders. 2. any person
supporting a great burden.*

American Heritage Dictionary

INTRODUCTION

Before reading about roles and tasks in the language classroom, pause to consider your own classroom language learning experiences. What role did you
play? The instructor? What did you do? And the instructor? Was the instructor
the center point of the interaction? Did he or she ask questions while you and
your classmates answered them? Did you ever work in pairs or groups? If so,
what did you do? Did you ask each other questions? Were there class discussions? Who discussed the issues? Everyone or the instructor and the two best
students? During discussions, did classmates address each other or only
address the instructor? We all have different learning experiences, but there
are probably more similarities than differences when it comes to classroom
language learning. Your past experiences may well serve as examples of roles
and tasks, but the purpose of this book is not so much to validate your past
experiences as it is to challenge them. By challenging the past and its tradi-
tions, we can open the way for innovation.

In this chapter, we explore the traditional roles of instructors and students
in language classes. By *roles,* we mean the ways in which instructors and students view their jobs in the classroom. What do instructors do and why do
they do it? Likewise, why do students do what they do? In our experience
as both instructors and educators of teachers, we find that instructors must
be conscious of—and then must understand—the roles played out in classrooms if language teaching is to be truly communicative. Instructors must
understand how these traditional roles arose, but they must also realize that
traditional roles might no longer be appropriate in the "communicative classrooms" that are often discussed in professional circles. If instructors do not
understand these roles, then much of communicative language teaching will
simply perpetuate older methods. Our purpose in this chapter then, is to cri-
tique traditional classroom roles and to suggest alternative ones. Our journey
into communicative language teaching begins with a connection between traditional classrooms and Greek mythology.

3

THE ATLAS COMPLEX: ROLES DICTATE TASKS

Teaching, in all subject areas, entails *roles* and *tasks*. Both instructors and students play out roles in the classroom, but what determines these roles? The role that instructors often assume (and that students very willingly grant to them) is that of the authority, the expert, the central figure in the classroom who transmits knowledge to the students. Because instructors are authoritative knowledge transmitters, the students become their passive audience, receptive vessels into which that knowledge is poured. It is not difficult to see how such a classroom is organized; Figure 1.1 captures this dynamic in schematic form. The physical setup of many classes reflects and codifies the instructor's (I) authoritative role and the students' (S) receptive role.

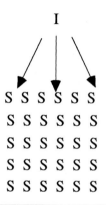

FIGURE 1.1. Knowledge Transmission in a Transmission-Oriented Class

Authoritative transmitter of knowledge and *receptive vessels* are the primary roles, respectively, that instructors and students play in many traditional classrooms. The tasks we most often associate with these roles are those of lecturing and notetaking. Other, secondary roles may be enacted in language classrooms. Depending on one's point of view, some of these secondary roles are neutral or positive, others negative. A partial list appears below.

Secondary Roles in a Transmission-Oriented Class

Instructor	Student
lecturer	notetaker
leader	follower
tutor	tutee
warden	prisoner
disciplinarian	disciplinee

*P*ause *to consider . . .*

whose responsibility it is to learn. If the instructor is the expert/authority, what happens when students do not carry out an assignment correctly or score poorly as a group on an exam? Would (and should) the instructor take it personally? Would (and should) the students blame the instructor for their performance?

The following description of an actual language class exemplifies the classroom dynamic characterized by the transmission-oriented roles of instructors and the receptacle roles of students.

1. Students were given ten minutes to complete individually a worksheet that contained a series of paragraphs. In each paragraph, various grammatical elements were deleted from sentences, with multiple choices provided for each blank. There were some twenty deletions.
2. At the end of ten minutes, students were instructed to work in groups of three. As a group they were to come to an agreement on the correct answers.
3. After about seven minutes, the instructor called for the class's attention. She then began going over the correct answers, one by one, in the order in which they appeared on the worksheet. She did not ask for volunteers but rather called on students to respond. She read each sentence to the class, pausing at the deletion to call attention to it, and then continued reading to the end of the sentence. The student who was called on supplied the word or phrase needed to complete the sentence.
4. On the second item, although the student gave the correct answer, the instructor offered a lengthy explanation of the particular grammatical item worked on (in this instance, comparisons such as *more than* and *less than*). On the fifth item, a student gave an incorrect answer and the instructor offered a lengthy explanation of the grammar point (in this instance, conjunctions). On the tenth item, a student gave an incorrect answer and the instructor gave a lengthy explanation of passive constructions. Just as the instructor was finishing the explanation, the bell rang. Ten items were left to complete.

The language instructor depicted above clearly exemplifies the role of authority or expert transmitter of knowledge. All action and interaction, as well as all explanations, were dictated by the instructor. The students' role is to be taught, to receive knowledge. Like the titan Atlas of Greek mythology, who supported the heavens on his shoulders, instructors such as the one described in the preceding example

assume full responsibility for all that goes on. They supply motivations, insight, clear explanations, even intellectual curiosity. In exchange, their students supply almost nothing but a faint imitation of the academic performance that they witness. [Instructors] so thoroughly dominate the proceedings that they are cut off from what the students know or are confused about. For their part, the students form a group of isolated individuals who have no more in common than their one-to-one relationship with the same individual. While [instructors] exercise their authority through control of the subject matter and the social encounter in the classroom, they lack the power to make things happen for their students. They are both caught in the middle of their classes by a host of mysterious forces—hidden assumptions, hidden expectations, and the results of their own isolating experiences. [This is] the Atlas Complex. (Finkel and Monk 1983, p. 85)

The Atlas Complex is not discipline specific; teacher-centered, knowledge-transmitting classrooms are the norm for many subject areas. In many chemistry classes, for example, students sit and take notes while the instructor lectures (except in lab sessions). Very often in history and political science classes, students listen to instructors give descriptions and explanations that will more than likely appear on subsequent tests. It often seems that much of American educational practice reflects the Atlas Complex.

To be sure, instructors have invested much time in becoming experts in their fields. In the classroom, they often (and perhaps rightly so) seek to share that expertise. Most instructors "assume that their principal task is one of improving the ways in which they express their expertise: Clear and precise explanations can always be sharpened; penetrating questions can always be made more penetrating" (Finkel and Monk 1983, p. 86). An implicit assumption here is that students actually do *learn* from the explanations instructors provide. Therefore, instructors think that by improving their explanations they will improve students' learning. Another assumption is that students learn by being asked questions: by improving the questions asked, instructors assume students will learn more. How valid are these assumptions for learning in general and language learning in particular? In Chapter 2, we will briefly examine some major findings of language learning research that challenge these assumptions. For the moment, let's examine the Atlas Complex in language teaching in more detail.

---

*P*ause to consider . . .

a possible parallel between classrooms and families. Do you see a parallel between a typical parent/child relationship and a traditional teacher/student relationship? What kinds of behaviors do the two types of relationships have in common?

Audiolingualism

In language teaching, the instructor as central figure has always been the norm. As the profession moved from grammar and text-translation methods to a more "oral" approach, the instructor-as-authority-and-expert was codified in a teaching method called Audiolingual Methodology, commonly referred to as ALM or audiolingualism.* Developed at military schools (where one did not question authority), ALM's teaching materials explicitly cast the instructor as drill leader, perhaps the ultimate manifestation of the Atlas Complex. With ALM, students were typically given a model sentence. The instructor then provided the cue that students would substitute into the sentence; some substitutions required that the sentence be altered in various ways while other substitutions did not. The students' role has been likened to that of a parrot since their task was to perform the substitution or transformation quickly and accurately. Note the following examples.

Activity A. Substitution Drill. Change the model sentence, substituting the cue word for its corresponding element in the model.

> MODEL: I don't want to eat anymore!

instructor's cue	*student response*
1. to sleep	I don't want to sleep anymore!
2. to study	I don't want to study anymore!
3. to drink	I don't want to drink anymore!

Activity B. Transformation Drill. Transform each sentence, substituting the past for the present.

1. I eat.	I ate.
2. He goes.	He went.
3. We sleep.	We slept.

What the ALM instructor did not usually provide was the opportunity for students to use the language in a meaningful or communicative way, one involving the exchange of messages. When students spoke they were *practicing patterns.* A premium was placed on students' accurate production of the second language so that, by and large, students were allowed to repeat only that which was said to them or that which they were cued to utter, a very limited and limiting task. ALM was firmly grounded in the psychology of *behaviorism:* its followers believed that language learning was a matter of *habit formation.* (We explain behaviorism more in Chapter 2.) The philosophy of the

---

*It often surprises many of today's students that language teaching has not always been aural and oral in practice. Before the first half of the twentieth century, much of language teaching was focused on developing the ability to translate written texts, especially literary texts. The idea was that language was best exemplified in its literature and that a firm grounding in literary studies made for a good background in humanities and the liberal arts. Thus, for many, language teaching was equal to getting students to read "the Great Works" of other nations in their original languages.

ALM era was that if a student were allowed to make an error in the second language, then the student ran the risk of forming a bad habit—and bad habits are hard to break. In order to prevent bad habits from forming, students were simply not allowed to say anything original that might lead them to produce an utterance with errors in it. Students were only to repeat and to substitute new elements into particular, preplanned structural patterns. Nothing that happened in an ALM classroom could be construed as an exchange of information because *output* (the actual production of language) was severely restricted. In fact, many thought that students did not need to know what they were saying; they needed to know only that what they were saying was correct.

---

*P*ause to consider . . .

the meaning and purpose of expressing oneself orally. Should learning be divorced from reality? Re-examine the drills in Activities A and B. Should a language learner be required to state something such as "I don't want to sleep anymore!" if it isn't true? How often in your language learning experience did you say or repeat things that had no basis in reality? Did you memorize any dialogs that you can still repeat to this day? In your experience, how often were you allowed to express real ideas, real thoughts?

Communicative Language Teaching

With the advent of *communicative language teaching* (CLT), the instructor's role changed. The instructor was no longer simply the drill leader but was also charged with providing students opportunities for communication, that is, using the language to interpret and express real-life messages. The Atlas Complex did not, however, disappear. ALM had so rigidly institutionalized it that we find a transition period in early CLT in which the classroom dynamic could not yet be characterized as "free" communication. In early CLT, many instructors equated communication with conversation—but conversation of a particular type: the authority figure asked the questions, the students answered them. The instructor's task was no longer just to drill but also to interact. Instructors often did attempt to personalize the questions, and these questions usually did not require patterned responses from students. The contrast between the open-ended question, "What did you do last night?" and the cued sentence pattern "——— went to the movies last night" illustrates the shift from ALM to early CLT. The students' task was no longer to parrot but to create an answer. (In Chapter 5 we will examine drills and drill types in some detail.) In short, although CLT may have caused a major revolution in the way that some people *thought* about language teaching, no major revolution occurred in the day-to-day *practice* of most language teachers.

As language teaching began its slow evolution away from methods such as ALM, the roles played by instructors and students changed very little, if at all. As we saw above, communication was seen merely as conversation, which took the form of a question-and-answer session with the instructor in charge. Atlas's burden was yet to be relieved or shared. An example of the Atlas Complex combined with a question-and-answer conversation can be seen in the following exchange (taken from Leemann Guthrie 1984, p. 45). As you read, note the role assumed by the instructor and try to imagine the exchange taking place in a classroom (for example, who was standing or sitting where? what was the rest of the class doing?).

(1) INSTRUCTOR: Pensez-vous qu'il y a vraiment une personnalité française, typiquement française?
(2)   Oui?
(3) STUDENTS: Non.
(4) INSTRUCTOR: Non? Pourquoi?
                 (Pause)
(5)   Claudia?
(6) STUDENT: *Um … Je pense qu'il y a une …*
(7) INSTRUCTOR: *(Interrupting)* Qu'il y a une personnalité française?
(8)   Bon, décrivez la personnalité française.
(9) STUDENT: *How do you say "pride"?*
(10) INSTRUCTOR: Oh … vous avez déjà eu deux mots.
(11)   *(Writing on blackboard)* Okay, «La fierté» est comme en anglais "pride," et l'adjectif, «fier.»
(12)   Je suis fier. *I'm proud.*
(13)   Bon, est-ce que les Français sont très fiers?
(14)   Ils ont beaucoup de fierté?
                 (Silence)
(15)   Est-ce que les Français sont nationalistes?

[translation]

(1) TEACHER: Do you think there is really one French personality, a typically French personality?
(2)   Yes?
(3) STUDENTS: No.
(4) TEACHER: No? Why?
                 (Pause)
(5)   Claudia?
(6) STUDENT: Um … I think that there's a …
(7) TEACHER: *(Interrupting)* That there's a French personality?
(8)   Good, describe the French personality.
(9) STUDENT: How do you say "pride"?
(10) TEACHER: Oh … You've already had two words
(11)   *(Writing on blackboard)* Okay, "la fierté" is like in English "pride," and the adjective, "fier."
(12)   *Je suis fier*, I'm proud.
(13)   Good, are the French very proud?

(14)   Do they have a lot of pride?
             (Silence)
(15)   Are the French nationalistic?

The instructor as central figure and authority is clearly evidenced in line 5, where she selects the next person who will speak rather than a conversational partner. In line 7, the instructor again asserts her role as authority figure by finishing the student's sentence for her. Claudia, the student, subsequently appeals to the instructor's expert knowledge of the French language, one of the forces that binds instructors to the Atlas Complex. The instructor obliges Claudia's appeal, yet offers a much more detailed account of the French language than Claudia requested, the assumption being that students learn from explanations. The instructor, incidentally, also assumes to know what Claudia's opinion is since she never gives Claudia the opportunity to express her opinion before interrupting her and completing her sentence for her. This instructor imposes herself on Claudia's self-expression. In lines 13–15, rather than waiting for Claudia to use the explanation provided, the instructor continues to ask questions. The result? Silence. When silence ensues, she asks another question using an altogether different adjective. In order to maintain her role as authority, this instructor assumed the responsibility of not only asking questions but also answering them. As Leemann Guthrie points out about this exchange, "... it is clear that the [instructor] defines her own role not as that of a conversational partner or facilitator, but as one responsible for telling her students how to speak" (1984, p. 46).

Pause to consider . . .

how different the interactional dynamic and resulting discussion between Claudia and her instructor might have been. Why do you think silence resulted from the instructor's explanation of *fier* and *fierté*? How might the interaction have been different if the instructor had responded to Claudia by saying nothing more than "fierté" in response to her question?

In the next phase of CLT, the instructor was not the only one to ask questions. In this phase, a novel classroom dynamic emerged: students were now allowed to work in pairs and to pose questions to each other. But for many, the basic assumed roles of transmitter and receptacles were played out in pair work as well. In the following exercise, aimed at fostering communication, a model is provided that clearly spells out the Atlas-like question-and-answer model of conversation, even though the instructor is not part of the exercise.

Activity C. What Did You Eat Last Night? With another student, ask and answer questions according to the model.

MODEL: french fries → Did you eat french fries last night?
                  → Yes, I ate them. (No, I did not eat them.)

1. tacos
2. hamburgers
3. a steak
4. tuna casserole

During this exercise students ask each other questions that they can answer truthfully, but the real intent is to practice producing direct-object pronouns. The instructor is most likely monitoring students' performance. Are they asking the questions correctly? Are they answering them in complete sentences? Is the respondent using the correct direct-object pronoun? This activity has a clear focus on form rather than on meaning or communication.

Thus, even though pair work was intended to provide speaking opportunities, the resulting speech did not necessarily entail true communication, namely, the interpretation and expression of meaning. Many paired exercises differed very little from the classic ALM pattern-substitution drills, with their rigid constraints on what could be said and how it could be said. In the evolution of language teaching, we find that practice did not keep up with theory: instructors might have wanted to take on new roles, but the classroom activities still emphasized formal correctness, not communication.

Theory and practice did begin to converge as instructors began to talk to their students. That is, in addition to providing controlled exercises such as Activities A–C, they also engaged in more open-ended conversations. In the next example (from a classroom whose instructor explicitly claimed to be teaching communicatively) the instructor is dialoging with the students. Many instructors use the technique of asking personalized questions to begin a class, perhaps incorporating grammar and vocabulary from the previous day's work. The resulting conversations have a much more natural feel than do the conversations examined previously. Does this instructor still carry an Atlas-like burden?

INSTRUCTOR: What did you do last week? Raúl.
    RAÚL: I went to Florida. To the beach. We ate in a lot of restaurants.
INSTRUCTOR: That sounds like a fun week. Gloria, what did you do last week?
    GLORIA: Not much. My husband and I read. We watched TV.
INSTRUCTOR: Did you go to Florida?
    GLORIA: No.
INSTRUCTOR: Did you go to Florida last week? John.
    JOHN: Me? No. I went to Bloomington to visit my parents.

In spite of the surface differences between this exchange and, say, the one Leemann Guthrie illustrated, the instructor is still the central figure. In a typical classroom, the instructor will call on a student to answer, probe the student's response, and let the student know when she has completed her turn by calling on another student. The students answering the question will most likely address only the instructor and not their classmates, as the instructor is controlling the interaction. The entire burden is on the instructor, who initiates, responds, follows up, keeps the interaction going, and assigns turns. We will see in the next section some alternative ways instructors can engage students in using the second language without being so Atlas-like.

> ## *P*ause to consider . . .
>
> the nature of conversations. Was the verbal interaction between the four speakers above a true conversation? Did any of the individual students carry on a conversation with the instructor? How conversational can the exchange be if the students merely answer questions but never ask any of either the instructor or each other?

In the activities and exercises we have examined, the instructor assumes an authoritative role and then asserts it in all situations. Both instructors and students accept the fact that instructors are language authorities/experts and ought, therefore, to be the central figures in the classroom. A central reason that instructors assume the authority role is the way in which many people view language learning. As we noted, ALM viewed language learning as the acquisition of correct habits, and correct habits were learned through repetition and reinforcement. The language instructor's role, then, was to ensure that correct habits were learned and that no one deviated from the path of accuracy. This focus on correct habit formation demanded absolute control not only over how students spoke but also over what students said. Thus, drills and pattern practices naturally became staple classroom interactional routines. As Finkel and Monk point out, hidden assumptions bind instructors and students to the Atlas Complex, among them the popular beliefs about how adults learn languages. But does language acquisition actually happen as the theorists of 1955 envisioned? In the next chapter, we briefly present some findings from second language acquisition research relevant to the nature of language learning.

RELIEVING ATLAS: WHEN TASKS DICTATE ROLES

Communicative language teaching has been evolving since its inception. Roles other than those of linguistic disciplinarian, authority figure, expert, and parent have become available to instructors based on what we have learned about language acquisition and on changes in instructional materials. When instructors shift their roles, so do their students. As we saw in the preceding section, under ALM and early CLT the role of the instructor dictated the tasks given to students. Since the instructor's role was that of central authority, the fundamental task for all students was to respond to the instructor. However, the contemporary communicative era is now incorporating tasks that encourage communicative language development. In a reversal of direction, the tasks now determine the roles that instructors and learners may take. The major roles that instructors are beginning to assume are those of *resource person* and *architect*. In order for an instructor to be a resource person, there must be a fundamental change in the conversational dynamic of the classroom, something we will see below in Activity D. As architects, instructors provide activities and tasks that allow for a distribution of teaching functions between instructors and students. As a consequence, when the instructor gives up the role of Atlas, the students are no longer mere receptive vessels; they must become more active, more responsible for their own learning.

Instructor as Resource Person

What is a resource person? The best way to describe this role is with an example. In the nonclassroom world, when you ask someone for directions, you assume responsibility for understanding those directions. The person giving directions makes no assumptions concerning what you did or did not understand. Rather, the person assumes you will ask if you have a question. The person giving directions actually responds to your specific needs; he or she will give you additional information, clarifying whatever you did not understand. This kind of give-and-take characterizes nonclassroom interaction.

But what happens in the classroom? Let's examine another example. The following listening activity is a fairly common one for practicing vocabulary. In essence, the instructor describes a visual and the students respond with the appropriate vocabulary word. In reading the activities, be sure to think about the roles that the instructor and the students play.

Activity D. What Food Is It? Look over the food chart, getting a sense of serving size, weight, and calories for the various foods listed. Your instructor will read a description twice. Listen carefully and then identify the food being described.

> MODEL: (you hear) A cup of this dairy product contains one hundred
>   twenty-five calories.
>   (you say) Yogurt.

While this activity might seem quite simple, it reflects the assumption that the instructor is responsible for teaching and learning. In Activity D, assumptions are made about what students will and will not comprehend. It is assumed that they will not comprehend the first time. The instructor should, therefore, automatically repeat all information. Is the assumption correct? Perhaps only a handful of students will be able to identify the items the first time; perhaps everyone will. Since either case is possible, the issue becomes one of responsibility. Whose responsibility is it to indicate a lack of comprehension? In the nonclassroom setting, those who receive information generally carry the burden of indicating a lack of comprehension and must ask for repetition, clarification, and so on. If instructors automatically repeat themselves, they have assumed a responsibility that typically would not be theirs in the nonclassroom setting. Automatic repetition is one sign of the Atlas Complex.

We know that the Atlas Complex is a difficult mindset to alter because both instructors and students are generally willing to allow this type of dynamic in the classroom. But in order to share responsibility with the instructor or to shift it entirely, students must be given certain tools, such as the questions below in Activity E. This activity is a version of Activity D in which the instructor acts as a resource person, not an authoritative Atlas figure. The instructor has the information and is willing to supply it—but only when asked. The instructor does not assume that everyone requires every item to be repeated. Thus, those who need repetition are responsible not only for asking for it but also for identifying that part of the item they did not comprehend. Students take on the burden of responsibility the instructor assumed in Activity D.

Activity E. What Food Is It? Look over the food chart, getting a sense of food groups, serving size, weight, and calories for the various foods listed. Your instructor will read a description of a food item. Listen carefully and try to identify the food.

> MODEL: (you hear) A cup of this dairy product contains one hundred
> twenty-five calories.
> (you say)   Yogurt.

If you can not identify the item, then you should ask any or all of the following questions, depending on what you did not understand.

> What quantity did you say?
> How many calories, please?
> What was the food group?

When instructors' roles change, so do those of students. The students negotiated meaning for themselves in Activity E: they initiated part of the interaction. When the instructor's role is that of a resource person, the student's role is that of information gatherer and negotiator of meaning. Their task is no longer simply to listen and respond but to signal if and where comprehension has not taken place. Whereas we previously defined communication as the interpretation and expression of meaning, we now add the concept of negotiation to the definition. *Communication is the interpretation, expression, and negotiation of meaning, both in and out of the classroom.*

---

*P**ause to consider** . . .*

the nature of responsibility. How attentive will students be if they know that instructors will repeat each item verbatim? Which of the two sets of directions to the instructor favors students being passive, receptive vessels? Which favors them being actively engaged in processing the language?

Instructor as Architect

In a nonclassroom setting, conversations are not directed by an individual. That is, one person does not choose who the next speaker will be. When three or four people talk, they talk among themselves. There is give-and-take as contributions to the topic are made from all sides. Information is gathered, checked, and built up among the participants.

In order to examine these issues within the context of the language class, let's compare and contrast the following two versions of the same activity. The first version, Activity F, resembles the traditional open-ended discussion question during which the instructor's tasks are to ask questions, select participants, and keep the interaction moving. The students' task is no more than to answer the question asked. The second version, Activity G, contains the same content as F, but the structure of the interaction has been radically altered. Activity G sets up a series of intermediate steps, each of which contains concrete tasks for students to perform: make lists, compare them, and discuss the information they generate. The end result of both versions is that students address the question, but the *process* is not the same for each. As you read, try to picture the interactions between instructors and students as well as those among students that result from each version of the activity.

Activity F. Changing Roles. Contrast the traditional roles men and women played in the family structure with their contemporary ones. In what ways have their roles in the family changed?

Activity G. Changing Roles

Step 1. With a classmate, make a list of the actions, attitudes, or qualities that characterize the traditional role played by men in the family structure.

Step 2. Compare your list with those prepared by the rest of the class. Do you all have the same ideas? Do you wish to modify your list?

Step 3. Make a list of actions, attitudes, or qualities that characterize the traditional role played by women in the family structure.

Step 4. Compare your list with those prepared by the rest of the class. Do you all have the same ideas? Do you wish to modify your list?

Step 5. Now, contrast the traditional roles men and women played in the family structure with their contemporary ones. In what ways have their roles in the family changed?

If you have observed many language classes, particularly more traditional ones, then you might have seen an example of the first version of the activity, namely, the open-ended discussion question. We can picture an instructor standing in front of the class. After the question is posed, silence would most likely ensue as students would not readily and eagerly volunteer. The instructor would then break the silence either by calling on a particular student or by restating the question. If a discussion of changing family structure ever got off the ground, the instructor would gather bits and pieces of the answer from those students willing to speak. One student might say something about male roles, the next about female roles. A cohesive response to the question would probably not result from this kind of teacher-fronted interaction (as was the case with the discussion Leemann Guthrie observed about the French personality). If asked, many language instructors will say that the purpose of Activity F is simply to get students to talk in the second language, to display what they already know about the topic, or even to practice particular vocabulary and grammar. In short, the open-ended discussion question format is not really designed for students to learn about the topic or from each other; it is simply a speaking exercise.

Pause to consider . . .

speaking for speaking's sake. Is it sufficient to have students speak just for the sake of having them produce language orally? Is such discussion meaningful in a communicative way? Should there be a greater purpose to language use in the classroom?

The second version, Activity G, attempts to circumvent some of the short-comings of the first by acknowledging that a discussion is a *multilayered communicative event*, that is, an interaction requiring various steps and tasks. Dividing the activity literally into steps is one way to bring out the layers and to assist the learners in tackling the topic. The instructor is the central figure only in Step 5 of the activity, but because all class members will have dealt with the prerequisite information, many more will likely participate in the discussion than would have in Activity F.

Pause to consider . . .

the specific classroom procedures involved in Activity G, which divides the discussion into steps. If you were carrying out this activity in class as an instructor, what would you be doing during each step? In other words, project yourself into the classroom. How would you enact Steps 2 and 4? Step 5?

When the instructor takes on the role of *architect*, the one who designs and plans but is not responsible for the final product, then students become *builders* or *coworkers*, who put it together. Just as discussions in nonclassroom settings allow for all participants to contribute to the construction of a message, so can discussions in a classroom setting. In order to achieve this goal, the instructor must make a decision about how to structure the interaction. In so doing, the instructor must relinquish the authority-figure role during class time. When roles depend on tasks, the instructor no longer assumes the sole, Atlas-like responsibility for all that happens in the classroom. Students begin to share some of the teaching functions that instructors ordinarily assume for themselves and that students typically concede to them.

THE SOCIAL DIMENSIONS
OF A LANGUAGE CLASSROOM

How instructors view themselves is inextricably linked to how they view students. If instructors see themselves as authoritative knowledge transmitters, then their students are necessarily their receptive audience. But when an instructor is a resource person for—or an architect of—interaction, then the students become information gatherers and negotiators as well as builders and coworkers. While the goal of classroom language instruction is language learning, it is not the only outcome. The classroom is *a social environment* in which there are social as well as linguistic outcomes. In the following description of language learning, note how responsibility is an underlying theme.

> Constructing social norms is a process of building expectations for how to behave and what to do.... The instructional and communicative processes that take place across time during classroom foreign language teaching and learning influence not only what occurs in the classroom and how it occurs, but also what is eventually learned. That is, as students are learning the pieces and parts of language, they are simultaneously learning how to be competent members of the classroom in order to participate in language learning activities.... As in learning a native language, learning a foreign language is also a tacit process of socialization that comes about through social interaction. (Brooks 1990, pp. 164–6)

The expert role for instructors and receptive-vessel role for students, as well as the notion that learning takes place through explanation and question answering, are comfortable roles and notions. We slip into them easily. Students walk into our classrooms assuming that we will transmit to them our knowledge. However, the assumption is clearly incorrect when it comes to learning another language. We need look no further than the students' knowledge at the end of the semester for proof of its inaccuracy. Students do not leave our classes knowing as much as we do or knowing everything that was in the book. In order to relieve the instructor of Atlas' burden and foster more active learning on the part of the students, instructors must reorient not only themselves and the materials they use, but also the students. They must change students' expectations of what happens inside the language classroom so that students know how to become "competent members" of the class.

We begin this process of change and reorientation by questioning a basic term: *student.* What's in a name? The term *student* has passive connotations.

---

*P*ause to consider . . .

surveys of student beliefs and attitudes. Let's say that you surveyed your class's beliefs and discovered that they believed the best teachers were of the gender you are not. Or that the best teachers provide lots of additional handouts but that you do not believe in doing so. Or that the best teachers are also all fun and games, but you are not. Would you try to change your teaching practices and your personality to fit their beliefs? Would you try to change their beliefs? Why?

"Student," "studious," and "study" all imply that there is a receptacle into which knowledge is poured. They also imply a very private, solitary, and quiet act. Even the *American Heritage Dictionary* implies nothing more than physical presence in its definition of *student:* "one who attends a school, college or university" (1992). Yet the nontraditional, more communicative student roles described in the present chapter are quite active and social, requiring more than mere attendance. Therefore, we suggest the term *learner* rather than *student* and use it in the remainder of this book. "Learner," "learn," "builder," "gatherer," "negotiator"—all imply an active participant.

Throughout this book, we explore ways in which instruction can work *in unison with* acquisitional processes rather than *against* them. We emphasize that what happens in language classrooms reflects the view that students are learners and instructors are resource persons and architects. Instructors must resist the constant temptation to display their knowledge of the language they teach. Instead, they must formulate tasks to maximize learners' contributions to the language-learning enterprise. To ensure that kind of result, the students who were put into groups in order to reach a consensus about the correct answer (p. 5) should be allowed to state their thought processes and to know that their work in groups counted for something. Likewise, Claudia (in the Leemann Guthrie example on p. 9) should have been allowed to state her opinion and not have it stated for her. Similarly, learners must be provided with opportunities to express real information and not merely the information in drills. And finally, learners must be given opportunities to construct communicative interactions in the classroom as they would outside the classroom—to interpret, express, and negotiate meaning. In short, to help "students" become "learners," we must give them both the responsibility and the appropriate materials. Most important, they must learn how to carry out that responsibility.

SUMMARY

The classroom is not only an academic environment with expected academic outcomes. It is also a social environment in which the participants learn how to behave. In this chapter, we presented the concept of the Atlas Complex, a metaphor that captures the traditional classroom dynamic in which the instructor's role is to transmit knowledge and the students' role is to receive that knowledge. This role was codified in the language teaching methodology called Audiolingualism, with its emphasis on habit formation and correct language production. With the shift from ALM to more communicative approaches, we saw communication taking place in the classroom in particular ways. First, we saw instructors communicating with a handful of students in question-and-answer conversations, a dynamic that still adhered to the traditional Atlas-like distribution of teaching and learning functions. Second, we saw the advent of paired work in which students asked each other questions. Yet the teaching materials themselves were scarcely different from those of the ALM era.

We proposed that the term *learners* be substituted for the term *students*. By breaking with traditional nomenclature, we hope to challenge the past. To encourage learners to be responsible for their own learning requires that an instructor *consciously decide* to adopt other roles and to inspire and teach learners to take on other roles as well. The instructor must consciously work toward a classroom dynamic that maximizes each individual's participation and contribution. With instructors adopting such roles as architect and resource person, students can take on the roles of builders, coworkers, and information gatherers. Furthermore, the materials that instructors use must permit these new roles. To that end, the traditional discussion question can be supplanted by a task-oriented activity in which each step identifies the layers involved in discussing a topic. By providing a series of tasks to complete, instructors give learners responsibility for generating the information themselves rather than merely receiving it.

Without work and effort on the instructor's part, communicative language teaching runs the risk of lapsing into older patterns of instruction and disappearing as just another fad, another fossil in the evolutionary record of language instruction.

KEY TERMS, CONCEPTS, AND ISSUES

Be able to define, discuss the significance of, or identify the issues associated with each of the following words and phrases.

Atlas Complex
classroom dynamic
roles dictate tasks
knowledge transmission and receptive vessels
secondary roles for instructors and learners
Audiolingual Methodology (ALM)
habit formation
pattern practices and substitution drills
Communicative Language Teaching (CLT)
conversation
    question and answer only
    paired work
    classroom versus nonclassroom
meaning, purpose, and reality
tasks dictate roles
distributing teaching functions
responsibility for learning
instructor = architect, resource person
students = builders, coworkers, information gatherers, negotiators
participation and contribution in the classroom
communication
multilayered communicative events
discussion questions versus intermediate tasks and steps
social dimension of teaching and learning
learners versus students

EXPLORING THE TOPICS FURTHER

You may wish to read further about the following topics. Each of the works we recommend also contains a bibliography providing further directions in which to explore your interests.

1. *Audiolingual Methodology.* A description and analysis of Audiolingual Methodology is offered by Richards and Rogers (1986, pp. 44–63). Several of the works they cite would also provide more insight into this methodology: Brooks (1964), Chastain (1970), Lado (1957), and Politzer (1965) (particularly Parts I and IV).

2. *Various language teaching methodologies.* Richards and Rogers (1986, pp. 64–86) offer an overview of communicative language teaching as well as a number of other methodologies. Other works that might prove interesting are Leemann Guthrie's article (in Savignon and Berns 1984) and Krashen and Terrell's work on the Natural Approach (1983). Also see the book by Savignon (1983).

3. *Social dimensions of language learning and teaching.* van Lier (1988) offers an ethnographic perspective on the workings of the classroom. Numerous article-length works also provide valuable insights. Among them are articles by Brooks and Wildner-Bassett (in VanPatten and Lee 1990). Also of interest in this regard is a more recent article by Brooks (1993).

CHAPTER 2

Research Insights

in-sight (*ĭn'-sīt'*) *n. 1. the capacity to discern the true nature of a situation; penetration. 2. an elucidating glimpse.*
American Heritage Dictionary

INTRODUCTION

When you were first learning a second language, did you ever notice a discrepancy between how well you did on class exercises, practices, and tests and how you struggled during conversations? Did you wonder why your grammar could be so good in one situation but seem to disappear in the other? Did you think the difference was because you didn't study enough? Because you didn't drill enough? What could you have done to get the grammar in your head better so that your conversations were as error-free as your tests?

In this chapter, we explore some of the major findings of second language acquisition research that should help you understand what it means to acquire a second language. We focus on three major areas of research: the acquisition of grammar; the limited effects of what is now called "explicit" instruction in grammar; and research on the development of communicative language ability. We present the findings of these research areas as insights or, as the definition above suggests, "elucidating glimpses" into the process of acquiring a second language.

THE ACQUISITION OF GRAMMAR

As you might recall from Chapter 1, the prevailing theories of language learning in the 1950s and 1960s were behaviorism and habit formation. Language acquisition was viewed as the progressive accumulation of good habits, and the goal was error-free production. The learner's first language (L1) was seen as a major obstacle to L2 (second language) acquisition since it caused *interference errors* (caused by habits in the L1) and *negative transfer* (from L1 to L2) of habits. Theorists believed that language learning proceeded from form to meaning; that is, the learner first mastered all the grammatical forms and structures of the language and eventually moved on to expressing meaning. When this theory was applied to language teaching, the result was Audiolingual Methodology (ALM), whose major characteristics can be summarized as follows:

- the instructor was central; all information flowed from the instructor to the students
- errors in grammar were to be avoided at all cost; thus, the instructor tightly controlled both what and how students spoke or wrote
- the essential teaching/learning techniques were (1) memorization of dialogues and (2) pattern practice involving transformation ("Change the sentence from present to past"), substitution ("Insert a negative into the sentence and make all necessary changes")
- the contrasts between L1 and L2 were highlighted and drilled in order to avoid interference from L1 habits

Given such a theory of learning and its accompanying methodology, language learners were not much different from wild horses in the Old West: they were to be tamed, trained, and forced into particular patterns of behavior.

But in the late 1960s and early 1970s, some theorists and researchers began seriously to question the basic tenets of language learning as habit formation and thus also questioned ALM as an approach to language teaching. Corder was one of the first to question habit formation theory openly. In particular, he questioned the insistence that errors be avoided and that errors are simply a result of L1 interference. He noticed that many students produced errors in the process of learning a language that could not be traced to L1 interference. Corder reasoned that if L1 was not the source of these errors, then they must have been due to some other more general cognitive or linguistic processes of learning. In his now famous essay, "The Significance of Learners' Errors," Corder wrote:

> [Errors] are indispensable to the learner himself, because we can regard the errors as a device the learner uses in order to learn. It is a way the learner has of testing his hypotheses about the nature of the language he is learning. The making of errors then is a strategy employed both by children acquiring their mother tongue and by those learning a second language. (Corder 1967, as reprinted in 1981, p. 11)

Corder openly challenged mainstream language teaching of his day by suggesting that we should actually allow learners to produce errors so that we could study them systematically. In that way, we could come to understand the processes that actually underlie second language learning. He concluded his essay with the following words.

> We have been reminded recently of von Humboldt's statement that we cannot really teach language, we can only create conditions in which it will develop spontaneously in the mind in its own way . . . When we know [more about the processes underlying language acquisition from having studied errors] we may begin to be more critical of our cherished notions. We may be able to allow the learner's innate strategies to dictate our practice and determine our syllabus; we may learn to adapt ourselves to *his* needs rather than impose upon

him *our* preconceptions of *how* he ought to learn, *what* he ought to learn and *when* he ought to learn it. (ibid, p. 13)

Researchers responded quickly to Corder's challenge and, based on the data they gathered, began to develop theories about the underlying processes.

---

*P*ause to consider . . .

the challenges posed by Corder's ideas. What popular beliefs have been similarly successfully challenged by research? For example, will you spoil a baby if you pick her up every time she cries? Do you catch a cold from being exposed to cold temperatures? Does practice make perfect?

In the 1970s, research began to confirm Corder's speculation that language learning (that is, the acquisition of grammar) was not like other kinds of learning and that habit-formation theory was woefully inadequate in accounting for language acquisition. Research on the language that learners produced led to three important constructs that challenged the cherished notions of the time: orders of acquisition, stages of development, and formulaic speech. At that time, we must remember, language acquisition was equated with only the acquisition of grammar; research on second language reading and writing would emerge later.

Acquisition Orders

Orders of acquisition (also called *acquisition orders*) refer to the sequential acquisition of various grammatical features over time. Certain elements of grammar are learned before others, and this progression can be observed and quantified in learners' oral production. The grammatical features studied in the 1970s were *morphemes* (pieces and parts of words, such as verb endings and noun endings) and *functors* (words such as *the, is, a,* and *an,* which have particular grammatical functions in sentences). In English, for example, it has been shown that the acquisition of verb morphemes tends to follow the following order:

1. *-ing*
2. regular past tense
3. irregular past tense
4. third-person present tense-*s*

In other words, if we studied the language produced by learners of English, we would first see the greatest accuracy in the use of *-ing* with verbs in our learners' output. The last thing we would see is accuracy in the use of third persons. This order would be apparent regardless of the learner's L1. In other words, Chinese, Spanish, and Arabic speakers of English follow the same acquisition order for verb morphemes. This order was thus believed to be universal for learners of English. To be sure, some learners might progress through the order faster than others; still others might never complete the acquisition process because they could not quite get third person *-s* into their speech. But we would nevertheless be able to see a universal pattern of acquisition. Acquisition orders provided the first empirical evidence that Corder was correct in suggesting that learners possessed "internal strategies" for organizing language data and that these strategies did not necessarily obey outside influences.

Stages of Development

Another major construct to emerge from research on the acquisition of grammar was the notion of *stages of development:* the systematic patterns of acquisition for a given structure. Unlike acquisition orders involving a variety of grammatical features, stages of development pertain to just one grammatical structure, not several. Researchers identified the stages that a learner traverses during the development of a particular feature of language. Each stage is characterized by the type of error(s) made as a learner acquires the structure.

One of the classic examples of stages of development involves the acquisition of negation in English. Researchers studying both classroom and non-classroom learners have observed a general tendency to pass through four stages of development for this one grammatical feature. The errors made at each stage do not seem to be influenced by any particular L1, since learners from a wide variety of L1 backgrounds all pass through these stages. (The examples below are taken from Ellis 1986, pp. 59–60).

Stage 1: no + PHRASE
No drink.
No you playing here.

Stage 2: negator moves inside phrase; *not* and *don't* added to list of negators, but *don't* is considered one word
I no can swim.
I don't see nothing mop.

Stage 3: negator attached to modals but initially may be unanalyzed as is *don't* in Stage 2
I can't play this one.
I won't tell.

Stage 4: auxiliary system of English is developed, and learner acquires correct use of *not* and contractions
He doesn't know anything.
I didn't said it.

As these patterns for the acquisition of negation in English suggest, learners make particular kinds of errors at particular stages in the acquisition of a structure. Each stage marks some kind of restructuring in the mind of the learner regarding that particular structure. That is, a structure does not just "pop into the heads" of learners; it *evolves* over time.

In a study of the acquisition of Spanish *ser* and *estar* (equivalents of *to be* in English), VanPatten also found stages of development in classroom learners. He found a tendency for learners to pass through five stages of development in their acquisition of basic uses of the Spanish copular (linking) verbs, with Stage 2 lasting some time for English speakers learning Spanish. (The following examples are taken from VanPatten 1987; asterisks indicate ungrammatical constructions.)

Stage 1: no copular verb
   *Juan alto. (John tall.)

Stage 2: acquisition of *ser* and its overextension in contexts where *estar* would be appropriate
   Maria es muy simpática. (Mary is very nice.)
   *Ella es estudiar. (She's studying.)
   *Mis padres son a Chicago. (My parents are in Chicago.)
   *Soy muy contento hoy. (I'm very happy today.)

Stage 3: acquisition of *estar* + progressive
   Está estudiando. (She's studying.)

Stage 4: acquisition of *estar* + location
   Están en Chicago. (They're in Chicago.)

Stage 5: acquisition of *estar* + adjectives of condition
   Estoy muy contento. (I'm very happy.)

Stages of development have been found for word order in German, WH-questions in English (that is, the structure of questions containing *when, who, why, where,* and so forth), tense and aspect in Romance languages and English, and case marking, among other linguistic structures. (Stages overlap; a learner may clearly be in Stage 2 of the acquisition of a structure but have residual patterns from Stage 1, for example.) As in the case of acquisition orders, stages of development suggest that learners actively organize language in their heads independently of external influence. Something causes them to make certain kinds of errors and not others, and something produces certain universal patterns of acquisition regardless of the L1. The research on acquisition orders and developmental stages clearly demonstrates that language acquisition could not be a result of imitation and the learning of "good habits."

Pause to consider . . .
_____

spontaneous/communicative speech. In the two examples just discussed, researchers engaged learners in conversation, asked them to interview native speakers, and got them to narrate or describe pictures, videos, movies, and other visual stimuli. Would the research results presented so far have been the same if researchers had not used spontaneous or communicative tasks? Do you think we would see the same or similar acquisition orders? Do you think the stages of development would look the same—or exist at all? What would the results be if fill-in-the-blank tests had been used? Or if learners had been given a task such as, "You must use the subjunctive at least five times in your answers"?

Formulaic Speech

The third major construct that undermined behaviorist theories of language learning was *formulaic speech:* routinized chunks of language that have no internal structure for the speaker. An example of formulaic speech is the phrase "May I take your order?" uttered by a non-native–speaking waitress. The phrase is formulaic because she has not really acquired the rules of word order that place *may* at the front of the sentence, nor has she acquired possessive pronouns. For example, this waitress might also say "I use pen?" instead of "May I use your pen?" "May I take your order?" is part of an interactional routine she is quite capable of carrying out. This same speaker might also be able to use appropriately the chunk "Idunno" (written here as all one word to indicate it is a chunk). She has acquired neither *do* support (that is, the ability to use *do*) nor the negator *not*, because she might also say "I no drive" instead of "I don't drive."

---

*P*ause to consider . . .

routines and formulaic speech in your native language. Can you list examples of such speech? You probably don't need to think beyond the most common exchanges.

But formulaic speech is not limited to whole chunks that stand by themselves. Some formulaic speech is used in sentences that are not themselves formulaic in nature. A speaker who says "Gimme a piece of that pie" might also say "Gimme a kiss" or "Gimme a chance." These examples suggest that "Gimme" exists as formulaic speech that can be used in the pattern "Gimme _____."

Second language research in the 1970s revealed that learners who are in language-rich environments, such as adults and children learning the language where it is spoken, often internalize and use formulaic speech that they hear. Sometimes they use it incorrectly, but it is clear that they are internalizing chunks of language and that not everything they say is rule governed (that is, the result of knowing rules of grammar). Child learners of English, for example, who are attending elementary school where English is the native language, often pick up formulaic speech such as "I wanna _____," "Can I _____?" and "Where's _____?" among others. To the learner, these chunks are like single words. In the last example, it is clear that the learner has no idea that the chunk of language he is using consists of a word plus the contracted copular verb *is*. To him, it is simply the way to begin an inquiry into location. He might thus produce both "Where's the teacher?" and "Where's butterflies live?" Even classroom learners of a foreign language (who do not use the language outside the classroom) pick up formulaic speech from their teacher. VanPatten reports that learners of Spanish often use *megusta* _____ to talk about anything they like and that *cómosedice* _____ is used to get English-to-Spanish word translations from teachers and yet the learner has no real idea—conscious or unconscious—of the individual parts of these phrases (VanPatten 1986).

> ### *P*ause to consider . . .
>
> formulaic speech in your second language. Can you think of any formulaic speech that might exist in your second language linguistic system? If not, listen to yourself and others speak in your second language and make note of any formulaic speech you encounter.

The fact that learners' speech contained elements of language that were not taught and drilled was a serious blow to behaviorist theory. On the one hand, formulaic speech clearly demonstrates that learners are sensitive to the linguistic environment in which they find themselves. In other words, input is important in language acquisition. Learners could and did get language in ways other than imitating the instructor. On the other hand, researchers found that not all language was rule governed. Language acquisition could not be as simple as replacing first language patterns with second language ones. We explore further the role of the L1 in the next section.

THE ROLE OF THE FIRST LANGUAGE IN SECOND LANGUAGE ACQUISITION

Interference and Transfer

Another major finding of contemporary research is the role of the L1 during second language acquisition. Habit-formation theory claimed that errors were a result of the L1 "interfering" in the learning process, and that learners would "transfer" their L1 habits to the L2. As researchers began to analyze the systematic errors that learners made, they found that interference errors or transfer errors were hardly so widespread. In 1976, for example, LoCoco found that only 13.2% of the errors of English-speaking adults learning Spanish could be attributed to L1 patterns. In a 1975 study, LoCoco also looked at English-speaking learners of German and found that interference errors accounted for only 23% of the errors in the earliest stages. (Her data revealed that this percentage dropped off considerably as the students progressed in the first few years of study.) In 1977, White found that 20.6% of the errors of her Spanish-speaking subjects learning English could be attributed to L1 interference. In short, learners do not seem to be simply transferring L1 habits, as originally thought by the behaviorists, because the L1 does not account for a considerable percentage of the L2 errors.

Currently, L1 transfer is seen as a part of language acquisition that is constrained by other processes that guide language learning. The greatest role attributed to L1 transfer is not when L1 and L2 patterns are different, but when they are similar. That is, the learner's L1 is more likely to cause interference in the developing system when the internal mechanisms note enough similarity between the L1 and L2 pattern or structure to permit the L1 pattern to be transferred. Recall that VanPatten (1985a, 1987) found that English-speaking learners pass through various stages in the acquisition of the Spanish copular verbs *ser* and *estar*. The first stage involves a tendency to simply omit the copula (*Juan alto* 'John tall'). This first stage cannot be attributable to L1 transfer because both languages require a copular verb. The next stage is a tendency to overgeneralize *ser* (probably due to its overwhelming frequency in Spanish when compared to *estar*). It is here that L1 transfer may be triggered. The internal mechanisms have begun to overgeneralize *ser*, nearly creating a "one-copula system" in the learner's mind. This system is now close to the English system of one copula. The result? The second stage (overgeneralizing *ser*) tends to be rather protracted for the L1 speaker of English. In short, L1 transfer is seen as a rather subtle phenomenon that influences the length of stages in development as well as the character of those stages; it is more likely due to *degree of similarity* rather than *degree of difference*.

To be sure, learners often produce utterances that resemble L1 sentences. The learner of French, for example, who says *Je suis vingt ans* instead of *J'ai vingt ans* for "I am 20 years old" seems to be transferring an L1 pattern. However, this type of error is generally due not to transfer, as just described above, but rather to a communication strategy of dressing up an L1 utterance in L2 vocabulary. This strategy is most prevalent with beginning learners who may not have a mental representation of a particular pattern because they have not had enough exposure to the language.

Input and the Brain

The research we have now seen on grammar acquisition and the influence of L1 began to undermine habit-formation theories of the acquisition of grammar. If both classroom and nonclassroom learners showed evidence of acquisition orders, stages of development, formulaic speech, and rather limited L1 transfer errors, how could simple habit formation be true? And if habit formation could not account for learner output, what could?

What is now generally accepted is that learners have internal mechanisms in the brain that organize and store language. These mechanisms are still not completely understood, although we will examine some in Chapter 5. But it is clear that these mechanisms have their own role in language acquisition. The question that arises is what kind of language data do these mechanisms need in order to operate? If drills and practices aren't responsible for acquisition orders, stages of development, and so forth, what do language learners need?

The concept of *input* is relevant to this question. Input is defined as language that the learner hears (or sees) and attends to for its meaning. It contrasts with output, or what the learner produces. In addition, input is useful to the learner only if it is comprehensible. A stream of speech that runs by the learner and sounds like jibberish is not good input. In short, every time a learner hears or reads an utterance, is actively engaged in trying to get the meaning of what the speaker or writer is conveying, and can understand most or some of the utterance, he is getting input for those internal mechanisms to work on.

Comprehensible Input and Acquisition

Krashen (1982 and elsewhere) has put forth the *Input Hypothesis*. His claim is very strong: comprehensible input *causes* acquisition. He believes that as long as there is motivation and the right affective environment (e.g., low anxiety), a person cannot avoid learning a second language if there is sustained comprehensible input. Others don't make as strong a claim and suggest that language acquisition is a complex process involving social, cognitive, linguistic, and other factors. Because not all language learners are equally successful, there must be more at work than comprehensible input. Nonetheless, almost everyone today believes that comprehensible input is a critical factor in language acquisition. Long (1990) puts it quite nicely when he says that comprehensible input is a necessary (but perhaps not sufficient) ingredient of language acquisition. What this means is that *successful language acquisition cannot happen without comprehensible input*. Classroom learners who get a steady diet of explanations and practice might appear to have some kind of language ability, but it is not the same as those who get consistent and constant exposure to comprehensible input. At the same time, learners need more than comprehensible input. As we shall see later in this chapter, learners also need opportunities to use the language in communicative interaction. Although input may be responsible for the evolution of the language system in the learner's head, having to use the language pushes the learner to develop what we call *communicative language ability*.

THE LIMITED EFFECTS
OF EXPLICIT INSTRUCTION

In this chapter, we have reviewed general findings about the acquisition of grammar regardless of context: foreign vs. second language, classroom vs. nonclassroom. As the evidence on acquisition accumulated, researchers began to turn their attention to the following question: Does instruction make a difference? That is, does *explicit instruction* in grammar, together with practice, error correction, and so forth, have any significant effect on how learners acquire a language? The findings have stirred quite a debate in the profession, for they delighted some theorists and bothered some instructors.

One of the first findings to emerge was that acquisition orders do not match instructional orders. That is, the emergence of verb inflections, noun endings, functors, and even syntactic patterns did not necessarily match the order in which they were taught and practiced. English third-person -s, for example, is a verb morpheme taught rather early in most ESL programs. Yet, as we saw in the previous section, it is one of the last verb morphemes to be acquired in speech. Lightbown (1983) reports that intense practice in the language forms she investigated resulted in *overlearning* (use in linguistic contexts where the item should not be used) but that this overlearning disappeared and the learners went right back to following the natural orders of acquisition. And Pica (1983) found almost the same orders of acquisition in three very distinct sets of learners of English: foreign-language learners in Mexico, classroom learners in Philadelphia, and nonclassroom learners in Pennsylvania. These and other investigations all yielded the same results: explicit instruction and practice did very little, if anything, to alter acquisition orders. Learners seemed to follow a particular path on their way to developing the second language system, regardless of the order in which grammatical features were taught.

A second finding of classroom-based research is that explicit grammar instruction does not circumvent "natural" stages of development. That is, explicit grammar instruction does not seem to affect stages of development. Learners still tend to pass through stages, make overgeneralizations (for example, generalize regular past tense endings to irregular verbs), and so forth, regardless of instruction. In a particularly notable study, Ellis (1984) found that learners of English in the classroom who were exposed to instruction and practice nonetheless exhibited the same stages of development in the acquisition of negation and other structures as did nonclassroom learners. In a later study, Ellis (1989) examined the acquisition of German word order in foreign-language learners in Great Britain. He found that even though they received explicit instruction and practice, their stages of development matched those observed in nonclassroom learners (of various L1s) who learned German "naturally" in Germany. Kaplan (1987) found that foreign-language learners of French in the U.S. exhibited patterns of development in the acquisition of the *passé composé* and the *imparfait* that were strikingly similar to those of nonclassroom learners (with a different L1) in France. And if you recall VanPatten's findings on the acquisition of *ser* and *estar* (pp. 24–25), it is notable that the very first stage of acquisition is the absence of copular (linking) verbs altogether. How could this be when the instructors clearly did not teach or practice with their students the erroneous omission of linking verbs? These studies and others all suggest that the learner is guided by some internal mechanisms and that instruction simply cannot override what these mechanisms do.

Pause to consider . . .

what other learning situations might or might not be affected by explicit instruction. In which of the following do you think instruction might make a difference? In which might the effects of instruction not significantly affect the stages that a person needs to go through to master the skill and internalize the intricacies of the behavior?

playing tennis	sewing
playing poker	writing a good term paper
riding a bike	jumping rope with children

In any of these learning situations, do you think that instruction might be a *hindrance*? In which of them do you think lots of input (seeing how others do it, watching the activity in real life contexts) might be the most critical ingredient in learning?

③ A third finding of classroom-based research is that language produced by learners on grammar-focused tests does not necessarily match that found in communicative speech. On tests, learners of English might be able to supply third person -s correctly on fill-in-the-blank and short-answer tests although they omit this verb inflection when using the language to communicate information outside (and often inside!) the classroom. Likewise, learners of Spanish might correctly write on a test *tuve* (I had) only to use later in conversation **tení* (an overgeneralization of the regular past tense forms) or even **tuví*. In one particular study of classroom learners of Spanish in Southern California, Terrell, Baycroft, and Perrone (1987) investigated what classroom learners could do with the subjunctive. Their subjects did quite well on the paper-and-pencil tests of the subjunctive that they gave, scoring an average of 23 out of 25 when asked to complete sentences such as *Juan José quiere que su hermana _____ en casa esta tarde (quedarse)* 'John Joseph wants his sister _____ at home this afternoon (to stay)'. But when given a communicative task, namely, to talk about topics such as "Who would you like to marry?" and "What are your plans for this summer?" the subjects produced utterances such as **Quiero que mi esposo a tener buen sentido de humor* 'I want my husband to have a good sense of humor', **Mi padre me quiere ir a la escuela* 'My father wants me to go to school', and **El no quiere que yo trabajo* 'He doesn't want me to work'. In fact, the scores on the communicative task revealed that only 12% of the utterances produced by the learners contained any uses of the subjunctive that were correct in both verb form and sentence structure. Why was there such a discrepancy between tests and speech?

Krashen (1982) has suggested that learners receiving explicit grammar instruction may develop a conscious *Monitor*, a kind of "grammar police" that can edit for correct use of grammar and syntax only under certain conditions. These conditions are (1) when the learner needs to produce a correct sentence and (2) when there is time to do it (such as on a written test as opposed to in naturally occurring conversation). Krashen posits the Monitor as responsible for the difference between the language produced on form-focused tests and other kinds of language production. Krashen has further suggested that the system used during communicative interaction is a system independent of the Monitor. This other system he calls the *acquired system,* which is built up over time from exposure to comprehensible input. It is now widely accepted that learners' grammatical accuracy depends on the kinds of tasks they are engaged in. [MONITOR]

To be sure, the overall picture of instruction is not completely negative. Classroom learners have been found to approximate normative (that is, native-like) use of grammar more than have nonclassroom learners. Thus, those who receive instruction seem to go further in terms of acquiring more of the grammar of the language. And the rate of acquisition of grammar seems to be speeded up by instruction. But we should examine just why classroom learners might do better in the long run compared to nonclassroom learners.

Is Classroom Learning Superior?

① Currently, three reasons may account for the so-called superiority of classroom learners. First, classroom learners tend to be exposed to a wider range of language data when compared to nonclassroom learners. The latter have often been immigrants of lower socioeconomic classes who move to another country for economic or political reasons, and their exposure to language in the new country is frequently limited to conversational language. Classroom language learners, on the other hand, get exposure not only to conversational language but also to the language of written texts, speeches, and other types of *planned discourse*. Planned discourse tends to contain more complex syntax (more clauses, conjunctions), broader vocabulary, and a wider range of grammatical structures. As one example, passive structures tend to be infrequent in spoken language. We have little reason to say "The food was consumed by Ginger" when talking about what the dog just did. We are much more likely to use an active structure: "Ginger ate the food." Planned and written discourse, on the other hand, contain more instances of passive sentences as exemplified in the following excerpt from *Newsweek*. (You will also probably notice the generally more complex sentences and broader vocabulary mentioned above.)

> The decision [by President Clinton] left gay activists puzzled and angry over the administration's rejection of an unpublished $1.3 million Rand Corporation study that proposed that homosexuals be permitted to serve openly under strict guidelines. (*Newsweek*, August 2, 1993, p. 4)

The second reason suggested for the apparent superiority of classroom learning is that instruction heightens learners' awareness of grammatical form and structure, perhaps making forms more salient in the input. In this way, learners are simply more apt to notice grammatical forms and pay attention to them in the language they hear and see. Sharwood Smith (1993) has coined a new term for grammar instruction, suggesting that it be thought of as *input enhancement*. Grammar instruction might thus help learners to perceive what is in the input. This term makes great sense given the critical role of comprehensible input. In Chapter 5 we will examine grammar instruction and input in more detail as we rethink explicit instruction as *structured input*.

A final reason for classroom learners going further and learning more in the long run may be that they "self-select." Those classroom learners who keep studying languages might simply be a special subset of learners with certain characteristics. Most people in the United States study languages because they have to, completing only those requirements that allow them to earn a degree or certificate. However, those who venture beyond the basic requirements could have motivation and an affinity for language learning that spurns them on *in spite of* the instruction. They continue to elect language classes, study more and more grammar, and even major in the language or study abroad. At this latter stage, it becomes hard to tell what happens to these learners: Are they better now because they have had so much explicit instruction? Or are they better because they have been exposed to so much input and have had a natural disposition to process more of it? This issue is not trivial since beginning (and even some experienced) instructors say, "Well, I learned the grammar that way. Why can't I teach it that way?" They do not recognize that they are special and that they may have acquired language in precisely the ways that we have been discussing here.

To summarize this section, we have examined some general findings from second language acquisition research as well as some conclusions about the effects of explicit instruction. In both cases we have seen that the acquisition of grammar does not lend itself to external manipulation but rather has its own agenda. Some aspects of language get learned later than others regardless of instruction, and learners tend to follow certain developmental paths as the grammar evolves in their heads. In general, the acquisition of grammar appears to be a result of some internal mechanisms that process, organize, and store language data. These data come from comprehensible input that learners hear and read.

LEARNING TO COMMUNICATE

Studies of the acquisition of grammar were not the only research to undermine habit formation and ALM. You might recall that, according to the theories of habit formation and ALM, communicating with the language was something that would happen as a result of internalizing grammatical habits: the learner had to learn habits before using them. In 1972, Savignon published a study that would have a major impact on the way in which professionals perceived the ALM classroom and its effect on developing communicative language abilities. In her study, she compared three groups learning French in a first-semester college classroom. The first received classical ALM training with four classroom days and one lab day per week. The second received the same ALM training, but on the fifth day lab practice was replaced by cultural studies: students saw films and slide shows, had discussions about their impressions of France, and participated in informal discussions with French students studying in the U.S., among other activities. The third group received ALM training, but lab day was devoted to training in communication: students first discussed what it meant to communicate and how nonverbal communication played a role in face-to-face interactions. They subsequently engaged in activities that focused on doing things in French: greeting, departing, information gathering, information sharing. Savignon subsequently gave students from all three groups a test of communicative competence that involved four different kinds of activities: (1) discussion with a native speaker of French, (2) information gathering with a native speaker of French (that is, the students interviewed a French person), (3) a monologue on a topic, with the learner alone in a room with a tape recorder, (4) narration (describing the activities of an actor who performed a nonspeaking series of actions).

Native speakers of French were trained to evaluate the first two tasks based on the effort to communicate and the amount of communication, and the second two tasks based on fluency and comprehensibility. In addition, all students were given the College Entrance Examination Board (CEEB) tests for listening and reading in French. The results from Savignon's study were quite clear; they are displayed in Table 2.1. The learners in the third group, the "communication" group, scored significantly higher than the others on the tests of communicative competence. More importantly, the control ALM

TABLE 2.1 Comparative Study of Communicative Competence in Three Groups

		Group Means			
Group	N	CEEB Listening	CEEB Reading	Instructor's evaluation of oral skills	Test of communicative competence
ALM only	15	6.67	6.00	14.80	34.27
Culture	15	6.20	6.67	15.87	44.27
Comm.	12	9.00	8.08	19.92	66.00
F-ratio		1.11	0.56	3.98*	8.54**

*p < .05
**p < .001

Source: Savignon (1972), adapted from Savignon (1983).

group scored quite low on the tests of communicative competence, suggesting that drill and practice were not effective in promoting communicative language ability. The communication group also scored as well if not slightly higher than the others on the CEEB tests. (Independent measures of aptitude and scholastic ability were used before the study began to be sure that all groups were of the same general language learning ability.)

Savignon's study was the first empirically based research to suggest a very important aspect of language acquisition: one learns to communicate by practicing communication. As Savignon states, "Those students who had been given the opportunity to use their linguistic knowledge for real communication were able to speak French. The others were not" (1983, pp. 78-79). Since Savignon's seminal study, others have gone on to study various aspects of both classroom and nonclassroom communication with similar findings. Some researchers have gone so far as to claim that learners actually learn language through communicating. Hatch (1978a), for example, suggests that during communication, learners "negotiate" and even "regulate" the kind of input they receive so that they obtain input suited to their individual needs. Swain (1985) argues that communicative production encourages learners to attend to input better since they themselves need to use language they are

Pause to consider . . .

what Savignon's study suggests about a lament often heard from classroom learners of a language. It is not uncommon to hear "I took four years of high-school French and can't speak a word," or "I was really good in Spanish and got A's, but I can't understand a thing when someone talks to me." What would you ask these people about their language classrooms? In what ways do these comments argue against habit-formation theory in language learning?

hearing around them. Others, however, suggest that some aspects of grammar and syntax are not acquirable through simple acts of everyday communication (see, for example, Sato 1986). While research continues on the relationship between communication and acquisition, one thing remains clear: communicative language ability—the ability to express one's self *and* to understand others—develops as learners engage in communication and not as a result of habit formation with grammatical items. (We offer an expanded treatment of communicative language ability in Chapter 8.)

SUMMARY

In this chapter we briefly reviewed three major areas of research that challenged the very core of ALM. We saw that the acquisition of grammar is more a function of the learner than of the instructor, instruction, or instructional materials. In other words, people apparently come to the task of language learning with some internal mechanisms that operate on language data. Requiring comprehensible input, these mechanisms organize linguistic data independently of the order in which grammatical items were taught and independently of explanation and practice. The effects of grammar instruction are limited at best, at least for the kind of instruction that has dominated classrooms for some time. In addition, we have seen that the development of communicative language ability is not a blossom that springs forth from the roots and stem of habit formation. Communicative language ability is something that develops as learners engage in communication, and there is reason to believe that communicative activities should be present from the earliest stages of classroom language learning.

In short, we are now ready to think again about Corder's challenge: we might not really be able to "teach" language, and we can only create conditions in which language can be acquired by the learner. In the chapters that follow, we examine such conditions, ranging from providing comprehensible input in the classroom to communicative and interactive tasks to grammar instruction that can be considered to be input enhancement.

KEY TERMS, CONCEPTS, AND ISSUES

the tenets of ALM
errors
acquisition orders
stages of development
formulaic speech
 routines
 chunks
L1 transfer
interference
the role of input in acquisition
 Input Hypothesis

explicit grammar instruction *debate is it useful?*
 limited effects *of explicit grammar instruction*
  acquisition orders versus instructional orders *don't match*
  instruction versus natural stages *are not circumvented*
  grammar focused tests versus spontaneous speech *no correspondance*
 the "superiority" of classroom learning *wider range of data*
  planned discourse *more complex*
  input enhancement *by heightening awareness of grammatical forms*
  the nature of the learner who goes on *he self-selects*
learning to communicate *by practising communication*

EXPLORING THE TOPICS FURTHER

1. *Second language acquisition research.* VanPatten (1992a and b) offers an overview of findings from second language acquisition research and a list of cited works that are relevant to the language classroom. Some of the chapters in Freed's book (1991) also contain overviews and discussion of second language research accessible to the novice reader of this material. For a comprehensive overview of second language research, see Larsen-Freeman and Long (1991). Before reading these works, however, you might want to put them into their historical context by examining Corder (1981).

2. *Communication.* Savignon's (1983) book is a very readable standard work in this area. See also some of the readings in the series by Savignon and Berns (1984, 1987).

CHAPTER 3

Comprehensible Input

com·pre·hen·si·ble *(kŏm'-prĭ-hĕn'sə-bəl)* adj. *capable of being comprehended or understood; intelligible.*

American Heritage Dictionary

INTRODUCTION

Think of your past experiences with announcements over public address systems. Such systems are used in train and bus stations and in airports as well as inside commuter trains to announce the next stop. Have you ever found yourself not able to understand such an announcement? Was it garbled? Did it go by too fast? Were you not paying attention when it began and then unable to make sense of it as it went on? Has this happened to you in both your first and second languages?

There are many situations in which we might not understand what someone else says. Perhaps we are sitting somewhere and overhear others speaking in a language that we don't know. Perhaps we are listening to an academic lecture for which we are not prepared, only to have the lecture go over our heads. Perhaps we are watching a news broadcast in our second language, only to struggle with the content of the broadcast as the commentator's words zip by our ears. In such cases, we cannot make the connection between the language and the meaning that it encodes. The language is, simply put, incomprehensible. From a language learner's point of view, if the language is incomprehensible, what good does it do the learner's developing system?

In Chapter 2, we reviewed some basic findings about classroom and non-classroom language acquisition that offer the language instructor insights into the learning process. As the research on second language acquisition accumulated, researchers and theorists turned their attention more and more to the role of input (especially comprehensible, meaning-bearing input) in the acquisition process. You will recall that researchers have claimed that comprehensible input is a necessary ingredient for successful language acquisition and that the language learner's internal mechanisms work on input data to construct a linguistic system.

In this chapter we examine two major issues: the characteristics of input that are most useful for the language learner and some examples of how instructors can add more input into the classroom.

WHAT IS GOOD INPUT?

Input is to language acquisition what gas is to a car. An engine needs gas to run; without gas, the car would not move an inch. Likewise, input in language learning is what gets the "engine" of acquisition going. Without it, acquisition simply doesn't happen.

Gas itself is a refined and filtered petroleum product; you simply cannot put crude oil into your gas tank and expect the car to run. And because gas is a refined petroleum product, some is better than others. High-octane gas makes many cars run more smoothly and efficiently than does low-octane gas. Likewise, some input is better than others, and the kind of input that is best for language learners is a kind of refined language. Imagine the beginning second language learner finding herself in the middle of a café in a country where the language is spoken. What would she understand? What use would the language environment be to this beginner?

There are several general characteristics of input that make it potentially useful to the learner. First, input has to be *meaning-bearing*. Stated another way, the language that the learner is listening to (or reading, if we are talking about written language) *must contain some message to which the learner is supposed to attend*. Thus, meaning-bearing input has some communicative intent; the purpose of the speaker is to communicate a message to a listener. When someone says to a learner, "I went out last night. And, boy! Did I have a good time!" the speaker is attempting to communicate a message about last night's events, and both speaker and listener understand that the learner-listener is supposed to focus on the message.

A second general characteristic of input is that it has to be *comprehensible.* This is perhaps the most important characteristic of input from the learner's point of view. It is also the characteristic that has received the most attention in second language acquisition theory and research. *The learner must be able to understand most of what the speaker (or writer) is saying if acquisition is to happen.* In other words, the learner must be able to figure out what the speaker is saying if he is to attach meaning to the speech stream coming at him. Why is this? Acquisition consists in large part of the building up of form-meaning connections in the learner's head. For example, the learner of French hears the word *chien* in various contexts and eventually attaches it to a particular meaning: a four-legged canine. As another example, a learner of Italian might hear *-ato* in various contexts and eventually attach it to a particular meaning: past-time reference. Features of language, be they grammar, vocabulary, pronunciation, or something else, can only make their way into the learner's mental representation of the language system if they have been linked to some kind of real-world meaning. If the input is incomprehensible or if it is not meaning-bearing, then these form-meaning connections just don't happen.

Input with Children

Return for a moment to the gas-car metaphor. What makes input "high octane"? And, given that we are concerned with getting learners *started* in acquisition, what kind of input is good for beginners? It is clear that learners cannot be spoken to in the way native-speaking adults talk to each other. Language learners—especially beginners—need input that is simplified compared to the free-flowing language that native speakers may use with each other (or what might appear on television or radio broadcasts, for instance). Most children get some kind of simplified input when learning their first language. They get this simplified input from parents, caretakers, siblings, and story books. Note, for example, the following interchange between a parent and a one-and-a-half-year-old child that is typical of interchanges during diaper changing or crib play. (Intonation and rhythm are not indicated in the interchange. You should try to imagine what this interchange would sound like.)

PARENT: Where's your nose?
  CHILD: (*Touches nose.*)
PARENT: Where's your mouth?
  CHILD: (*Grabs for parent's face.*)
PARENT: Come on. Show me your mouth. Your mouth. Where is it?
  CHILD: (*Giggles and puts finger on mouth.*)
PARENT: That's it. That's your mouth! Oh! You're so smart! How'd I get such a smart baby, huh? Are you smart? Yes you are, aren't you? Aren't you?

Now contrast the speech used above with the following conversation between the same parent and a friend.

PARENT: I'm pretty fed up with my job these days. I mean, I can't believe that the company thinks we will take a cut in pay and not say anything. I mean, it's just—I don't know.
  FRIEND: But it's like that everywhere! Last week I read in *Newsweek*—at least I think it was *Newsweek*. We get both *Newsweek* and *Time*—but anyway I read where IBM is cutting another 500 jobs this next week. I bet those people wouldn't mind a cut in pay just to keep food on the table.
PARENT: Come on! It's not that easy and you know it . . .

As you can see, the speech the infant heard and the speech used by that infant's parent with a friend are different in a number of ways: breadth of vocabulary, length of utterance, repetition, and clarity. And even though we have not included indications of intonation, articulation, rhythm, and pitch, these too would vary in the two communicative situations. Work on child language acquisition in the 1960s and 1970s revealed that the speech addressed to first-language acquirers was generally simpler and more redundant than speech addressed to older children and adults. In arguing against many linguists' position that children receive degenerate input—input full of false starts, incomplete sentences, and even grammar mistakes—Snow summarizes her research findings by stating that

Snow

> children such as those included in [this] study do not learn language on the basis of a confusing corpus full of mistakes, garbles, and complexities. They hear, in fact, a relatively consistent, organized, simplified, and redundant set of utterances which in many ways seems quite well designed as a set of "language lessons." (Snow 1978, p. 498)

Another important aspect of speech directed to children is that adults often rephrase what children say to them, thus providing the children with target models of what the children intend to say. Focusing on the child's message, an adult often expands the child's utterances as illustrated in the following example. [Note: Peter is the child; all others are adults.]:

PATSY: What happened to it [the truck]?
PETER: (*looking under his chair*) Lose it. Dump truck! Dump truck! Fall! Fall!
  LOIS: Yes, the dump truck fell down.
(Lightbown and Spada)

In the example above, Lois expands Peter's child utterance *Fall! Fall!* to its full adult form *The dump truck fell down*. Researchers have suggested that these *expansions* provide input data that the child's internal mechanisms may use to compare the current state of his language with what a full-fledged grammatical utterance might sound like. What is important about Lois's expansions—and most expansions in adult-child interchanges—is that the adult is *not* correcting the speech of the child; the adult is merely confirming what the child says. The adult echoes the child's utterance to let him know that she understands the message.

Input with Second Language Learners

The research on input addressed to children prompted second language researchers to examine second language input in the same way. A number of characteristics of simplified second language input have been enumerated by various researchers. Larsen-Freeman summarizes the research in this way:

> Input to [nonnative speakers] is shorter and less complicated and is produced at a slower rate than speech between adult [native speakers]. This input tends to be more regular, canonical [that is, typical] word order is adhered to, and there is a high proportion of unmarked patterns. There are fewer false starts and there is less repair. High-frequency vocabulary is used . . . There is a limited use of pronouns . . . There are more questions. Question tags and alternative questions occur more frequently. There is less pre-verb modification, presum-

---

*P*ause to consider . . .

Larsen-Freeman's description of typical simplified second language input. Look at her description and then compare it to the adult-child exchanges above. Would you say at this point that the input directed to child language acquirers and the input directed to second language acquirers (as described by Larsen-Freeman) undergo some of the same modifications compared to native-to-native adult language?

ably so new information can be highlighted at the end of the utterance, where it is more salient. The input is higher-pitched, it shows more intonation variation in pitch, and it is louder in volume. It contains fewer reduced vowels and fewer contractions. (Larsen-Freeman 1985, p. 436)

Perhaps the most comprehensive list of the characteristics of simplified input in second language situations was made by Hatch (1983), who examines simplified input in terms of five general categories: (1) rate of speech, (2) vocabulary, (3) syntax, (4) discourse, and (5) speech setting. With these characteristics, she also suggests possible *benefits* derived from those characteristics. That is, each characteristic presumably has some impact on how the language is perceived and/or processed by the language learner. In Table 3.1 we reproduce Hatch's list. From Hatch's point of view, it is clear that simplified input provides learners with language that is, overall, easier to process: the ability to make form-meaning connections is enhanced because

TABLE 3.1 Characteristics of Simplified Input to Second Language Learners

General Characteristic	Examples
Slower rate	1. Fewer reduced vowels and fewer contractions. 2. Longer pauses. 3. Extra stress on nouns. Half-beat pauses following topic noun.
Vocabulary	1. High-frequency vocabulary, less slang, fewer idioms. 2. Fewer pronoun forms of all kinds; high use of names for "one," "they," "we." 3. Definitions are marked (e.g., "This is an X," "It's a kind of X.") 4. Lexical information in definitions that provide extra information related to derivational morphology (e.g., "miracle—anything that's miraculous"), form class (e.g., "funds or money"), or semantic features (e.g., "a cathedral usually means a church that has very high ceilings"). 5. Use of gestures and/or pictures (drawings).
Syntax	1. Simple propositional syntax, short sentences. 2. Repetition and restatement. 3. Less pre-verb modification; more modification after the verb. 4. Expansion of learner's utterance.
Discourse	1. Speaker gives the learner a choice of responses within a posed question (e.g., "Where did you go? Did you go to the beach or to the mountains?"). 2. Speaker uses tag questions (e.g., "What did he want? A book?"). 3. Speaker offers correction (e.g., "You mean he left?").
Speech setting	1. Repetition of scenarios (e.g., daily encounters in a particular place).

Source: adapted from Hatch (1983)

the language is structured in such a way as to make certain features of language *acoustically more salient*. The forms and structure of the language are more easily perceived, and the learner has a greater chance to hear and process the form-meaning connections that are contained in the input. For example, speech with fewer contractions results in the learner being able to hear whether the language has a copular verb or not, or what the auxiliary verbs are. Simpler syntax reduces the burden on processing and increases the chance that the learner will hear certain forms and structures. Some simplifications—or, better yet, modifications—of input aid the acquisition of related words and their morphology (form). When someone defines a word using another word with the same root, for example, the learner receives evidence as to word endings related to nouns, verbs, and adjectives.

Pause to consider . . .

some of Hatch's descriptions of input modifications. Reread and consider the examples related to syntax. Can you give concrete examples of each? Can you think of a specific benefit for each type of modification? What might be the specific benefit of repetition and restatement?

INTAKE

The idea of processing input and linguistic data has led researchers and theorists to posit another construct: *intake*. While input is the language the learner is exposed to, intake is the *language that the learner actually attends to and that gets processed in working memory in some way*. Thus, not all input—no matter how comprehensible or meaningful—automatically makes its way into the learner's head. Intake, then, can be considered a subset, or filtered version, of the input. Recall from Chapter 2 that learners possess certain internal mechanisms that operate on input and that just because a learner hears something in the input does not mean that she will automatically acquire it. Acquisition is not instantaneous! What this means is that while the source of the input is external to the learner, what happens to the input is largely in the learner's hands—or brain, to be precise. In Chapter 5 we will examine in some detail the processes that learners use to derive intake from input. For now, it is sufficient to understand that comprehensible, meaning-bearing input is necessary for successful second language acquisition but that not all input becomes intake.

Interaction and Negotiation

We have been discussing input as though the learner's interlocutor is in complete charge of the language that the learner hears. The speaker makes adjustments or modifications and thus simplifies the input that the learner receives. This picture is, however, a bit one sided. While it is true that speakers generally modify their speech to make themselves more comprehensible to language learners, it is equally true that language learners often get the speakers to *make* specific modifications. To put this in other words, language learners often *negotiate* the flow and quality of input directed to them when they are engaged in some kind of conversational *interaction*. Learners may ask for repetitions and clarifications, or they may use some other device to signal that comprehension is problematic. These signals cause the other interlocutors to modify their speech in some way in an attempt to facilitate the learner's comprehension. This negotiation is most clearly illustrated in the following four examples taken from another investigation by Hatch (1978a):

Example 1

NATIVE SPEAKER: Did you have a nice weekend?
        RICARDO: Huh?
NATIVE SPEAKER: Friday, Saturday . . . did you have fun?

Example 2

NATIVE SPEAKER: Did you ride the mules?
        RICARDO: Mules?
NATIVE SPEAKER: The horses around. The pack mules.
        RICARDO: Pack mules?

Example 3

NATIVE SPEAKER: Do you wear them every day?
        RICARDO: Huh?
NATIVE SPEAKER: Do you put them on every day?
        RICARDO: Wear?
NATIVE SPEAKER: Yeah, do you [*adds gesture here*] put them on every day?
        RICARDO: Ah! No!

Example 4

NATIVE SPEAKER: I see. Well, is it typed?
        LEARNER: Type? Yes . . . uh . . . for the . . . I don't . . . I don't type.
NATIVE SPEAKER: Is it handwritten?
        LEARNER: Uh. Pardon me? Excuse me?
NATIVE SPEAKER: Is your thesis now handwritten?
        (*later*)
NATIVE SPEAKER: Is your thesis now typewritten or did you write it by hand?
        LEARNER: Ah, yes, by hand.
NATIVE SPEAKER: By hand.

In each interchange, the learner caused the speaker to modify utterances. *Interaction*, then, may enhance the availability of comprehensible input because interaction pushes the learner to indicate what he does and does not understand. This, in turn, can cause the interlocutor to modify her input in the ways suggested by Hatch in Table 3.1. Comprehensible input derived from interaction, then, may be quite different from, say, input from the radio or the TV, where the speaker *is* in absolute and complete control of both what is said and how it is said, and the learner has no opportunity to negotiate comprehension.

P_ause to consider . . ._

how the speaker modified her speech in the four examples above. Use Hatch's list of the characteristics of simplified input (Table 3.1) to analyze what the speaker did each time. Also, reflect on how the learner actually signaled a comprehension problem. Did all learners use the same devices to get the speakers to modify their language? What kinds of devices or phrases might you teach learners early on to help them negotiate comprehension and, thus, the input they receive? Make a list of at least five phrases that your learners would find useful.

INPUT AND THE CLASSROOM

Many beginning instructors (and even some experienced instructors!) who have not been in communicative classes frequently ask, "But how can you use the language with beginning learners. They can't understand anything!" Indeed, this belief is reflected in some of the research on foreign language classrooms in the United States. In one study, for example, Wing (1987) found that the average instructor used the second language about 50% of the time in a second-year high school class. Of that 50%, only about half of the language was communicative in nature. That is, only about a quarter of _teacher talk_ (the specialized input that instructors often use with beginners) could be considered meaning-bearing input. And much of this was language used to solicit or confirm the speech of learners in the class ("Enrique, do number 3, please." "Good." "Excellent!"). In short, it was language used to manage the classroom exercises. To the extent that Wing's subjects represent instructors in general, learners may not be getting much comprehensible meaning-bearing input during class time in the early stages. If the class period is forty minutes long, then learners are at best getting approximately ten minutes of comprehensible input a day. And given the restricted range of language functions exhibited by the instructors in Wing's study, the input might not be very broad in terms of the linguistic data it contains.

The belief that beginning learners cannot understand anything is simply that—a belief. Imagine what life would be like if parents believed the same thing about their one-year-olds: no one would ever acquire language! There are, however, instructors for whom talking to beginning language learners is as natural as talking to a baby. These instructors may or may not be consciously aware of Hatch's and Larsen-Freeman's descriptions of simplified input; they simplify their language as a natural part of trying to make themselves understood. How do they do this? These instructors first make use of as many _nonlinguistic means_ as possible to make themselves understood. They use drawings, photos, diagrams, objects, gestures, and other visual aids to accompany their speech. These nonlinguistic means serve to anchor the input in the "here and now"; that is, they provide a mechanism for making the subject of conversation _concrete rather than abstract._

In the following example, a first-semester language instructor points, uses gestures, and draws on the blackboard. All these actions (indicated with all-capital letters) facilitate learner comprehension. Not indicated are the pauses, use of stress, slower articulation, and other strategies that would also form an important part of the spoken version of what you are about to read. As you read it over, you should consider what you would sound like if you were the instructor. What words would you emphasize with added stress? How long would your pauses be?

> Instructor: Let's draw a face. This is a face. [POINTS TO HER OWN FACE AND MAKES A CIRCLE AROUND IT WITH FINGER.] Let's draw a face, O.K.? [DRAWS AN OVAL ON THE BLACKBOARD.] You draw a face on your paper, too. Go ahead. Draw an oval to begin the face. [POINTS TO PAPERS AND MAKES AN OVAL MOTION WITH FINGERS.] Good. That's the first part of the face. The most important features on a face are the eyes. The eyes. [POINTS TO HER OWN EYES.] Eyes are very important. With eyes we see the world. Eyes are also the first thing someone sees on your face. What kind of eyes shall we put on this face? Big eyes? [MOTIONS BIG WITH HANDS.] Or little eyes? [GESTURES WITH HANDS.] Let's give this face two big eyes. [DRAWS EYES ON THE BOARD.] You draw two big eyes on your paper, too.

In addition to nonlinguistic means, language instructors who use a good deal of the second language in the classroom exhibit another trait: they tend to focus on topics that the learners already know something about. Such "high-input-giving" instructors tend to put learners into *familiar situations* (drawing a face, playing a card game) so that learners can make use of what they know about the real world in order to comprehend better. For example, an instructor might talk about his dog, drawing on the fact that learners already know certain things about dogs and dog behavior: they bark, wag their tails, have four feet, and so on. This instructor expects that learners' background knowledge will help them anticipate vocabulary and topics that he, the instructor, is talking about. In hearing about dogs, for example, learners would not expect the instructor to talk about milking, feeding them hay, or riding them. The instructor knows that learners will rule out a whole set of possible topics and words because of what they know about dogs. Using familiar themes and situations, good instructors allow their learners to process for language alone and do not push them to struggle with the topic itself. Imagine a first-semester Japanese course in which the instructor talked about particle physics! Just what background knowledge would the non-physics student be able to draw on in order to comprehend the message? (In Chapter 10 we explore making use of learners' background knowledge in further detail as it relates to reading comprehension.)

In short, good high-input-giving instructors follow the advice that Brown has given to parents:

> Believe that your child can understand more than he or she can say, and seek, above all, to communicate . . . . There is no set of rules of how to talk to a child that can even approach what you unconsciously

know. If you concentrate on communicating, everything else will follow. (Brown 1977, as cited in Krashen 1982, p. 65)

Let's turn to another example of teacher input, from an introductory
Spanish lesson on vocabulary related to family. In introducing the new vocabulary, the instructor chose to tell the class about his own family. The instructor's purpose then was both *didactic* and *communicative*. It was didactic because the instructor was actually presenting vocabulary related to the family,
and it was communicative because he was also attempting to have his class
understand as much about his own family as possible. As you read the description, note what the instructor does to make himself comprehensible. Also
ask yourself at what point in the course of study this presentation might have
occurred. As in the case of the face-drawing episode presented earlier, the following example is a sterilized presentation of input. False starts, stops, learner
clarification requests, and other interruptions are omitted for presentation
here. (We give an English translation here; the original teacher input was, of
course, in Spanish.)

Today we are going to talk about my family. I have a most interesting
family. (*Displays* "My Family" *chart on board or overhead.*) Here is me.
These are my parents. This is my father and this is my mother. Father
. . . mother. My father's name is Bill. My mother's name is Juanita.
They are divorced. This is my stepfather, Joe. My stepfather. And this
is my sister . . . my only sister. Her name is Gloria. (*Turns off the overhead or covers visual.*)

Let's see what kind of memory you have. What is my father's
name—Joe or Bill? (*responses*) What is my mother's name—Juanita or
Gloria? (*responses*) Right. Gloria is my sister, not my mother. And do I
have any brothers? (*responses*) No. (*Shows visual again.*) All right, to
summarize, my family consists of my father, Bill, my mother, Juanita,
and my sister, Gloria. I have no brothers. Oh, I also have a stepfather,
Joe. My parents have been divorced since 1972. (*Writes date on board.*)
Now, that was easy, but here are some other family members. (*Now reveals grandparents.*)

These are my grandparents. My grandparents. These are my maternal grandparents and these are my paternal grandparents. This
man here, Dick, is my paternal grandfather. And this woman, Bridgette, is my paternal grandmother. Grandfather . . . grandmother.
But Bridgette passed away many years ago; Bridgette is dead. (*Points
to tombstone.*) These are my maternal grandparents. Domingo is my
paternal grandfather . . . and Concepción is my maternal grandmother. Domingo passed away in 1985; Domingo is dead. Just to review, Dick and Bridgette are my paternal grandparents, and Domingo
and Concepción are my maternal grandparents. Grandfather . . .
grandfather . . . grandmother . . . grandmother. Both Bridgette and
Domingo are dead. By the way, Dick lives in Indiana and Concepción
lives in California. (*Removes or covers visual.*)

Ready for a real memory test? (*Shows new overhead, or distributes
ditto.*) In the left column are names; in the right column are relation-

ships. You have two minutes to match the name to a relationship. (*After two minutes, teacher calls time and quiz is reviewed with original drawing exposed; teacher engages in some light conversation in which students answer with one word, "yes/no" responses, such as, "Did you know that I was half Mexican? How does your family compare to mine—do you have more brothers and sisters?"*)

Now, here is the real interesting part. (*Reveals visual of extended family with aunts and uncles, some cousins, and so on. Instructor continues presentation using same format as before.*) (VanPatten 1991, pp. 59–60)

Many beginning instructors think that this scene must have taken place in the second semester or late in the year. In actuality, this lesson on family occurred during the first week of instruction! What makes the input comprehensible? The visual display of the family tree establishes the topic, and learners then know that the instructor is talking about family. This instructor thus draws on the background knowledge of the class in order to facilitate comprehension. By locating himself first in the family tree, learners know that the other people are his relatives. Learners are thus engaged in matching names to relationships: Juanita = mother, Gloria = sister. Thus, they are engaged in the didactic aspect of the lesson as mentioned earlier, that is, vocabulary acquisition. But note at the same time that they are processing far more than vocabulary related to family. As part of their attempt to comprehend, they may be picking up certain phrases such as "name is", "my _____", "I have _____" and they may be starting the process of acquiring gender markings on nouns and adjectives. Instructors who use the second language to teach vocabulary expose the learner to much more language—and provide richer input—than merely the vocabulary of the lesson.

*P*ause to consider . . .

the nature of the simplified input in the above interchange. After reviewing Larsen-Freeman's and Hatch's descriptions of simplified input to language learners, determine which aspects of simplification this instructor seemed to do naturally. See if you can find the following:
   1. lack of contractions
   2. repetitions
   3. reformulations of an utterance (i.e., saying one thing in various ways)
   4. simple syntax (i.e., sentence structure)
   5. frequent and/or "concrete" vocabulary
   6. comprehension checks (e.g., "Do you follow?" "Are you with me?")

To be sure, the second language learners in the above two examples may not be understanding every word their instructors utter. It would be surprising if they were! Instead, learners are most likely catching bits and pieces of the language. In the very beginning stages, they may catch only content words and repeated chunks or formulas ("I have _____," "name is," "Draw a _____," "Who is _____?"). Most likely the learners are not attending to certain grammatical features of the language, such as articles and case endings, as they concentrate on getting the message. Some learners, however, may notice verb endings, noun endings, and other features early on, but these are the exceptional learners. Or, these learners might notice that endings vary, but they are unable to pick up on the systematic nature of the variation. With time, however, learners are able to comprehend the input with greater ease. Ease of comprehension brings with it a greater likelihood that learners will attend to grammatical features in the input that they missed previously, a topic that we discuss in Chapter 5.

INPUT AND VOCABULARY

We have presented comprehensible input as it relates to language acquisition in general. That is, we have not referred to specific aspects or features of a language that learners acquire through input and interaction. In Chapters 5 and 6, we describe how learners acquire grammar through input and interaction. But to prepare the stage for those concepts, we turn now to the acquisition of vocabulary through input and interaction. Can you cite specific instances in your own language development where you acquired words from the contexts in which they were used?

Vocabulary Lists and Visuals

If you think back to one of your beginning language classes, you probably had a textbook with vocabulary lists. The vocabulary may have been presented in bilingual lists as in the following example from a French book:

la maison	the house
la chambre	the room
la cuisine	the kitchen
le boudoir	the bedroom
la salle de bain	the bathroom
les muebles	furniture
la chaise	the chair
le lit	the bed

Very often such lists suggest to learners that vocabulary acquisition is a matter of memorizing second language equivalents of first language words. Some textbooks even have study hints for learning vocabulary and recommend that learners make flashcards with the second language word on one side and the first language word on the other. Other study hints include covering the first language side of the list with a piece of paper and giving the first language equivalent of each second language word. Or, it is suggested that one cover the second language side of the list and give the second language equivalent of each first language word. While these study hints can be helpful for the specific purpose of studying for a test in which one may have to give first or second language equivalencies, these types of practice are no substitute for meaning-bearing comprehensible input in learning vocabulary.

We saw in the previous section a vocabulary lesson that was built around an attempt to communicate about one person's family. The vocabulary was initially presented and practiced with significant comprehensible input. Learners actively attended to the teacher's input for its meaning and were learning words during the process. Many professionals advocate the introduction and learning of vocabulary via comprehensible input whether they call it "vocabulary learning" or not. Krashen and Terrell, for example, advocate the use of topics around which input activities can be developed. The following list of selected topics form natural vocabulary groups; you can think of others as you read the list.

description of students

clothing

colors

objects in the classroom

favorite activities

sports and games

climate and seasons

weather

seasonal activities

holiday activities

family and relatives

physical states

emotional states

daily activities

holiday and vacation activities

pets

(adapted from Krashen and Terrell 1983, pp. 67–68)

Most textbooks have similar vocabulary groups. Some still make use of bilingual lists, but others have moved toward the use of visuals (drawings, photographs, cartoons) to present vocabulary. In Figure 3.1, German vocabulary words related to clothing are accompanied not by English translations but by drawings. As learners study vocabulary in this way, they are encouraged to make direct form-meaning connections similar to those that they would make if the vocabulary were presented within the context of comprehensible, meaning-bearing input. Terrell refers to the process of making direct form-meaning connections as *binding*.

Binding is the term I propose to describe the cognitive and affective mental process of linking a meaning to a form. The concept of binding

FIGURE 3.1. Presentation of German Clothing Vocabulary in a Contemporary German Textbook.

> is what language teachers refer to when they insist that a new word ultimately be associated directly with its meaning and not with a translation. (Terrell 1986, p. 214)

How can we encourage binding during vocabulary acquisition? We have already explored the nature of simplified or modified input and the use of visuals as means by which instructors can make input comprehensible. These can also be used to encourage binding of vocabulary: we saw how visuals such as photos and drawings "anchor" the input in the here-and-now, making the idea and references to it more concrete. As one more example of binding new vocabulary, the instructor in the following classroom excerpt uses photos to introduce vocabulary related to clothing. Her speech is anchored in the here-and-now because both she and the learners have the concrete reference of the photo before them; this photo serves as the common ground between them. The italicized information in brackets represents the instructor's or students' actions while the nonitalicized information represents what learners say.

> Look at this picture. What do you see? A woman? [Yes.] Yes, that's right. There is a woman in the picture. [*The instructor points to the hat.*] What is this? [*Learners shake heads, indicating they don't know.*] This is a hat. This picture of the woman who is wearing the hat is for Yvonne. O.K.? Now, who has the picture of the woman who is wearing the hat? [*Yvonne.*] Good. Now here is another picture. Is this a man or a woman in the picture? [*A man.*] Right. Yvonne has a picture of a woman with a hat, but this is a picture of a man. Is he wearing a hat? [*No.*] Right. He's not wearing a hat. What is he wearing? Well, he's wearing a suit. [*Instructor points to suit.*] This is a grey suit. And he's also wearing a tie. [*Instructor points.*] So, this man is wearing a suit and a tie. Let's give this photo to Dave. Now, who has the picture of the man in the suit and tie? [*Dave.*] And who has the picture of the woman with the hat? [*Yvonne.*] Does the man with the suit also have

on a hat? [*No.*] Does the woman have on a tie? [*No.*] Here's another photo. This woman is wearing a blouse and pants . . .

(adapted from Terrell 1991)

But anchoring input is not limited to visuals. In the remainder of this chapter, we examine some other ways in which instructors can anchor their speech in the here-and-now to promote vocabulary acquisition.

Using Learners and the Classroom

The classroom is rich in resources for teaching common vocabulary. Indeed, instructors can make use of learners, their features, and their belongings to teach vocabulary. Involving learners heightens attention and adds a personal element to the class as learners become active participants in the teaching process. The following is an example of an instructor using learners in the classroom to teach the vocabulary associated with physical descriptions.

> [*Instructor points to a learner.*] What is your name? [Barbara.] Barbara, come here please. [*Gestures to Barbara to approach.*] That's right, come here. [*Barbara approaches.*] Good. Thank you. Class, look at Barbara. She has long, brown hair. [*Instructor points and gestures to assist comprehension.*] Her hair is long and brown. Her hair is not short, it is long. What is the name of the person with long brown hair? [Barbara.] Now, let's see. What's your name? [Sharon.] OK, Sharon, please come here. [*Sharon approaches.*] Class, look at Sharon. She has short blond hair. Her hair is not long, it is short. [*Gestures "long" and "short" with palms facing each other as he moves them close to each other or away from each other.*] It is not brown, it is blond. What is the name of the person with short blond hair? [Sharon.] Right. And what is the name of the person with long brown hair? [Barbara.] Right again. Now, what's your name? [Steve.] Come here, please. Class, this is Steve. Look at Steve's hair. Is it blond? [No.] Is it brown? [Yes.] Then Steve has hair like Barbara's. But is it long? [No.] Is it short? [Yes.] Then Steve has hair like Sharon's. He has the same color hair as Barbara. But he has the same length [*gestures in an up and down motion with palms facing each other*] of hair as Sharon. The color is brown. The length is short.
>
> (adapted and expanded from Krashen and Terrell 1983, p. 76)

Pause to consider . . .

the roles of instructor and learners in the classroom during these initial input activities. At first glance, the presentations may seem Atlas-like since the teacher is shouldering the burden of communication and is doing all the work. But is this so? Are the learners mere receptacles? What are the instructors doing to keep the learners active and attentive during the lesson? What distinguishes what learners are doing during these activities from what they would do during a drill?

Total Physical Response ⟵

Another technique for providing input that has actually been formalized as a method is *Total Physical Response*, generally referred to by practitioners as TPR. Developed by James Asher of San Jose State University, TPR in its simplest terms refers to learners carrying out the actions commanded by the instructor. The instructor first performs the actions while learners listen and watch. Then the learners perform the same actions with the instructor. The instructor subsequently "tests" the binding of the commands by stopping her simultaneous performance of the command and allowing learners to do it as a group on their own. For example, on the very first day of class an instructor might begin with the following. (Italicized words are in the second language; nonitalicized words are in the native language. The information in parentheses indicates the physical action(s) occurring.)

In this class, you are going to learn language by performing actions based on my commands. To help you learn the commands, I will say them and demonstrate each one. You will then act out the action with me. Ready?

> *Stand up.* (Instructor stands up.)
> *Sit down.* (Instructor sits down.)
> *Stand up.* (Instructor stands up.)
> *Sit down.* (Instructor sits down.)
> Now do it with me. *Stand up.* (Instructor and class stand up.)
> *Sit down.* (Instructor and class sit down.)
> *Stand up.* (Instructor and class stand up.)
> *Sit down.* (Instructor and class sit down.)
> Watch and listen again.
> *Stand up. Walk to the blackboard. Walk to your seat. Sit down.* (Instructor acts each out as she says it.)
> *Stand up. Walk to the blackboard. Walk to your seat. Sit down.* (Instructor acts each out as she says it.)
> Now do it with me. *Stand up. Walk to the blackboard. Walk to your seat. Sit down.* (Instructor and learners act each out as she says it.)
> *Stand up. Walk to the blackboard. Walk to your seat. Sit down.* (Instructor and learners act each out as she says it.)
> Robert, you try it. *Stand up.* (Robert stands up while teacher simply stands to the side.) *Sit down.* (Robert sits down.) *Stand up.* (Robert stands up.) *Walk to the blackboard.* (Robert walks to the blackboard.) *Walk to your seat.* (Robert walks to his seat.)
> *Sit down.* (Robert sits down.)
> *Excellent.* Who else wants to try? (Instructor does this again with another learner.)
> Now, watch and listen again. *Stand up. Walk to the blackboard. Touch the blackboard. Walk to your seat. Touch your seat. Sit down.* (Instructor acts each out as she says it.)
> [The activity continues as above.]

Correct performance of the actions demonstrates learners' comprehension. If a learner makes an error (performs the wrong action) or hesitates, the instructor simply repeats the command, acts it out again, or gives some other clue to the learner. Note that TPR qualifies as both meaning bearing and comprehensible. It is meaning bearing because the input contains a message and comprehensible because the instructor demonstrates the actions. The instructor's own actions, then, serve a similar function to the drawings, photos, and other visual aids mentioned previously. Very quickly, learners begin to make the connections between what is said and what they are supposed to do. It is also worth noting that TPR contains many of the characteristics of simplified input discussed earlier in this chapter: shorter sentences, pauses, concrete vocabulary. Many instructors find TPR an ideal way to introduce vocabulary once learners know the commands "show," "take," "touch," "hide," "draw," "give," and "pick up." A great deal of vocabulary can be introduced during the course of 30 minutes! As instructors introduce vocabulary with objects and/or visuals, they can instruct learners to carry out the following actions:

> Hide the picture of the house.
> Walk to the drawing of an apartment.
> Give the brown dog to Emily.
> Draw a tree on the board.
> Pick up the history book and give it to Robert.
> Pick up the math book and show it to the class.

In a lesson on body parts, an instructor might ask learners to manipulate photos of various body parts. With the photos arranged in the chalktray and on his desk, he could call learners to the front of the class and gave them commands such as:

> Put the photo of the nose on top of the photo of the mouth.
> Take the two ears and put them on top of the eyebrows.

The instructor might subsequently have the class "build a face" on the blackboard. With tape added to the back of the visuals, he might tell learners:

> Robert, put a nose on the board.
> Now, Jane, put a mouth on the board.
> Stan, select an ear and place it on the board.

and so on until the class completed a somewhat Picasso-like face and head.

---

*P*ause to consider . . .

the importance of visuals in language instruction. Why is it a good idea for beginning instructors to start a "picture file"? (A picture file is a file of photos from magazines that have been cut and mounted onto construction paper.) What are the qualities of "good" visuals for the language classroom? How large should a picture be? Should it be simple and straightforward or contain a complex scene? Why do some consider the overhead projector to be a language instructor's best friend?

Inexperienced instructors often see TPR as consisting of only simple commands. But as learners progress, the instructor can combine commands and declarative statements, thus increasing the quality of the input that learners receive. For example, after several days of TPR, instructors can push their learners into comprehending "if-then" statements by simply giving the second language equivalents for *if, but,* and *then* and then giving commands of the following type: "If Susan walks to the blackboard, then stand up. But if she walks to the door, just raise your hand."

Vocabulary Activities

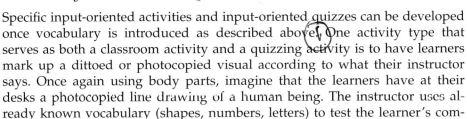

Specific input-oriented activities and input-oriented quizzes can be developed once vocabulary is introduced as described above. One activity type that serves as both a classroom activity and a quizzing activity is to have learners mark up a dittoed or photocopied visual according to what their instructor says. Once again using body parts, imagine that the learners have at their desks a photocopied line drawing of a human being. The instructor uses already known vocabulary (shapes, numbers, letters) to test the learner's comprehension of body parts in context.

1. Draw a circle around the nose.
2. Write the number 15 on the left eye and the number 14 on the right eye.
3. Place an X over the mouth.

If learners already know colors, then they could be given crayons or colored pencils and told to:

1. Color the eyes red.
2. Color the left ear blue and the right ear green.

1. Learners could play games such as Bingo, using cards with body parts rather than numbers (each card would be slightly different). The instructor would reach into a bag and pull out the name of a body part and read it. Students would place a marker on each body part and the first learner to obtain a row of body parts vertically, horizontally, or diagonally would win.

2. Another type of input activity requires visualization. Learners are given crayons and colored pencils for drawing. They then close their eyes and listen to a brief description that uses current vocabulary. As they listen, they should develop a mental picture of what is described. Once the description is complete, they open their eyes and draw. Visualization activities could be used for vocabulary such as physical descriptions, clothing, weather, family members and relatives, physical states, and emotional states. Following is an example of one such visualizing activity used as an end-of-class quiz. It uses vocabulary related to rooms and furniture.

> I am going to describe a room in a house. I want you to close your eyes and listen. Try to picture the house in your mind. Visualize it as I describe it. After I complete the description, you will draw it! Ready? O.K., close your eyes. Now listen carefully—and visualize the room. [*The instructor lowers her voice and speaks slowly and dramatically, using many pauses.*] This is a living room. Not a

kitchen, not a bedroom, and not a dining room, but a living room. This room has two large windows. Through the windows you can see some trees. Between the two windows is a small green sofa. Above the small green sofa is a painting. It is a painting of a woman. To the left of the sofa is a chair. It is a large chair. The chair is blue and green. Next to the chair is a small round table. The small round table is made of wood.

Some textbooks have begun to incorporate input-oriented work as part of the initial vocabulary presentation, making the first-time instructor's task a bit easier if her goal is to provide as much input as possible. Activities include matching (vocabulary-visuals, vocabulary-statements, vocabulary-definitions), true-false (likely-unlikely, possible-impossible), and others. As an example, the following textbook activity uses vocabulary related to moods and feelings (*happy, sad, bored, tired*). Learners first glance over the expressions in their textbooks as the instructor pronounces them. Then they complete the subsequent matching activity.

Following is a list of thoughts that Claudia [the person in the visual display of emotions and feelings] had during the three days described above. Match each feeling your instructor mentions to one of Claudia's thoughts.

> MODEL: INSTRUCTOR: She's nervous.
>   CLASS: That goes with number 2.

1. "I would like to sleep ten hours tonight!"
2. "Gee whiz! I only have four hours left to study. I'm gonna fail!"
3. "They are going to think I'm dumb."
4. "Didn't this prof learn about public speaking? How monotonous."
5. "Yippee! I got an A! I got an A!"

[Instructor reads: She's very happy.
She feels embarrassed.
She's nervous.
She's tired.
She's bored.]

A related input-oriented activity would be the following, in which the instructor states a mood or emotion about typical students and the learners select the reason for that mood.

Your instructor will read some moods that are common among students. Choose the activity that might cause that mood in the typical student.

1. **a.** He is studying in the library.
   b. He has three exams today.
   c. He slept fine last night.

2. **a.** She has to study but a roommate is playing the stereo loud.
   b. She received a letter from a good friend this morning.
   c. She is going shopping after class.

3. **a.** He is attending classes.
   b. He is going to the cafeteria to eat.
   c. He won $1,000,000 in the lottery.

4. **a.** She is going to a party with some friends.
   b. She ate in a great restaurant last night.
   c. She got an F on a test.

[*Instructor reads:* 1. The student is very tense. 2. The student is upset. 3. The student is happy. 4. The student is depressed.]

---

*P*ause to consider . . .

. . . using the previous five examples of activities as tasks on a short vocabulary quiz. Are they equal in difficulty? For example, how does the task of coloring body parts compare in difficulty to the activity in which a learner has to visualize and then draw a room? How do both compare, say, to the activity about students' moods and their possible causes? If these tasks are not equal in difficulty, how would you determine point value and assign a grade to each?

SUMMARY

We have explored a number of issues related to comprehensible input and second language teaching. First, we saw that the necessary characteristics of good input are that it be

1. meaning bearing (it carries a message that the learner attends to) and
2. comprehensible

In both first and second language acquisition, people who speak to learners modify their speech in certain ways to facilitate learner comprehension. Learners, when actively engaged in attempting to comprehend, can get their interlocutors to make modifications in what they said. These modifications include simplification of vocabulary and syntax, reduction of speed, increased use of pauses, shorter sentences, repetition and rephrasing, and others. These modifications enable learners to attend to form-meaning connections in the input, which in turn translates into better acquisition. In short, it is not native-like discourse that fuels acquisition in the early stages but rather discourse that is tailored to the learner. This tailoring may adjust over time as the learner builds up a linguistic system and becomes increasingly skilled in comprehension.

We also explored examples of teacher talk in classrooms, showing how some instructors provide comprehensible input in large doses to their learners. Focusing on the here-and-now, anchoring the input in topics with which learners are familiar, using visuals, and drawing on the board, these instructors provide classroom learners with the kind of high-octane input their internal mechanisms need in order to succeed in language acquisition. These instructors are providing opportunities for binding to take place.

Finally, we examined some specific uses of comprehensible, meaning-bearing input in the teaching of vocabulary: visuals, Total Physical Response, visualization techniques, and matching activities. These activities are also easily adaptable for quizzing in an input format, thus linking instructional techniques with testing techniques.

It is important to remember that vocabulary acquisition is not the only critical use of input. In this chapter, we have seen various examples of input useful for vocabulary acquisition, and it would be easy to infer that input provision equals vocabulary acquisition. But it should be clear that comprehensible meaning-bearing input is crucial for *all* domains of language: syntax, verbal morphology, nominal morphology, pronunciation, and semantics, in addition to vocabulary. In Chapter 5, we explore in detail the relationship of input to the acquisition of grammar. For now, you should understand that, while learners are reaping the benefits of vocabulary acquisition from the input they are exposed to, they are also acquiring grammar.

KEY TERMS, CONCEPTS, AND ISSUES

input *gas in a car / key to acquisition / most of it*
  comprehensible *The learner must understand most of it to be attended to*
  meaning bearing *must contain a message*
  simplified *To be comprehensible / below native speaker standards*
expansions in adult-child interactions *To compare the current state of child's language*
simplified input in second language acquisition *beneficial, easier to process, more salient*
  linguistic characteristics *slow rate, vocabulary, simple syntax, discourse, repetition features*
intake *The part of input that is processed and "sticks"*
learner negotiation of input *control of flow of input when engaged in interaction*
  interaction *communicational, signals and asking for clarification/repetition*
how to make input comprehensible in the classroom *non linguistic, previous learning*
  nonlinguistic aids *visual, realia*
    concrete versus abstract referent *here and now, aids*
  familiar topics *such as family*
  familiar situations *such as the student can relate to*
binding in vocabulary acquisition *making direct form meaning connection*
form-meaning connections *binding / better acquisitional process*
  direct versus indirect *visuals better*
    bilingual lists *not good, memorizing*
    visuals *connection*
TPR *Total physical responses*
activities and quizzes *input oriented*
  drawing
  games
  visualization *non linguistic responses, negotiation of meaning*
  matching

EXPLORING THE TOPICS FURTHER

1. *The role of input in language acquisition.* For discussions of input in the second language context, see Hatch (1978a) and Krashen (1982). Ellis (1986: Chapter 6) presents a very nice overview of input and interaction in both classroom and nonclassroom contexts. For a good research and theoretical perspective on comprehensible input, the book by Larsen-Freeman and Long (1991, Chapter 5) is useful. For those wishing to understand comprehension-based approaches to instruction (that is, curricula in which language teaching is largely that of providing comprehensible input to learners), see Winitz (1981).

2. *Input-oriented activities.* You might wish to examine textbooks that have an input orientation. The Terrell books for Spanish (*Dos mundos*), French (*Deux mondes*), and German (*Kontakte*) offer many examples, especially in the introductory chapters, which incorporate the technique of Total Physical Response. *¿Sabías que...?* (VanPatten et al. 1992) and *Il Carciofo* (Musumeci 1990) also feature input-oriented activities. VanPatten (1991) offers suggestions for intermediate- and advanced-stage input-oriented activities in addition to the early-stage activities presented in this chapter. This essay also gives a global perspective on input within a language curriculum.

Listening Comprehension

lis-ten (lĭs´-ən) v. 1. *to apply oneself to hearing something.* 2. *to pay attention; give heed.*

American Heritage Dictionary

INTRODUCTION

[handwritten note: Yesterday was the day of the world's worst terroist attack. (Sept. 11)]

Sit back and think about yesterday and all the things you did. In how many situations were your first language listening skills called upon? Did you have conversations with friends, colleagues, and other people? Did you conduct any business transactions (at the bank, in a store, over the phone)? Did you watch TV? Go to the movies? Play a game with someone? In any of these situations, did you have to ask someone to repeat something said? Did your mind wander and did you have to say "I'm sorry. Could you say that again?"

Now think about listening in your second language. Do you have days during which you perform the same listening tasks you reflected upon above? Do you always understand everything you hear in the second language? What factors make your listening in a second language as easy as, or more difficult than, listening in your first language?

In this chapter, we explore various aspects of listening comprehension as it relates to skill development. Whereas in the previous chapter we examined the use of comprehensible input for acquisition in the classroom, here we focus on listening as communication. We briefly describe the nature of listening as a psycholinguistic process and follow this with a discussion of listening as a communicative act. We then focus on listening tasks in the classroom and language laboratory. We conclude with an examination of issues related to testing listening comprehension in a second language.

LISTENING AS A PSYCHOLINGUISTIC PROCESS

[handwritten note: Not true]

Listening, like reading, has often been referred to as a "passive" or "receptive" skill. These terms stand in contrast to "active" or "productive," used to refer to speaking and writing skills. The term *passive* is an unfortunate one for it suggests that the listener is a mere bystander during communication, a submis-

59

sive individual, unable to act, who does not participate and merely accepts whatever is thrown her way. Despite the persistence of the terms *passive* and *receptive* for listening skills, scholars agree that listeners are active participants during the communicative act and that listening is a dynamic process drawing on a variety of mental processes and knowledge sources. Wolvin and Coakley (1985) divide the act of listening into three very broad sets of processes:

1. perceiving aural stimuli
2. attending to aural stimuli
3. assigning meaning to aural stimuli

At each step of the way, learners are actively engaged in processing what they hear. We now examine each set of processes in turn, spending most of our time on the third.

 Perception of aural stimuli refers to the physiological aspects of listening. Sound waves enter the ear canal, causing the ear drum to vibrate. These vibrations are converted into electrical impulses that trigger the release of chemicals, which in turn react with what is called the acoustic nerve (analogous to the optic nerve in vision), which transmits a signal to the brain. Clearly, the ear drum must be a sensitive organ, sending the vibrations and electrical impulses that represent the differences between *ship* and *sheep*, *cad* and *cat*, and *talk* and *talked* correctly to the brain. Perception, then, is a necessary aspect of listening comprehension, but it cannot be equated with it.

Attending to aural stimuli involves active concentration by the listener. The listener must be focused on the aural stimuli and must select what to pay attention to and what to disregard. At any given moment, a listener could be talking on the phone with the TV or radio on, birds singing in the trees, children playing and screaming in the backyard, and cars zooming down the street. If the purpose is to carry on the phone conversation, the listener must tune out the background noises and attend only to the incoming sounds on the telephone in order to be successful. This ability suggests that we all have some internal mechanisms responsible for filtering incoming stimuli; we can (and do) perceive all the sounds around us, but we attend only to some of them. Like perception, however, attending to stimuli is a necessary aspect of listening but, by itself, not a sufficient one.

Once stimuli are attended to, they must be assigned meaning. For the present discussion, this is perhaps the most important set of processes in listening for comprehension. Interestingly, assigning meaning is not a straightforward phenomenon and is perhaps trickier than perception and attention. Why is this so? *Assigning meaning to perceived and attended stimuli* is an interpretative act that involves personal, cultural, and linguistic matters interacting in complex ways. The word *run*, for example, can mean one of the following (and perhaps more):

1. a fast, forward movement involving the legs
2. nose dripping
3. the act of seeking a political office
4. not turning something off (e.g., He left the water running.)
5. a snag in a pair of pantyhose
6. massive sales (e.g., We have a run on size 8 shoes. They're all gone.)

7. a trip (e.g., making a run to Chicago)
8. a race

But the likelihood of a listener misassigning meaning to the word *run* is greatly diminished if the word is used as a noun instead of a verb; if the speaker is a truck driver rather than a political pundit; if the occurrence of the word happens as part of the development of a single topic; or if the speaker and listener share the same cultural and personal backgrounds.

However, assigning meaning is not limited to the word level. Whole sentences must be interpreted, and sometimes individual words can be assigned meaning only after the entire sentence has been heard. Richards (1983) outlines the complex nature of assigning meaning to attended aural stimuli in six steps:

1. the speech event or interactional set is determined (e.g., this is a lecture, this is a debate, this is an interrogation, this is a job interview)
2. scripts (episodic prototypes) relevant to the situation or context are recalled (i.e., the listener brings forth a master scheme of how the interaction or set is to play out and what kind of language will be used)
3. the speaker's goals are determined by way of the situation, the script, and the position of the utterance in the flow of discourse (e.g., during an interview a listener might determine that at this point the speaker is trying to find out about his experience)
4. the propositional or referential content of the speaker's utterance is determined
5. an illocutionary meaning is assigned to the speaker's utterance (e.g., that utterance was a compliment, that utterance was a request, that utterance was a slur)
6. the meaning is retained and acted upon but the actual form in which it was encoded by the speaker (and received by the listener) may not be remembered (e.g., the listener may say "39" but not subsequently remember whether the question was "How old are you?" "What is your age?" "And your age?" "Please state your age," and, when reporting the conversation later, may say that the person asked him how old he was)

As an example of how this complex act of listening occurs, let's take an example from a TV commercial for Taco Bell. First, we determine the situation: this is a commercial on TV. We then call forth from our memory similar TV commercial scripts ("They're going to show me something. They're going to have a catchy line. They may have a cute song, and the whole thing will last ten seconds or so."), and we determine the goal ("They want me to like their food. They want to sell me on their tacos."). We catch the zingy line (*"Make a run for the border!"*) and assign referential meaning to it. Finally, we assign the line its illocutionary meaning ("Even though the utterance is a command form, they do not really expect me to hop in my car and drive to El Paso/Ciudad Juarez. This line is a metaphor.").

It is interesting that, although speakers might share a common culture and language that direct them to assign particular meanings to particular streams of speech, this is no guarantee that they will always assign the *same* illocutionary meanings to utterances they hear in conversations. Because of personal and individual psychological makeup, what is understood as a compliment by one person might be seen as a snide remark by another. What is interpreted as a mere suggestion or opinion by someone might be interpreted as a command by someone else. Thus, meaning assignment during listening is not as purely linguistic act or even a social act; it can also be an individual act.

Assigning meaning to aural stimuli can also involve the construction of meaning even though something specific was not said. This is called *inference*. We "infer" whenever we project beyond the referential meaning encoded in someone's utterance. Assigning illocutionary meaning to an utterance is a type of inference, but one can also infer meaning *when no utterance was uttered*. Note the following interchange.

A: Are you free this evening?
 B: What time?
A: 8:00.
 B: Pick me up at 7:45.

Now compare it to an expanded version.

A: Are you free this evening? I'd like us to go out.
 B: It depends when. What time do you have in mind?
A: 8:00. Is that O.K.?
 B: 8:00 is fine. Pick me up at 7:45.

In the first version, both speakers are projecting beyond the concrete referents of their utterances. B knows that A is asking for a date even though A never uses the words *date* or *go out*. A knows that B has accepted in the end even though B has not said *I accept, Yes I will go out with you*, or any other response. Such things were simply inferred.

Inference for second language learners is as important as it is for first language speakers and can take on characteristics that do not normally occur during native-to-native interactions. One additional characteristic is that inference can actually include deducing meanings of novel or unfamiliar words and phrases, that is, inferring the referential meaning of words during the act of listening. In this case, the learner fills in lexical gaps based on contextual and pragmatic cues. In the conversational exchange we just saw, B says, "Pick me up." There are a variety of ways of saying this in colloquial English: *Come by, Swing by, Buzz by,* among others. Imagine the second language learner who hears *Swing by* or *Buzz by.* She very well might not be familiar with these expressions, but does that mean she cannot complete the act of setting up the

---

*P*ause to consider . . .

the kind of listening involved in "channel surfing." Can you describe channel surfing in terms of perceiving, attending, assigning meaning, and inferring? Are you equally able to channel surf in your second language?

date? The learner can infer the meaning of *swing by* or *buzz by* given the situation and the script already understood by both speakers for setting up a time to get together.

LISTENING AS COMMUNICATION

Although some people tend to equate communication with speaking, it is clear that a communicative act involves both expression and interpretation of meaning. In oral interactions, interpretation refers to listening as well as speaking, and in everyday life both native speakers and second language speakers engage in a variety of communicative situations during which they listen. Broadly speaking, there are two types of listening situations: *collaborative* and *noncollaborative*. Collaborative situations are those in which both speaker and listener work together to negotiate meaning. The listener actively collaborates in the construction of the discourse. Nodding, furrowing the brow, asking questions, commenting on what was said, adding to what was said, saying "Yeah, yeah" or "Huh!?"—all of these allow the listener to play an active role in shaping what the other speaker says and how she says it.

Noncollaborative situations are those in which the listener does not participate in the construction of discourse and is merely an observant listener. The speaker is the sole person who determines the nature of the discourse. Listening to a song is an example of noncollaborative listening, as is listening to the President's State of the Union Address.

Listening situations also fall along another dimension: *modality*, aural versus visual perception. Although it is true that listening involves aural stimuli, it is not the case that listening deals exclusively with the aural mode. In many, if not most cases, listeners *see* the other interlocutor and receive information on how to interpret messages via facial expressions, body posture, gestures, signs, slides, and other visual features. For example, students sitting in a large lecture hall listening to a professor's formal lecture might very well be attending to overhead transparencies, handouts, or other visual clues in addition to the visual cues provided by the professor. The opposite case would be a telephone conversation in which accompanying visual stimuli are absent (at least, until the time when pictaphones become the staple of every household and business): the modality here is aural only.

Thus, we can say that listening situations can be categorized according to two sets of features: the presence or absence of collaboration and the presence or absence of accompanying visual stimuli. This relationship is illustrated in Figure 4.1.

---

*P*ause to consider . . .

other listening examples. Can you add other situations to each of the boxes in Figure 4.1? To do so, review what listening you have done in the last week.

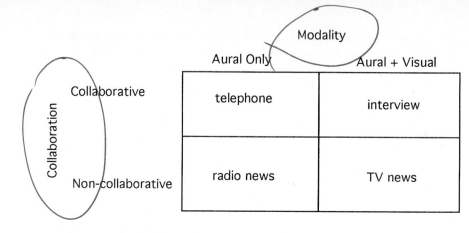

FIGURE 4.1. The Dimensions of a Listening Situation

*Strategies
may change*

Let us now consider listener performance. What strategies or tactics do skilled listeners use during communication? It seems intuitively obvious that strategies may change depending on the collaborative/noncollaborative nature of the situation. For collaborative situations, Rost summarizes a number of what he calls *"strategic responses* that constitute effective listener performance in collaborative discourse" (1990, p. 115). (Since a listener cannot interact with the speaker in a noncollaborative setting, there are no strategic responses to be discussed for the latter.) Rost lists eight skills and eleven strategic responses.

Skills

1. recognizing indicators used by the other speaker to (a) introduce new ideas, (b) change topics, (c) provide emphasis and/or clarification, or (d) express contrary points of view
2. maintaining continuity of context in order to assist the prediction and verification of propositions in the discourse
3. identifying an interpersonal frame that suggests what the speaker's intent is toward the listener
4. recognizing changes in prosody—pitch, speed, pauses—and identifying both patterns and inconsistencies in how the other speaker uses these
5. identifying ambiguity and contradictions in what the other speaker says; identifying places where inadequate information is given
6. distinguishing between fact and opinion; also, identifying uses of irony, metaphor, and other "non-referential" use of language
7. identifying needed clarifications of topics and ideas
8. providing appropriate feedback to the other speaker
(based on Rost 1990, p. 115)

Strategic Responses

Skilled listeners will . . .
1. try to identify points at which they can switch to the speaker role;

2. look for those places in the discourse where they are to participate in socially appropriate ways (i.e., listeners recognize those cues in which they should obligatorily take a turn at speaking);
3. provide appropriate cues to the speaker that they are following the discourse;
4. provide prompts to the speaker to continue the discourse;
5. provide cues to indicate how they align with the speaker's intent;
6. evaluate the speaker's contributions and reformulate them when they conflict with listener goals;
7. be aware of power asymmetries in the discourse and recognize when a "superior" party is enforcing interpretative rules;
8. identify a plausible speaker intent when interpreting an utterance;
9. afford recognition to the speaker's intent in participating in unequal encounters;
10. identify parts of discourse needing repair and query those points when appropriate;
11. utilize gambits (set phrases and other linguistic patterns that promote interaction) for checking understanding when appropriate.
(based on Rost 1990, p. 116)

What is clear from the above skills and strategic responses is the role that the listener plays in *maintaining the discourse*. The listener is not a bystander but a co-constructor of the discourse. The listener provides cues as to how well he understands and must signal the other speaker in various ways about how the topic is developing. Another important job of the listener is to signal nonunderstanding through global, local, and transitional queries (Rost 1990, p. 112). A *global query* functions at the broad level of the entire discourse: "I don't understand. Could you start from the beginning and speak a little more slowly?" "Do you want me to remember all of this? Should I take notes?" A *local query* identifies a particular point in the discourse that the listener has not understood and requests clarification of that point: "What do you mean by 'strategic response'?" and "Strategic response?" (with rising intonation) both signal that the listener has not understood a specific point. *Transitional queries* indicate difficulty with a hypothesis or prediction made by the listener. "Why did she do that?" and "I don't see the problem with that" are indications that the listener has understood but cannot integrate the information with previous knowledge or with predictions already made about the topic.

To summarize this discussion of listening as communication, we see that listening acts can vary along two major dimensions: type of collaboration and aural-visual modality. Listeners can be collaborative listeners during face-to-face interchanges and telephone conversations, or they can be noncollaborative listeners while listening to the radio. They can be engaged in aural-only situations (radio, telephone) or aural plus some other kind of visual stimulus (watching TV). In addition, we see that listeners are active (not passive) participants in the act of communication. Listeners must understand when to take on the role of speaker and add to the topic. They must understand when to confirm what they've heard and support the speaker's discourse, and they must know how to signal nonunderstanding to the other speaker. It goes

---

P*ause to consider . . .*

how conscious we are of our skills and strategies. Reread Rost's lists of skills and strategic responses. Do you think we engage these skills and strategies consciously or unconsciously? In other words, are these things we just do or are they things we have to think about and then do? Are you able to engage these skills and strategies equally in your first and second languages?

---

without saying that skilled listeners develop these abilities through communicative interaction itself and not through guided, manipulative practices. This is the focus of the remainder of this chapter, in which we examine ways to develop communicative listening skills.

LISTENING IN THE SECOND LANGUAGE CLASSROOM

What kinds of listening tasks do classroom learners generally engage in? Are they given opportunities to listen in a wide variety of situations? Do they have the opportunity to develop the skills and strategic responses described in the previous section? Classrooms are limited environments when it comes to providing learners a full range of everyday listening tasks and situations. If we take Figure 4.1., for example, and attempt to place into it typical classroom and formal listening activities, what activities can go in each box? We offer some suggestions in Figure 4.2; you should think of activities to complete the remaining boxes.

The classroom second language learner tends to be engaged in only two kinds of listening situations: collaborative aural + visual situations (classroom discussion where there is use of the blackboard, overheads, or other presentation devices) and noncollaborative aural-only situations (lab practice). Although there is increased interest in the use of video and TV in language classrooms, which represent noncollaborative aural + visual listening situations, the use of these media is far from being everyday. If we probe even further, we see that the two situations which do present themselves might not always offer learners opportunities to develop the full range of skills and strategic responses used by skilled listeners. We examine classroom discussions first.

Classroom Discussion

A comparison of classroom and nonclassroom discussions suggests that maximal active participation of the learner as listener is limited in a number of ways. Table 4.1 lists some of the basic differences between listening in class and listening outside of class. First, in the classroom learners "share" the

	Aural Only	Aural + Visual
Collaborative	???	classroom "discussion"
Non-collaborative	lab materials	???

Collaboration

FIGURE 4.2. Common Listening Situations in the Second Language Classroom

instructor with everyone else during the discussion and, given the public nature of the discourse, might be unwilling to show nonunderstanding. In the nonclassroom setting, language learners often get the chance to interact one-on-one with a native speaker, who will signal nonunderstanding, will confirm, and will readily take turns. The native speaker can thus provide the learner with a variety of appropriate models of listening performance. Classroom learners, however, cannot do this with each other; only the instructor can provide a model of the fullest range of skilled listener behaviors. Because instructors tend to control the topic of the discussion and also make great use of question asking, learner-listeners may not be given the opportunity to function as co-creators in the discourse and to develop appropriate listener responses. On the other hand, roles outside the classroom vary as learners act as listeners in conversations with friends, clerks, doctors, telephone solicitors,

TABLE 4.1. A Comparison of Classroom and Nonclassroom Collaborative Listening

Classroom	Nonclassroom
tends to be group participation, guided by a teacher	often only two participants
learners interact with teacher and other learners	learners interact with natives
teacher tends to control topic development	learners participate in topic development
setting is always the classroom	settings are varied
social roles are fixed	social roles vary
purpose includes evaluation (either immediate or delayed)	purpose is largely communicative (informational and/or social)

bus drivers, and other individuals with whom they may have equal or non-equal status relationships. In the classroom, learners are in an unequal power relationship with their instructors. Finally, whereas the purpose of listening in the nonclassroom situation is either informational (receiving a message) or social (establishing and maintaining relationships), the purpose of listening in the classroom is often evaluative (the instructor keeps an eye out for who is having problems and who isn't, who is paying attention and who isn't, with the intent of providing feedback or assigning a grade).

The classroom, then, may not be an ideal place for the development of all listening skills and strategic responses. Nonetheless, it is the place where such skills and responses *can begin to develop.* Instructors can take steps toward maximizing class time for the development of listening. Here are some suggestions.

1. Use the second language to conduct business. Making announcements, describing what will be on a test, and assigning homework all push learners toward purposeful listening. Because learners have a great stake in comprehending the business at hand, they will be more likely to question, confirm, and signal nonunderstanding in order to get the message.

2. Allow learners to nominate topics and structure the discourse. They are much more likely to get involved in active participatory listening if they help control the topic. One teaching technique would be to reserve five minutes a day or ten minutes every other day during which a learner can nominate a topic. The class can decide on Monday, for example, who will nominate a topic on Wednesday, and then on Wednesday another who will nominate a topic on Friday, so that all eventually are involved in nominating topics during the term. The learner in charge can solicit opinions from classmates about what to discuss (for example, "We would like to know about where you are from. What was it like growing up there?").

3. Be a participatory listener yourself. When learners attempt to express themselves, you need to respond as a listener, not an instructor. That is, as a listener the instructor should engage in appropriate listening performance. In this way, learners see and hear how to perform as listeners in the second language. model

4. Set aside telephone time. Instructors can increase the scope of listening opportunities by encouraging biweekly phone calls. Learners must call another instructor or a native speaker and interview that person over the phone. Or, an instructor might set aside a block of time during which she receives telephone calls in the second language from her learners, who ask questions, get information, or simply "chat."

5. Provide some good listening gambits to learners. In addition to simply allowing more opportunities for collaborative listening, instructors can also point out to learners typical listening gambits for signalling nonunderstanding, confirmation, and so forth. The instructor can

place signs around the room with second language equivalents of gambits such as:

I didn't catch that.

Could you speak more slowly, please?

What is _____?

Did you say _____? What's that?

I don't understand _____.

Really?

No kidding!

O.K., O.K.

Oh, I'm sorry. My mind was wandering.

In addition to discussions and conversations, the classroom can also provide opportunities for the learner to listen in noncollaborative aural + visual–stimuli situations. Language instructors sometimes forget that academic listening is a very common type of communicative listening. If learners continue their education in the second language, they will no doubt need to attend lectures and presentations. The instructor can thus include an occasional listening situation that functions like academic listening: delivering a lecture or presentation (complete with use of blackboard, overhead, slides, and photos) and having learners take notes. Learners are then asked to do one of several things with the information they have heard:

- summarize it in written form
- make a visual representation of the information (charts or posters, for example, depending on the information)
- take a test on the information
- some combination of the above

Such opportunities provide a different type of listening situation in which the strategies required may be different from those used in more "conversational" listening. Since students may not be able to interrupt and may have to wait until an appropriate time to ask a question or receive a clarification, they are thus pushed to process language far beyond the sentence level.

---

*P*ause to consider . . .

the relevance of classroom listening to nonclassroom listening. Think back to the first time you listened to the second language in a nonclassroom setting. What were the characteristics of that listening situation? Did your classroom experiences prepare you for the nonclassroom experience?

LISTENING IN THE LANGUAGE LABORATORY

We now examine the use of the laboratory for developing listening abilities. It is probably fair to say that traditional language laboratory materials offer non-collaborative, aural-only types of practice. The exercises in these practices contain sentence-level, dialogue-level, or monologue-type discourse, but they are noncollaborative in nature. Typical examples appear below. (Note: When we refer to laboratory listening, we do not suggest that the learner has to sit in a laboratory booth to complete the exercises. It is increasingly common for learners to do these kinds of activities in isolation at home with a personal tape machine.)

Activity A. Sentence-Level Listening Practice. Listen to each sentence and determine whether it is true or false according to the visual clue.

Activity B. Dialogue-Level Listening Practice. Listen to Alphonse and Christine make plans for this evening. Then indicate who said what.

ALPHONSE	CHRISTINE	
☐	☐	1. This person wants to go out to eat.
☐	☐	2. This person wants to get home early.
☐	☐	3. This person offers to drive.

Activity C. Monologue-Type Practice. Listen to the speaker as he talks about Holy Week in Spain. Then answer the questions that follow.

1. What city in Spain is most famous for its celebration of Holy Week?
2. How many tourists visit that city every year for this religious event?

How do these noncollaborative situations in the laboratory compare with other nonclassroom, noncollaborative listening? First, let's recall what other noncollaborative listening situations exist. One can listen to the radio for news, weather, music, and announcements; to songs, books-on-tape, and other prerecorded material; to recorded messages on phones. One can watch TV, a movie, or a play or watch-listen to a commencement speech or political debate. There are, of course, other situations, but what these all have in common is that listeners have some control over the topic. They often decide what radio station to listen to, whether or not to listen to the news, whether to listen to a murder mystery or a science fiction book-on-tape, and so forth. In addition, listeners approach their task with a purpose: getting the message regarding some specific news story, finding out where a sale is taking place, determining who did what to whom. We may listen for purely entertainment reasons. We listen to certain songs not for information but simply because we like the song; likewise, we may watch a particular TV show simply because we like it. Finally, in the nonclassroom setting noncollaborative listeners generally determine when they are done listening. They may change the channel, turn off the radio or TV, fast forward to a different song, or simply tune out.

TABLE 4.2. A Comparison of Noncollaborative Listening in and out of the Laboratory

Laboratory	Nonclassroom
topic is predetermined	learner controls the topic
purpose is often to practice	learner listens for information
(same as above)	learner listens for entertainment
initiation and termination of listening is determined by another	learner initiates and terminates listening

In Table 4.2 the characteristics of out-of-laboratory noncollaborative listening are contrasted with those of the laboratory. In the laboratory the learner does not control topics; these are predetermined. Nor does the learner initiate and terminate listening: listening is completed when the task is completed. Finally, in the laboratory the learner listens as part of language-learning practice and is very often evaluated on his performance.

It is difficult to imagine learners controlling the topic or the initiation and termination of the listening act itself while in the laboratory (except, of course, when the listener chooses to walk away before finishing the lesson!). But it does seem possible that we can increase the communicative purpose of listening, that is, listening for information. Laboratory activities A, B, and C presented earlier all lack informational purpose: the learner listens in order to answer questions. But in real life, we often listen in order to report to someone or to summarize information. We listen to the weather report only to tell someone else later what the weather is going to be like or to use that information to make a decision. We listen to the news and then discuss it with friends. We listen to a speech and then report on it or summarize it for someone else. In short, listeners take information and then transform it into their own words for others. How often do learners get the opportunity to do this in the second language? It seems that the language laboratory could provide useful opportunities. Here are some possibilities for noncollaborative purposeful listening.

1. Listen to a radio broadcast, lecture, monologue, story, or some other oral text and prepare:
   a. a written summary
   b. an oral summary
   c. an outline
   d. some combination of a, b, and c.
2. Listen to a conversation/dialogue and then report it as a narrative.
3. Listen to a set of directions (instructions) and then perform a task.

Tasks 1 and 2 are rather straightforward and have begun to appear in laboratory materials. As one example, here is the task assigned to students in one activity based on listening to a short text about the increase in multiple births (i.e., giving birth to twins, triplets, quadruplets). The selection presented here is actually the final section of the listening task.

Activity D. Synthesis.

Step 1. The speaker mentioned four principal factors that have contributed to the increase in multiple births. Complete the following chart, identifying the factors and how each contributes to this increase.

Factors That Lead to Increased Multiple Births

Factors	How They Contribute
1. Many women wait to have children.	1.
2.	2.
3.	3.
4.	4. This increases the chance of multiple fertilized eggs surviving in the womb.

Step 2. In a short composition, use the information from your chart to explain why there has been an increase in multiple births. You might want to use the following sentence to begin your composition: "Different factors contribute to the recent rise in multiple births. These factors are the following:"

These kinds of activities encourage learners to synthesize information (that is, distill ideas) they have listened to and report on it in their own words. The chart in Activity D requires learners to select ideas and to organize them in a coherent way. The follow-up writing activity then asks learners to pull these ideas together using connected discourse. Thus, listening is not an activity in and of itself but, rather, part of a more complex communicative activity that goes beyond listening. In a sense, *listening is a means to an end;* it is not the end itself.

The third task type (listening to a set of directions and then performing a task) is rarely found in language teaching materials. It is usually limited to the lesson on giving and receiving directions, in which learners demonstrate comprehension by starting at point A on a map and winding up at a predetermined point B. But in real life oral directions and instructions are given to listeners in a variety of situations. The following list illustrates actions that might require following oral instructions:

- following a recipe
- entering a contest
- filling out forms
- building something
- putting something together
- playing a game
- analyzing some kind of data
- using an electronic device
- taking or administering medicine
- playing a sport or performing an athletic activity

The above list is partial, but note how far we have gone beyond the usual giving and receiving directions for getting somewhere. Laboratory materials can offer more of these kinds of listening opportunities. For example, the following activity could easily be performed in a lab or as a homework assignment.

Activity E. Playing a Card Game. In this activity, you will learn how to play a card game. On the tape, one person will be giving instructions to another. Listen and pay attention to the instructions as best you can. It is helpful to have a deck of cards handy to act out the instructions as you receive them. Afterwards, you will answer some questions about the rules of the game, and tomorrow in class you will need to show that you have understood the rules by actually playing the game! Listen to the tape as many times as you like. (Note: You will encounter a number of new words and phrases as you listen, but you should be able to guess these based on the context and the situation. Keep in mind that you are learning a card game. What are typical expressions and words used in playing cards that you use in your first language?)

Text of the tape

ROB: O.K. First, I deal out five cards.
GERRI: O.K. Why five?
ROB: Hold on, hold on. O.K., pick them up and organize them according to numbers. Say, fours, fives. Like this. If you have two fives, put them together, if you have . . .
GERRI: What if I have more than two?
ROB: Well, then put them all together. The idea is to group your cards by numbers. You done?
GERRI: Yeah, uh huh.
ROB: O.K. Now . . . (the instructions continue)

Follow-up Questions

1. How many cards are dealt at the beginning?

    a. five   **b.** seven   **c.** ten

2. Cards are supposed to be grouped. Are they grouped by number or suit?

Note that comprehension in this activity is examined in two ways. First, the learner answers some questions about the game itself, demonstrating how well he has understood its basic elements. Second, the learner is asked to play the game in class, demonstrating how well he integrated what he heard on the

Pause to consider . . .

some other examples. Can you think of additional activities that could be used for listening outside of class?

tape into long-term memory, a part of listening performance that is essential in everyday life.

GETTING READY TO LISTEN

Prelistening activities

Currently of special interest to language teachers is the use of what are called "prelistening" activities. *Prelistening activities* are those that are designed to help orient learners before they actually begin listening to something. This orientation helps maximize learners' comprehension. Recall that in listening, attention requires that we focus on aural stimuli and that we make decisions about what to attend to and what to ignore. When we attend to aural stimuli, we often have scripts in mind and make predictions about what we are going to hear. This facilitates comprehension, but we generally do this unconsciously. In second language situations, on the other hand, particularly in the beginning stages, *consciously* orienting learners before a listening task has been shown to increase comprehension. Prelistening activities fall into three general groups that are not necessarily mutually exclusive:

1. vocabulary preparation
2. review of existing knowledge
3. anticipation of content

We examine each in turn.

Vocabulary preparation is the simple task of acquainting learners with unfamiliar words and expressions that will be either useful or necessary for the listening excerpt. The goal is not to have learners memorize words and produce them but to recognize them and attach meaning to them when they hear them. Thus, most prelistening vocabulary preparation is limited to input-oriented activities. Instructors can make use of visuals, TPR, definitions, and even lists. But another way (and perhaps a better one because the vocabulary is linked with content) is to embed the new words and expressions in either a review of existing knowledge or in an anticipation of content.

Review of existing knowledge requires learners to reflect on what they already know. For example, in Activity E with the card game instructions, most learners know a great deal about card games even if they don't play cards themselves. They probably know that

there is a dealer;

cards are shuffled, dealt, shown, discarded, and so on;

people sometimes bet;

players can either win or lose;

cards have numbers or faces (jack, queen, king); and

cards have suits.

A review of existing knowledge explicitly calls forth some of these concepts to check what learners actually know about some topic in its most general sense. As mentioned above, vocabulary preparation can be combined with a review of knowledge. For example, prior to listening to the instructions on the card game, learners might be given a quiz on what they know about cards and card games, with new vocabulary and expressions glossed.

Activity F. Before Listening. Before listening, what do you already know about cards and playing cards? See if you can determine whether the following statements are true or false.

1. Card games may involve one or more persons.
2. When two or more people are involved, one person must deal.
3. A person always deals from right to left.
4. Cards are always dealt face down.

Note that learners might or might not know the answers to the above questions, so it is irrelevant if they get them all right or all wrong when they answer. What is important is that, after completing the activity and checking their answers, they have either confirmed or developed some knowledge of cards and card playing before they begin listening *and* they have begun to bind meaning with form (in this case, related vocabulary and expressions). A review of existing knowledge can take a variety of forms and can be teacher led, textbook led, or on the actual tape that learners listen to. Table 4.3 lists some examples of activity types for a review of existing knowledge. Of course, any combination of activities can be used, since there is nothing wrong with variety!

Some activities (like brainstorming) might need to be conducted in the first language, especially in the early stages. The role of the instructor, then, is to take the concepts expressed in the first language and transform them into the second language.

TABLE 4.3 Examples of Activity Types for a Review of Existing Knowledge (Prelistening)

Quizzes

true-false-"don't have a clue"
multiple choice
short answer

Teacher-led discussion

The instructor leads a discussion in which she explains and asks questions, using the blackboard and other visual devices.

Short Reading

Learners read a short text before listening. They then answer questions, participate in a teacher led discussion, or perform some other task.

Learner Brainstorming

Either in groups or with the instructor, or a combination of the two, learners brainstorm what they know about the topic. They might create a semantic map, make lists of concepts, or trade experiences.

Anticipation of content directs learners to predict some of the things that a speaker might say. When we listen to a weather report while driving, for example, we expect to hear certain phrases and expressions and not others. And we expect the report to be about our local area. "Thirty percent chance of thunderstorms," "High in the low 90s this afternoon," "Grab an umbrella if you're leaving your house because . . ." are samples of expressions that we expect to hear. We do not expect to hear such things as "It's *coooold* in Moscow today" or "Next year should bring us more rain." In the card-game listening activity, what would one expect to hear? What would one expect to hear if the listening activity specifically involves instructions on how to play a game? One would expect to hear the rules of the game, the objective of the game (how one wins), what a winning hand is, how to score points, and so forth. The same activities used to review existing knowledge can be used to anticipate content (see Table 4.3): learners can be quizzed in some way, they can be taken through a teacher-led discussion (question-and-answer session), they can read a short text (say, the rules for another game and can then make a list of things they expect to be told), or they can brainstorm.

What does one expect to hear?

TESTING LISTENING COMPREHENSION

It would seem redundant to say that a test of listening comprehension must test listening comprehension, but it is nonetheless important to remember. Why? In some formal testing situations, aural testing of vocabulary or grammar has been equated with listening comprehension. Just a few years ago it was not uncommon to find the following as a standard listening section on a foreign language exam in the United States.

Section 1. Oral Questions. Listen to each question carefully and then answer in a complete sentence.

1. Did you call your mother last night?
2. Did you eat eggs for breakfast this morning?
3. What time did you get up today?
4. Where did you go last night?
5. Did you arrive at class on time today?

Exam sections such as this one (used to test past tense) cannot be classified as "listening comprehension" as we have been developing that concept in this chapter. Although it is true that the test takers are listening to sentences that they must then respond to, the actual section itself bears little resemblance to the kind of listening that happens in real life. And because the section asks for written responses in complete sentences, the nature of performance in listening is severely compromised. What, then, should a listening test look like?

A good listening test considers at least the following three factors:

1. content (topic domain)
2. task (how the learner is asked to demonstrate comprehension)
3. language of performance

Content

For content, we can develop a listening test that is topic specific (listening to a description of someone's family) or not (listening to a news report). Whether or not to restrict the content of a listening test is determined by the purpose of the test. In certain professions, for example, a listening test that is content specific might be preferred but not necessary. Can the doctor understand the patient's description of her symptoms? Can the counterperson at the social services office understand the routine requests of clients? In other professions, specificity of content in listening tests will not be appropriate. We would expect, for example, that a U.N. interpreter could successfully comprehend in the second language a wide variety of topic domains. In these situations, the nature of test content is dictated or suggested by the nature of the profession or job.

In the typical second language classroom, however, it is clear that professional concerns rarely can be considered for the purposes of testing. In a given classroom, an instructor may have a wide array of future professionals engaged in language learning, and testing cannot be tailored to each individual in any practical manner. Listening tests can nevertheless still be either content specific or broad in content, depending on the purpose of the test. If the listening test is part of a quiz or lesson test, then content can be restricted as in the following example, which might be used on a test that focuses on family and family relationships.

Section 2. Families and Relationships. You will hear two people talk about their families. Select one of the two speakers and, after listening, draw his or her family tree using all the information you can. The connection of lines should demonstrate family relationships and each face should have a name under it.

If the listening test is part of an exit exam or placement test, then a wider variety of topic domains might be sampled. Or, the test might utilize a short section from a movie or some other speech sample that does not focus on any one topic domain.

Tasks

The task that a learner is asked to perform to demonstrate comprehension can fall into one of two categories: tasks that require a linguistic response and those that require a nonlinguistic response. Samples of each are listed in Table 4.4.

Basically, a *linguistic response* is any kind of response that requires the use of language on the part of the learner to demonstrate comprehension. That is, comprehension can only be assessed based on the language that the learner *produces.* This language can be words (labeling things, filling in blanks), phrases (outlines, tables, answering questions), sentences (answering questions, writing summary statements), and connected discourse (summarizing in paragraph form). *Nonlinguistic responses* are those that do not require the production of language for comprehension to be assessed: the learner indicates comprehension visually, not verbally. In the family-tree example, the

TABLE 4.4 Sample Linguistic and Nonlinguistic Tasks for Assessing Listening Comprehension

Linguistic	Nonlinguistic
creating an outline	making a graph
filling in a chart	creating a drawing
labeling things in a visual display	selecting a visual
making a table	indicating something on a visual with numbers, arrows, circles, etc.
creating a quiz	filling in missing parts in a drawing
answering questions	arranging items or objects
summarizing in written or oral form	performing a physical task (e.g., cooking something, acting something out)

[handwritten: words whether written or spoken]   *[handwritten: no words either written or spoken]*

learner demonstrated comprehension nonlinguistically by drawing the family tree. Here are other tasks that could be used with the same test stimuli (the description of the family) to assess comprehension.

[handwritten in margin: I can't see a clear difference yet?]

Sample Linguistic Tasks

1. The learner answers a number of questions about the various family members.
2. The learner is asked to write a brief paragraph in which he describes the family.
3. The learner is given a list of names and is asked to write next to each the relationship of that person to the speaker.

Sample Nonlinguistic Tasks

1. The learner receives names and faces as cut-outs and must place them into the family tree; the lines that represent the tree are already drawn in.
2. The learner receives the family tree with missing members and must add faces for those who are missing.
3. The learner receives four different family trees with only slight variations among them and must select the family tree that best represents the description he heard.

If an instructor teaches more than one class, then she might have learners help her create quizzes for another class. For example, after listening, learners could create five true-false statements about the family, five multiple-choice statements, or a column-matching activity (names on one side, relationships on the other in mixed order). The instructor could then grade each quiz (and the answer key that each learner provides) that night and use one or a combination of them in another class the next day.

Selection of task depends mostly on the level of the learners and the point at which the quiz or test is administered. Can the learners handle a summary? Would a word-level linguistic task be the best demonstration of their comprehension? These are the types of questions that an instructor must ask in developing listening quizzes and tests.

The *language of assessment* may seem an odd point to bring up. After all, isn't it obvious that learners are listening to something in the second language? The issue of language of assessment is not about the stimulus, however; it refers to the language used by learners when the task requires a linguistic response. Some instructors claim that everything should be done in the second language and that use of the native language in testing situations goes against this philosophy. However, research in second language reading (Lee 1986a; Wolf 1993b) demonstrates that language of assessment is a significant variable when testing reading comprehension. In Lee's and Wolf's studies, comprehension scores were significantly higher for those subjects who were allowed to respond in English (their first language) compared with those who took the test in Spanish (their language of study). Thus, learners' demonstration of comprehension was impeded when they had to write their answers in Spanish. We would expect the same to be true for listening comprehension as well.

What this means for instructors, then, is that if the actual test (including instructions and test items) is presented in the second language and if learners also have to *perform* in the second language (write answers, summarize, and so forth), then the test results are confounded by performance variables. An instructor needs to be aware of this problem and make judicious decisions based on the purpose of the test and comparison to real-life listening situations. For example, in everyday situations one engages in collaborative listening in the second language, and comprehension is demonstrated as learners use strategic responses as part of their communicative responsibilities. But when one listens to a weather report or news, watches a TV program, or engages in other noncollaborative listening situations, there may be no obligation on the part of the learner to demonstrate immediate comprehension by performing in the second language in some way.

TESTING GLOBAL LISTENING PROFICIENCY

Increasing attention has been paid to so-called global proficiency testing in the last twenty years. Whereas content-specific listening tests evaluate only limited areas of a learner's total performance, *global proficiency* tests measure the learner's ability to function—holistically—out of the classroom. Proficiency test makers generally develop a set of criterion-referenced norms against which to judge an individual's performance. This means that idealized descriptions based on research and experience are developed for different levels of skills: beginning listeners, intermediate listeners, advanced listeners, and so on. The American Council on the Teaching of Foreign Languages (ACTFL) has developed a set of criterion references for listening that comprise five major levels plus sublevels within several of the major levels. Listeners may be classified as Novice, Intermediate, Advanced, Superior, or Distinguished. Within the Novice and Intermediate levels, one can also be classified as Low, Mid or High, and, within Advanced, one may be classified as Advanced-Plus. Figure 4.3 provides the full descriptions of the listening guidelines as published by ACTFL.

These guidelines assume that all listening tasks take place in an authentic environment at a normal rate of speech using standard or near-standard norms.

Novice-Low Understanding is limited to occasional words, such as cognates, borrowed words, and high-frequency social conventions. Essentially no ability to comprehend even short utterances.

Novice-Mid Able to understand some short, learned utterances, particularly where context strongly supports understanding and speech is clearly audible. Comprehends some words and phrases for simple questions, statements, high-frequency commands and courtesy formulae about topics that refer to basic personal information or the immediate physical setting. The listener requires long pauses for assimilation and periodically requests repetition and/or a slower rate of speech.

Novice-High Able to understand short, learned utterances and some sentence-length utterances, particularly where context strongly supports understanding and speech is clearly audible. Comprehends words and phrases from simple questions, statements, high-frequency commands and courtesy formulae. May require repetition, rephrasing and/or a slowed rate of speech for comprehension.

Intermediate-Low Able to understand sentence-length utterances which consist of recombinations of learned elements in a limited number of content areas, particularly if strongly supported by the situational context. Content refers to basic personal background and needs, social conventions and routine tasks, such as getting meals and receiving simple instructions and directions. Listening tasks pertain primarily to spontaneous face-to-face conversations. Understanding is often uneven; repetition and rewording may be necessary. Misunderstandings in both main ideas and details arise frequently.

Intermediate-Mid Able to understand sentence-length utterances which consist of recombinations of learned utterances on a variety of topics. Content continues to refer primarily to basic personal background and needs, social conventions and somewhat more complex tasks, such as lodging, transportation, and shopping. Additional content areas include some personal interests and activities, and a greater diversity of instructions and directions. Listening tasks not only pertain to spontaneous face-to-face conversations but also to short routine telephone conversations and some deliberate speech, such as simple announcements and reports over the media. Understanding continues to be uneven.

Intermediate-High Able to sustain understanding over longer stretches of connected discourse on a number of topics pertaining to

As one moves up the scale, the characterization of listening changes in both quantity and quality. There is a move from words and memorized phrases to connected discourse; from limited concrete topics to a broad range of topic domains, both concrete and abstract; and from effortful listening (ask-

different times and places; however, understanding is inconsistent due to failure to grasp main ideas and/or details. Thus, while topics do not differ significantly from those of an Advanced-level listener, comprehension is less in quantity and poorer in quality.

Advanced Able to understand main ideas and most details of connected discourse on a variety of topics beyond the immediacy of the situation. Comprehension may be uneven due to a variety of linguistic and extralinguistic factors, among which topic familiarity is very prominent. These texts frequently involve description and narration in different time frames or aspects, such as present, nonpast, habitual, or imperfective. Texts may include interviews, short lectures on familiar topics, and news items and reports primarily dealing with factual information. Listener is aware of cohesive devices but may not be able to use them to follow the sequence of thought in an oral text.

Advanced-Plus Able to understand the main ideas of most speech in a standard dialect; however, the listener may not be able to sustain comprehension in extended discourse which is propositionally and linguistically complex. Listener shows an emerging awareness of culturally implied meanings beyond the surface meanings of the text but may fail to grasp socio-cultural nuances of the message.

Superior Able to understand the main ideas of all speech in a standard dialect, including technical discussion in a field of specialization. Can follow the essentials of extended discourse which is propositionally and linguistically complex, as in academic/professional settings, in lectures, speeches, and reports. Listener shows some appreciation of aesthetic norms of target language, of idioms, colloquialisms, and register shifting. Able to make inferences within the cultural framework of the target language. Understanding is aided by an awareness of the underlying organizational structure of the oral text and includes sensitivity for its social and cultural references and its affective overtones. Rarely misunderstands but may not understand excessively rapid, highly colloquial speech or speech that has strong cultural references.

Distinguished Able to understand all forms and styles of speech pertinent to personal, social and professional needs tailored to different audiences. Shows strong sensitivity to social and cultural references and aesthetic norms by processing language from within the cultural framework. Texts include theater plays, screen productions, editorials, symposia, academic debates, public policy statements, literary readings, and most jokes and puns. May have difficulty with some dialects and slang. (Omaggio Hadley 1993; pp. 504–6)

FIGURE 4.3. ACTFL Proficiency Guidelines: General Descriptions for Listening

ing for lots of repetition, requiring speaker to slow down, and similar listening skills) to listening which requires little or no effort.

The ACTFL Guidelines are not the only criterion-referenced guidelines that have been developed. Rost offers a set of guidelines quite different from

Competent listener

- able to understand all styles of speech that are intelligible to well-educated native listeners in the target community and able to seek clarification smoothly when speech is unintelligible;
- able to understand abstract concepts expressed orally;
- able to note areas where own knowledge is lacking to achieve an acceptable understanding and to note where speaker is vague or inconsistent;
- able to understand and display appropriate listener responses in a wide range of social and specialized contexts in the target culture setting;
- able to adopt an appropriate risk strategy to respond to task demands.

Listener of modest ability

- able to understand most styles of speech that are intelligible to well-educated native listeners in the target community and attempts to seek clarification when speech is unintelligible, although attempts are not always successful or appropriate;
- able to understand some abstract concepts expressed orally, but often requires repetition or re-explanation;
- able to note areas where own knowledge is lacking to achieve an acceptable understanding and to note where speaker is vague or inconsistent, but occasionally is confused about the source of difficulty in understanding;
- able to understand enough of the linguistic/pragmatic input to

those proposed by ACTFL; they are included in Figure 4.4. Rost's classification of listener ability is divided into three broad categories: competent listener, listener of modest ability, and listener of limited ability.

Although there is some overlap between Rost's classifications and those in the ACTFL Guidelines (see, for example, how they compare in terms of content), what stands out as a major difference is the attempt by Rost to include skills and strategic responses in his classifications. For example, the listener of modest ability is able to note where his own knowledge is lacking as well as where a speaker is inconsistent or vague when speaking; he can also adopt appropriate risk strategies in response to a task, albeit not consistently. If we compare this to ACTFL's Advanced listener, we find that there is no mention of skills or strategies in the ACTFL description. The ACTFL Advanced profile describes what the learner can comprehend successfully in terms of content and linguistic demands, but it does not describe any mental or interactional abilities that pertain to listening performance.

We have suggested that content-specific listening tests are perhaps those that language instructors will use the most. But global proficiency scales are useful to language instructors for two general purposes: for placement and for determining overall ability upon exit from a program or sequence of

infer the gist of the communicative event; displays listener responses in a wide range of social and specialized contexts in the target culture setting, but often not appropriately;

- able to adopt an appropriate risk strategy to respond to task demands but often adopts an ineffective strategy which detracts from successful listening.

Listener of limited ability

- able to understand limited styles of speech that are intelligible to well-educated native listeners in the target community and is most often not successful or appropriate in attempts to seek clarification when speech is unintelligible;
- not able to understand unfamiliar abstract concepts expressed in the TL without considerable non-linguistic support; usually requires repetition or re-explanation or multiple clarification exchanges;
- usually not able to note areas where own knowledge is lacking to achieve an acceptable understanding and to note where speaker is vague or inconsistent, often expresses confusion about the source of difficulty in understanding;
- usually not able to understand enough of the linguistic/pragmatic input to infer the gist of the communicative event, displays limited range of listener responses;
- usually does not adopt an appropriate risk strategy to respond to task demands, most often opts for a high-risk strategy which detracts from successful listening. *Source: Rost 1990, pp. 186–87*

FIGURE 4.4. Rost's Classification of Listening Ability

courses. However, any global scale suffers from one major drawback: What does a test of global listening comprehension look like? While we can envision a test that is content specific, task specific, or restricted to a noncollaborative situation, how can a test of listening comprehension measure the multifaceted skill of listening? To find out if a learner was in Rost's category "Listener of Modest Ability," we would have to have a test that does at least the following:

- examines listening in a variety of collaborative and noncollaborative situations
- examines the ability to comprehend concrete and abstract concepts in a variety of content domains
- examines the ability to comprehend (and react appropriately) in a variety of social contexts
- encourages learners to inform us of what they are understanding and not understanding as they listen
- provides opportunities for taking risks to deal with challenging tasks

Under these requirements, constructing a valid listening test would be a monumental job. Until testing instruments for global listening proficiency become available, guidelines are best used by instructors as rough indications of program goals.

SUMMARY

In this chapter, we examined four major areas of second language listening: the psycholinguistic processes, listening as a communicative act, listening activities for second language classrooms and laboratories, and some issues in testing listening comprehension. We saw that listening is far from a passive skill. Indeed, the learner-listener is actively engaged in mental computations that are linguistic and nonlinguistic in nature. The listener is an active co-constructor of meaning in collaborative situations, and even in noncollaborative situations her mind is busy inferring, guessing, anticipating, and integrating meaning as she attends to the aural stimuli. We also saw that listening is not just aural but, in everyday life, is generally part of communicative situations in which visual and other stimuli are present. Thus, few are the cases where real-world listening is purely "ear only." In examining language-teaching practices, we considered the nature of listening in order to ask ourselves what range of listening practices learners get both in and out of the classroom. Our conclusion was that opportunities to listen in the second language are generally restricted to a small set of types, but that there are ways to increase both the opportunities to practice listening and the variety of situations in which listening is used. We ended with a brief examination of issues related to testing, drawing the distinction between content-specific and nonspecific tests, as well as examining tasks and language of assessment as variables in testing.

Before we conclude, let us reflect on this chapter and the chapter that preceded it (Chapter 3, Comprehensible Input). In essence, aren't both chapters about the same thing? Aren't they both concerned with issues of comprehension and aural stimuli? In a certain sense this is true, but at the same time it is not. Our discussion of the role of comprehensible input in second language acquisition dealt exactly with that: *acquisition*. Comprehensible input is a factor related to the acquisition of a linguistic system—vocabulary, morphology, syntax, phonology, and other linguistic features. As such, comprehensible input is a factor external to the learner; it consists of the linguistic data that he relies on to build a linguistic system.

Listening comprehension, on the other hand, deals with skill development. It refers to what learners understand and don't understand as they interact in a communicative setting, and how they signal comprehension and help to maintain the flow of discourse (in collaborative situations). Thus, listening comprehension is about factors internal to the learner.

Clearly the two concepts are related. If input is to be of any acquisitional use, it must be comprehended, which in turn suggests issues of listening. However, it is intuitively obvious that learners can make sense of and grasp main ideas in a speech stream that contains incomprehensible input. They might thus be able to "function" in a communicative interaction but not receive the right kind of input for acquisition. We will continue to explore these and related issues in future chapters.

85

CHAPTER 4
Listening
Comprehension

KEY TERMS, CONCEPTS, AND ISSUES

psycholinguistic processes *perceiving, attending, assigning meaning, active*
  perceiving *physiological aspect*
  attending *active concentration*
  assigning meaning *interpretative act*
inference *assigning meaning even though something specific was not said*
listening as communication ✓ *expression + interpretation/informational outcome*
  collaborative versus noncollaborative listening *speaker and listener work together to negotiate meaning*
  modality *aural vs. visual perception*
  skills *making sense of speakers message through all aspects of expression p.64*
  strategic responses *conversational skills to maintain communication*
  maintaining the discourse *through skills and strategic responses*
  gambits *set phrases for checking understanding when appropriate*
classroom versus nonclassroom listening *collaborative aural-visual vs. non-collaborative aural only*
listening in the language laboratory *no control of the listener*
listening as a means to an end *to complete tasks, not an end in itself*
prelistening activities *help orient learners before listening*
  vocabulary preparation *acquainting learners with unfamiliar words/expressions*
  review of existing knowledge *reflection on the already known*
  anticipation of content *directs learners to predict what speaker might say*
testing listening comprehension *good: content task, language*
  content *information the purpose of the test*
  specificity *depending on the purpose of the test*
  task *to demonstrate comprehension*
  linguistic versus nonlinguistic response *requires the use of language or not*
  language of assessment *depending on purpose of test*
global listening proficiency *ability of learner of functioning holistically outside the classroom*
comprehensible input versus listening as communication

external to
the learner
linguistic data

skill development
internal to the learner
practical setting

EXPLORING THE TOPICS FURTHER

1. *Listening processes.* Richards (1983) is a very readable work that describes in detail the processes involved in listening, with particular emphasis on listening in a second language.
2. *Listening skills and strategies.* Rost's 1990 book is an excellent examination of the role of listening in language learning and teaching. While some of the content is technical, his book was written with teachers in mind.
3. *Testing listening.* Chapter 7 of Rost's book treats several issues in testing only lightly touched upon here. He also includes samples of three standardized listening tests.

Grammar in Communicative Language Teaching

In Part II, we continue our examination of traditional assumptions, approaches, and classroom practices with a particular focus on grammar. The debate about grammar instruction is one of the major conflicts in language teaching today, but the debate centers on whether or not to teach grammar—whether teaching grammar has a role in communicative language teaching. In this unit, we concentrate on how (not whether) to teach grammar.

In Chapters 5 and 6, we propose to teach grammar via processing instruction, in which structured input activities teach learners to process grammar for meaning. We then explore parallel activities for language production: structured output activities in which learners produce meaningful language while focusing on specific forms. In Chapter 7, we provide suggestions for testing grammar consistent with processing instruction and examine the idea of using the content of classroom interaction on tests.

Grammar Instruction as Structured Input

struc-tured (strŭk' chərd) adj. *1. highly organized: a structured environment. 2. Psychology. having a limited number of correct
or nearly correct answers; said of a test.*
Compare **unstructured.**
American Heritage Dictionary

INTRODUCTION

Think back to when you were learning a second language—or reflect on
some of the instructional practices and techniques current in today's classrooms. Does the following scenario seem familiar? An instructor enters the
class and says,

> Today we are going to learn about direct objects and direct object pro-
> nouns. Does anyone know what a direct object is? [*Silence from the
> class.*] Well, a direct object is also called an object of the verb, and it
> refers to a thing upon which an action is performed. [*Quizzical looks
> from students.*] For example, in the sentence [*reveals overhead*] "John hit
> the ball," *the ball* is the direct object of *hit*. Here's another sentence [*re-
> veals overhead*], "Mary plays the piano." What's the direct object? [*One
> student ventures an answer.*] That's right, *piano. Piano* is the direct object
> of *plays*. Languages also have direct-object pronouns, which can sub-
> stitute for direct-object nouns.

And the explanation continues for about ten minutes, after which the
instructor leads the class through a set of drills and exercises designed to help
the learners master direct-object pronouns. The learners transform, substitute,
combine elements in slash sentences, fill in blanks, and eventually answer a
few personalized questions. The lesson on object pronouns is then considered
successfully completed.

If the description above looks or sounds familiar to you, it is because it is
the prototypical scenario for grammar instruction in classrooms in the United
States, if not around the world. It is the format that a great number of instructors follow whether the grammatical item is adjective endings, past-tense
inflections and uses, the subjunctive, or case marking.

As we saw in the first four chapters of this book, language classrooms are becoming more and more communicative. Instructors are increasingly using the second language to interact with students, and students are getting more and more comprehensible input from their instructors, textbooks, and other sources. In short, classrooms are becoming increasingly context- and acquisition-rich, with a greater focus on meaning. Ironically, at the same time that classrooms have begun to embrace communicative approaches, explicit grammar instruction has hardly changed at all.

In this chapter, we examine traditional grammar instruction and the tenets that underlie it. We discuss why it is not congruent with current communicative approaches, using second language acquisition theory to point out a basic flaw in traditional grammar instruction. We then explore an alternative approach to grammar instruction, one that seeks constantly to link meaning with structure or form, moves the learner from input to output, and is more learner centered than what we see in traditional grammar instruction.

TRADITIONAL APPROACHES TO GRAMMAR INSTRUCTION

If we glance at language textbooks (including those that are described as "communicative" and/or "proficiency oriented"), it appears that instruction in grammar adheres to several tenets rooted in *behaviorism* (the belief in "reinforcing good habits") and *historical inertia* ("That's the way it's been done for years and years and years"). The first tenet is that textbooks should follow a particular grammatical sequence, emphasizing verbal paradigms (for example, all of the present tense forms presented first, followed by all of the past tense forms), nominal morphology, and other grammatical units. Rooted in Latin grammars hundreds of years old, the sequence in today's textbooks reveals only slight modifications from the grammar sequencing of books published a century ago. Perhaps because of this persistence, many instructors justify adopting textbooks based on the sequence of grammar: "I don't like this textbook because the subjunctive comes too late," or "I like this textbook because the grammar is sequenced logically." Such reasoning leads publishers to be concerned about sequencing (as evidenced by questionnaires that explicitly ask instructors about the sequencing of grammar), which in turn reinforces instructors' concerns. Thus is born a cycle of consumerism and marketing in language teaching materials.

Pause to consider . . .

how important you think sequencing of grammar items is. Do you think particular items should precede/follow others? Why? Do you think your current abilities in your second language reflect the order in which you were taught present, past, and future tenses?

Exercise Sequencing

The second tenet of traditional instruction—and the one that is most important to our discussion—is that exercises for all grammatical features should be sequenced in a particular way. Thus, most textbooks sequence grammar practice in the following manner:

mechanical practice → meaningful practice → communicative practice

The classification of drills as *mechanical, meaningful,* or *communicative* is based on the degree of learner control over the response: whether or not there is one right answer, and whether or not the answer is already known to those participating in the interaction (see Paulston 1972 for the origin of this classification). The classification is based also on whether or not learners need to understand either what is said to them or what they themselves are saying in order to complete the drill successfully.

Mechanical drills

Mechanical drills are those during which the student need not attend to meaning and for which there is only one correct response. A classic example of a mechanical drill is the following, which is the first exercise in a series to practice object pronouns.

Change the sentence, substituting object pronouns for the direct object.

Juan pone los vasos en la mesa. → *Juan **los** pone en la mesa.*
(*las copas, la comida, el plato, la cafetera, las tortillas*)

John puts the glasses on the table. → John puts **them** on the table.
(the wine glasses, the food, the plate, the coffee pot, the tortillas)

As you read over the drill, it should become clear that the learner need not understand what she is saying in order to complete the drill. You can test this idea by substituting nonsense words for any content word in the drill. For example, if you substitute the fictitious Spanish words *gaga, momos,* and *posa* for *pone, vasos,* and *mesa,* respectively, you can still perform the drill: *Juan gaga los momos en la posa* → *Juan los gaga en la posa.* (It is important to note in this classification that the learner *may* understand what is being said; the point is that the learner does *not have to.*) In addition to an absence of meaning in this drill, there is one and only one response; anything other than making the correct substitution with an object pronoun is simply wrong.

Meaningful drills

The difference between mechanical and meaningful drills is that the learner must attend to the meaning of both the stimulus and her own answer in order to complete the meaningful drill successfully. Yet there is still only one right answer, and the answer is already known to the participants. For example, in the following meaningful drill, the learner must understand what is being said to him in order to respond to the instructor, but everyone knows what the answer will be since there is no new information contained in it.

Answer each question using an object pronoun.

1. *¿Dónde pone Juan sus libros al entrar en la clase?*
   (Instructor points to where Juan's books are.)
2. *¿Dónde pone María su chaqueta?* (Points to chair.)
3. *¿Dónde pongo yo mis cosas al entrar?*

1. Where does John put his books when he arrives in class?
2. Where does Mary put her jacket?
3. Where do I put my things when I come in?

While there is a focus on meaning in this type of practice, the actual message contained in the learner's utterance is restricted to one response; everyone can see where John's books are as the teacher points to them, so the only possible answer to the question "Where does John put his books when he arrives in class?" is "He puts them on the floor." Note that the quality and quantity of meaning are not considered in these classifications. Although there is meaning involved in meaningful drills, we can question just how "meaningful" they really are, given these constraints on learner responses.

Communicative drills

Unlike the previous two drill types, communicative drills require attention to meaning, and the information contained in the learner's answer is new and unknown to the person asking the question. Thus, the answer cannot be deemed right or wrong in terms of meaning conveyed. Here is an example of a communicative drill to practice object pronouns.

Working with a partner, ask and answer "Yes/No" questions using the cues as guides. If you are answering a question, use an object pronoun in your answer.

MODELO: *tocar/el piano*
          A: *¿Tocas el piano?*
          B: *No, no **lo** toco.*

1. *padres/llamar por teléfono*
2. *hacer/la tarea*
3. *ver/al profesor*

MODEL: to play/the piano
         A: Do you play the piano?
         B: No, I don't play **it.**

1. parents/call on the phone
2. to do/the homework
3. to see/the professor

As you can see in this example, a learner cannot complete the practice without understanding the message in the stimulus questions. He must know what *¿Tocas el piano?* means in order to answer the question. In addition, his response is not anticipated; while we are expecting a "Yes" or "No" as an answer, we do not know which it will be because the answer is presumably based on his own life.

93

CHAPTER 5
Grammar Instruction
as Structured Input

> **Pause to consider . . .**
>
> just how communicative most communicative drills really are. Do learners always pay attention to the meaning of utterances in these drill types? Examine the items listed for the partner activity just described. How much communication is really taking place? Rate the activity on a scale of 1 to 5 with 1 being not very communicative and 5 being very communicative. Explain your rating.

We summarize this section by noting that, although learners are always speaking or writing when engaged in traditional grammar practice, a great deal of grammar instruction is neither meaningful nor communicative. Traditional grammar practice is largely mechanical, with the focus exclusively on using a grammatical feature to *produce* some sort of utterance. A focus on message and a focus on input are simply absent when it comes to grammar. That traditional grammar instruction has not focused on input is the basis for the discussion in the next section.

> **Pause to consider . . .**
>
> the debate surrounding mechanical drills. Some have argued that mechanical practices are a necessary first step in learning a grammatical feature; the drills simply must be done. Others reject mechanical practices as having no value for language learning whatsoever; devoid of meaning, they are only exercises in rote memory, which plays no cognitive role in language learning. Still others claim that mechanical drills can have a positive psychological effect on learners, who, by successfully completing a mechanical drill, *feel* they can go on to more spontaneous communication. Which of these positions do you agree with?

INPUT AND TRADITIONAL
GRAMMAR INSTRUCTION

The debate about grammar instruction is one of the major conflicts in language teaching today. On the one hand, instructors are encouraged to make their classrooms as communicative as possible and to incorporate as much comprehensible input as possible. On the other hand, grammar instruction is typically mechanical, lacking in meaning and context, and hardly communicative. The "problem with grammar" has led some to abandon grammar instruction all together and to fashion more free-form communicative classes where explicit instruction in grammar is simply absent. The problem has led others to question the validity of communicative and input-based approaches. Faced with textbooks full of grammar and mechanical practice, they often say, "How am I supposed to cover all this material and be communicative, too? Forget it!"

However, there *is* a way to incorporate explicit grammar instruction into classes without sacrificing either communication or learner-centered activities. We can actually increase the amount of comprehensible input in classroom materials and activities and still get learners to "practice grammar." Before describing this approach, we must first review what we believe to be true about second language acquisition in and out of the classroom. We begin with the role of input.

Recall from Chapter 2 that, over time, learners build an internal system or representation of the language they are learning. Learners tap this system to create utterances. We construct the following schematic to illustrate our model of the acquisition process.

developing system → output

Recall also that comprehensible, meaning-bearing input is a necessary ingredient for successful acquisition. To put this in other terms, input is the raw data that learners use to construct their systems. Using input data, learners make "form-meaning" connections that become part of the developing system.

input → developing system → output

We know, however, that learners process input as they attempt to comprehend the message(s) contained in it. Processing the input involves "filtering" it in various ways. What learners actually wind up with after processing the input is a reduced, sometimes slightly altered set of input data that theorists call *intake*. The brain uses intake, and not raw input data, to create a linguistic system.

input → intake → developing system → output

What intake data actually look like may or may not resemble what we, as language instructors and advanced speakers of the language, think that learners are "perceiving" in the input. We will return to the concept of intake shortly, for it is an important one.

Note the contradiction between traditional grammar practice and our model of acquisition. The development of an internal system is input dependent; it happens when learners receive and process meaning-bearing input. Traditional grammar practice, on the other hand, is exclusively output oriented. That is, learners get an explanation and are then led through output practices; all of the drill types reviewed in the previous section require learn-

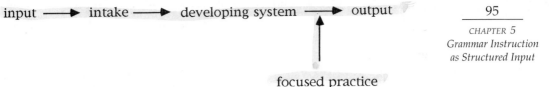

FIGURE 5.1. Traditional Practice in Grammar

ers to produce the language. Under this traditional scenario, how is the developing system provided with relevant input data that is both comprehensible and meaningful? Because it focuses on output, traditional grammar instruction engages those processes involved in *accessing* a developing system rather than those involved in forming the system. (We return to the topic of access and output in the next chapter when we discuss structured output activities.) The development of an internal system does not happen because learners practice output. While practice with output may help with fluency and accuracy in production, it is not "responsible" for getting the grammar into the learner's head to begin with. In short, traditional grammar instruction, which is intended to cause a change in the developing system, is akin to putting the cart before the horse when it comes to acquisition; the learner is asked to produce when the developing system has not yet had a chance to build up a representation of the language based on input data. In Figure 5.1, we see the point at which traditional grammar practice has its effect: it acts on output, not on input.

As seen in Figure 5.1, there are processes earlier in the sequence of events that should be addressed by instruction. It is reasonable to wonder whether grammar instruction focusing on input is more appropriate than traditional approaches to grammar instruction, in which learners are immediately engaged in production. What would happen if explicit instruction in grammar involved the manipulation of both input and input processing in some way? What if the input were structured to encourage richer grammatical intake?

Pause to consider . . .

the output-based nature of traditional grammar instruction, especially the use of mechanical drills. Why do you think drilling and output are so entrenched in the minds of many language instructors and materials developers? (Hint: Think about the theoretical underpinnings of Audiolingual Methodology from Chapters 1 and 2.)

SOME OBSERVATIONS ON HOW
LEARNERS PROCESS INPUT

If we are to employ grammar instruction as the manipulation of input rather than only output, we first need to examine the nature of input processing. In this section, we briefly review some of the more important processes and mechanisms that work on input.

It is important to remember that we are talking about learners processing *meaning-bearing* input: input containing information or a message that the learner is attempting to understand. Although related, comprehension and input processing are not the same phenomenon. We define *comprehension* as making or creating meaning from the informational content in the input. We define *input processing* as making form-meaning connections from the linguistic data in the input for the purposes of constructing a linguistic system: for example, connecting the meaning "past-time reference" to the ending *-ó* in Spanish and connecting the meaning "he drank" to *tomó.* (This distinction will become clearer as the chapter progresses.) While early-stage learners can quite possibly create meaning and make form-meaning connections at the same time, they have a limited attentional capacity with which to do so. In any situation, we have only so much attention to allocate—we can watch TV and talk on the phone, but we'll miss some of what's happening on TV and some of what's being said over the phone. We can read while the radio is playing in the background, but we have to tune out the radio in order to follow what we're reading. Or we tune out what we're reading in order to hear what's on the radio. In each scenario, the two events (or tasks) compete with each other for our attention.

Likewise, making meaning and making form-meaning connections compete for learners' attention. Whereas it would be desirable to turn off the TV to hear better on the phone or turn off the radio while we read, it is *not* desirable to separate making meaning and making form-meaning connections; otherwise, we have once again reduced language learning to mechanical drilling, where there is no meaning, only form. Learners must have access to comprehensible meaning-bearing input for second language acquisition to take place. And, certainly, creating meaning requires that learners have some knowledge of form-meaning relationships. So, how do these two pieces of the language-acquisition puzzle go together?

First, and most important, learners actively seek ways to maximize how much meaning they can get. Based on several L2 research studies as well as an examination of work in child L1 acquisition, VanPatten (1985b, 1990, and 1995) has developed a set of hypotheses about the relationship between input processing and second language acquisition. These hypotheses help us understand the competition between attention to form and attention to meaning and attempt to explain the trade-off inherent in a system characterized by learners' limited attentional capacity (see Table 5.1). We discuss two of these hypotheses in depth. It is important to understand them because we use them in the next section as the basis for re-thinking grammar instruction.

Hypothesis 1(a) states that "Learners process content words in the input before anything else." In other words, when driven by the need to understand the informational content of input, learners direct their attention to lexical

TABLE 5.1 Some Hypotheses about L2 Input-Processing Strategies

H1. Learners process input for meaning before they process it for form.
   H1(a). Learners process content words in the input before anything else.
   H1(b). Learners prefer processing lexical items to grammatical items (e.g., morphology*) for semantic information.
   H1(c). Learners prefer processing more meaningful morphology before less or nonmeaningful morphology.
H2. In order for learners to process form that is not meaningful, they must be able to process informational or communicative content at no or little cost to attention.
H3. Learners tend to process input strings as agent-action-object or subject-verb-object, assigning agent or subject status to the first noun phrase they encounter.
H4. Learners may process phrases and recurring patterns as whole unanalyzed chunks, especially if phonological properties (e.g., melodic contours, intonational patterns) help to delimit these phrases.

*Morphology includes verb inflections, inflections on nouns, inflections on adjectives; in other words, morphology refers to the "shape" of the grammatical item itself.

items. Sometimes informational content is encoded grammatically as well as lexically. That is, grammatical forms may convey some meaning. When the same meaning is encoded both lexically and grammatically, learners may simply ignore the grammatical item; it isn't necessary in order to capture what someone else is saying. Let's examine a few examples in which lexical and grammatical features compete for attention.

   a. He walks.
   b. Yesterday I went to the store.
   c. I bought two books.

In sentence *(a)*, both the subject pronoun and the person number marker *-s* provide the same information (third-person singular). In sentence *(b)*, the temporal adverb *yesterday* signals tense, as does the verb form. In sentence *(c)*, the quantifying adjective *two* signals plurality as does the noun inflection *-s*. Because processing is slower and more effortful for early-stage learners, and because their ability to comprehend is more easily taxed, obtaining meaning from the input must be economical and efficient. The most efficient way for learners to get meaning is to process the lexical items and "skip over" the grammatical items (number markers, verb forms, and noun inflections). They can do so because lexical items have a rather high informational value, or what VanPatten calls *communicative value* (VanPatten 1984a and 1985), defined to be the relative value a form contributes to overall sentence meaning. (Note that communicative value refers to input processing and not to language production.) The grammatical markers in sentences *(a)*, *(b)*, and *(c)* are very low in communicative value: learners can ignore them and still understand the utterances. On the other hand, the roots of the content words are high in communicative value; *walk* is essential for getting overall sentence meaning in *(a)*. The third person *-s* marker is low in communicative value in contrast to the progressive marker *-ing*. In the early stages of language acquisition, learners' processing of grammatically encoded information will be limited unless that information has a relatively high level of communicative value. In other words, although an instructor might be providing considerable comprehensible input, what learners actually process and attend to might be different from what the instructor *thinks* they are processing.

P*ause to consider . . .*

the concept of communicative value and the competition between meaning and form when a learner is attending to input. Can you think of grammatical items in the language you teach that learners might easily skip over as they attend to the meaning in the input? As you think of items, consider what else in the input might give learners the same information (i.e., convey the same meaning).

Another hypothesis explored by VanPatten addresses word order. Research on both first and second language learners in a variety of languages reveals that learners tend to process Noun-Verb-Noun strings as subject-verb-object. Passive structures, for example, are often misinterpreted as active by children and L2 learners in the early and intermediate stages of acquisition. A sentence such as

The horse was kicked by the cow.
N   V   N

is often misinterpreted as

The horse kicked the cow.
N   V   N

VanPatten (1984b) showed that learners of Spanish misinterpret direct-object pronouns as subjects of the verb if they are the only noun that directly precedes the verb. Learners overwhelmingly misinterpreted the sentence

Lo	*saluda*	*la mujer.*
him-OBJ	greets	the woman-SUBJ
'The woman greets him.'		

as 'He greets the woman.' Further evidence for the word-order strategy was found by LoCoco (1987), Lee (1987a), and Binkowski (1992). These results contributed to the formulation of the following processing-strategy hypothesis:

H3. Learners tend to process input strings as agent-action-object or subject-verb-object, assigning agent or subject status to the first noun phrase they encounter.

As VanPatten and Cadierno (1993) have argued, this word-order processing strategy most likely influences the acquisition of a variety of features. Since learners are misinterpreting utterances, they cannot be making the appropriate form-meaning connections. What intake could they be deriving from this input? What information is being fed to the developing system? By using this processing strategy, learners certainly delay their acquisition of direct-object pronouns because these object pronouns are misused as subjects. This processing strategy can also account for other acquisition patterns: the lack of fronted object-noun phrases in learners' speech; the difficulty in acquiring the case marker *a*; and the pervasive use of subject nouns and pronouns in contexts in which they would normally be omitted in Spanish (in linguistic terms, *null subjects*). In short, this one strategy potentially affects the acquisition of a wide range of grammatical features in Spanish (and, by extension, other languages that allow variations in word order). When this strategy is combined with the other processing strategies listed in Table 5.1, we can see precisely how learners manage to "miss" a variety of grammatical features in the input.

RETHINKING GRAMMAR INSTRUCTION: STRUCTURED INPUT

We now have some idea of what learners are doing with input when they are asked to comprehend it. With this knowledge, we can begin to develop a new kind of grammar instruction—one that will guide and focus learners' attention when they process input. Figure 5.2 visually captures our new conceptualization of grammar instruction. We suggest that grammar instruction should *first* occur at the level of processing input. It should be directed to the following questions: (1) Are forms being processed in the input? Are learners attending to grammatical information? (2) Are correct form-meaning connections being made when attending to input data?

An Example of Relating Processing Strategies to Instruction: Verb Morphology

We turn our attention now to activities that focus learners' attention on verb endings; the goal is for learners to use these morphological endings to comprehend tense rather than rely solely on lexical items. After learners receive a brief explanation of how past-tense endings work, they might first practice attaching the concept of past time to verb forms in an activity such as the following. The purpose is to circumvent the strategy described in H1(b) in Table

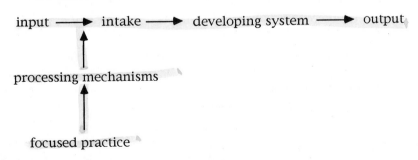

FIGURE 5.2. Processing-Oriented Grammar Instruction

5.1: learners prefer processing lexical items to processing grammatical items for semantic information.

Activity A. Listening for Time Reference. Listen to each sentence. Indicate whether the action occurred last week or is part of a set of actions oriented toward the present.

(sentences read by instructor or heard on tape)
1. John talked on the phone.
2. Mary helped her mother.
3. Robert studies for two hours.
4. Sam watched TV.
5. Lori visits her parents.

Learners might then be given sentences and told to match each to a particular adverbial.

Activity B. Matching. Once again, listen to each sentence. Select the appropriate time-related adverbials that can be added to the sentence you hear.

MODEL: (you hear) John deposited money in the bank.
(you select from)
   a.   Last Monday
   b.   Right now
   c.   Later this week
(you say) Last Monday

Further activities could be developed that involve what the learners themselves did or didn't do at a particular time.

Activity C. Did You Do It, Too? Listen to the speaker make a statement. Indicate whether you did that same thing last night.

MODEL: (you hear) I studied for a test.
(you say) Me too.
or   I didn't.

Note that, in each of these activities, only the verb ending encodes tense in the input sentence. Lexical items and discourse that would indicate a time frame are not present, thereby encouraging learners to attend to the grammatical

*P*ause to consider . . .

how the language you teach encodes past tense. Does this language's morphology or syntax present any particular problems for creating structured input activities? What would the previously outlined activities look like in the language you teach? Can you rewrite them for your class and include 8-10 items for each activity?

markers for tense. Thus, we have *structured* the input so that grammatical form carries meaning and learners must attend to the form in order to complete the task.

Another Example of Relating Processing Strategies to Instruction: Adjective Agreement

Let's examine another of VanPatten's processing strategies and develop some structured input activities that would encourage learners to get better intake from the input. This time, we focus on the following strategy:

> H1(c). Learners prefer processing more meaningful morphology before less meaningful or nonmeaningful morphology.

Some features of language do not have inherent semantic or communicative value. Quite simply, they are meaningless. In the Romance languages, for example, adjectives must agree in number and gender with the nouns they modify, but this feature of grammar contributes little or nothing to the meaning of the utterance in most cases (which is why mistakes in gender agreement rarely yield breakdowns in communication). In the following Spanish-language activity, learners' attention is directed toward proper adjective form by a task in which the adjective endings *must be attended to.* At the same time, the entire sentence must be processed for its meaning, for the learners need to know what is said in order to agree or disagree. These sentences are focused on gender agreement only, because the subject pronoun is not obligatory in Spanish (unlike French and English).

Activity D. Who Is It? Listen to each sentence in which a person is described. First, determine which person is being described. Then indicate whether you agree or disagree with the statement.

1. a. ☐ David Letterman   ☐ Madonna
   b. ☐ agree   ☐ disagree
2. a. ☐ David Letterman   ☐ Madonna
   b. ☐ agree   ☐ disagree
3. a. ☐ David Letterman   ☐ Madonna
   b. ☐ agree   ☐ disagree

(Sentences heard by learner)

1. *Es dinámica.* (She's dynamic.)
2. *Es comprensivo.* (He's understanding.)
3. *Es reservada.* (She's reserved.)

Although grammatical gender in Activity D is restricted to humans and thus is confounded with sexual gender, it is an activity in which grammatical gender must nevertheless be processed for meaning. Note that the same kind of activity can be developed for inanimate objects such as skyscrapers versus suburban homes, or ideas such as country versus city living. Simply select any pair of items that have different grammatical gender and create statements that must be applied on the basis of processing the grammatical marker. Instead of having learners agree/disagree with the statement, you might have them indicate true/false or likely/unlikely. (You are asked to create such activities in the activities and materials portfolio assignments in the Workbook.)

> ## *Pause to consider . . .*
>
> what would happen if the sentences in Activity D contained subject pronouns. Spanish, for example, does not require *él* (he) or *ella* (she) in a sentence the way English, French, and other languages do. It is enough to say *Es dinámica.* What would happen in terms of processing for the form of the adjective if each sentence began with a pronoun: *Ella es dinámica; El es comprensivo?* Would learners need to attend to the adjective ending to complete the task? Explain.

Research on Structured Input Activities

We refer to the activities just examined as *structured input activities,* and we refer to this overall approach to grammar instruction as *processing instruction.* The goal of processing instruction is to get learners to attend to grammatical data in the input and to process it. It does so by the use of structured input activities. In these activities, particular features of language are concentrated or "privileged" in a structured set of input utterances or sentences. A structured input activity, then, has the following key characteristics.

- The activity requires that the learner attend to the grammatical item in the input sentences while focused on meaning.
- Learners are asked *not* to produce the grammatical item, only to process it in the input.

The second characteristic of structured input activities is important. One of the criticisms of traditional grammar instruction is its emphasis on manipulating output. A structured input activity, on the other hand, focuses the learner on attending to grammatical form in the input. Thus, structured-input activities can be thought of as manipulated, comprehensible, meaning-bearing input—the ideal building material of second language acquisition.

How do we know that structured input activities (and thus processing instruction) are any better than traditional approaches to grammar instruction and practice? VanPatten and Cadierno investigated the effects of processing instruction in the teaching of direct-object pronouns in Spanish. In a carefully designed study (1993), they compared three groups: no instruction, traditional instruction (explanation + output practice), and processing instruction (explanation + structured input activities). Two assessment tasks were given in a pretest/posttest format: (1) a meaning-based interpretation task to see if subjects could correctly identify subjects and objects in a series of utterances by matching what they heard to a picture, and (2) a meaning-based production task in which subjects had to create a sentence based on a visual stimulus. Instruction for both the traditional group and the processing group lasted for two days, with no outside homework. The research incorporated a number of tight controls: equivalence in vocabulary, number of items for practice, instructor, and equivalence of ability on the target grammatical item before instruction among others. The results can be summarized as follows.

- The processing group made significant gains on the interpretation task after instruction, while the traditional group did not. The traditional group and control group did not differ from each other in terms of performance on the interpretation task.
- The processing group and the traditional group made equivalent significant gains on the production task after instruction.

A similar investigation was carried out by Cadierno (1992), using the preterit tense in Spanish. The results were exactly the same. The processing group made significant gains in both comprehension and production of preterit forms; the traditional group made gains only in production and was not significantly better at production than was the processing group. Another study was recently performed to determine whether the results of processing instruction would appear on more communicative production tasks. VanPatten and Sanz replicated the VanPatten and Cadierno study but added two other production tasks: a question-answer interview and a video narration task. They found that processing instruction had a significant effect on learners' ability to use direct object pronouns in their output (VanPatten and Sanz, in press).

The results of the research so far are clear: processing instruction has a significant impact on learners' developing linguistic systems, and that impact is observable in both comprehension and production of target items. The same cannot be said of traditional approaches to grammar instruction. What is especially exciting is that, in the research studies just cited, processing subjects never once produced the grammatical item during the experiment; their instruction was confined to structured input activities. Yet, they were able to produce the grammatical items *after* instruction as well as, if not better than, the subjects in the traditional groups could. This is a clear indication that we are on the right track in looking at grammar instruction from the viewpoint of input and input processing.

Before continuing, the reader might ask, But what of output? What does a "processing lesson" look like? What we propose is that structured input practices be a (crucial) first step in the acquisition of grammar but not the final step. In a given lesson, learners can and should be moved from input-based activities to output-based activities that focus on grammar; output activities are useful in developing accuracy of access as well as fluency. (Output and production activities with a grammar focus are considered in the next chapter.) We also encourage instructors and materials developers to examine the possible use of structured-input activities for use outside the classroom. Instead of drills and other mechanical practices, homework would be an ideal opportunity for learners to obtain additional structured input activities for building up their linguistic systems.

GUIDELINES FOR DEVELOPING STRUCTURED INPUT ACTIVITIES

It is appropriate now to establish some guidelines for the construction of structured input activities and provide examples of the many different types of activities that can be utilized in presenting structured input. Since most current textbooks and commercial materials do not contain input activities, instructors will need to develop their own as part of a grammar lesson. We present and explain each of the following principles that guide the construction of structured input activities.

Present One Thing at a Time

Structured input must be delivered to the learner's developing system in an efficient way. Maximum efficiency is achieved when one function and one form are the focus at any given time. This involves breaking up verb and noun/adjective paradigms or focusing on only one rule of usage at a time. Breaking up paradigms and lists of rules is useful for two reasons. First, it allows the explicit presentation and explanation of the grammatical structure to be kept to a minimum. The learner is not mired in a complex presentation and explanation of the grammatical item, as all forms and all functions are not being presented at once. Second, breaking up a paradigm is more likely to result in attention *directed* toward the targeted item. In other words, because there is less to pay attention to, it is easier to pay attention. Learners can be made aware of the rest of the paradigm and can be told that they will learn it over several days. The same is true for functions and uses of a grammar item. One possibility is to create overhead transparencies illustrating the paradigm or list of functions and to highlight (by circling and boxing) what is in focus during the lesson. As each new piece is presented, a different part of the transparency is highlighted.

Keep Meaning in Focus

Learners should not engage in the mechanical input activities of traditional grammar instruction. Remember that input should be attended to for its message so that learners can see how grammar assists in the "delivery" of that message. In the adjective-agreement example presented earlier (the "David Letterman and Madonna" activity), meaning was kept in focus by having

TABLE 5.2 Guidelines for the Development of Structured Input Activities

a. Present one thing at a time.
b. Keep meaning in focus.
c. Move from sentences to connected discourse.
d. Use both oral and written input.
e. Have the learner 'do something' with the input.
f. Keep the learner's processing strategies in mind.

Source: adapted from VanPatten (1993), pp. 438–39.

> ***P**ause to consider . . .*
>
> the teaching of past tense. Does the language you teach have a different past-tense form for each person (first-person singular, second-person singular, and so on)? What does this mean for the principle "Present one thing at a time"? With which form do you think you might begin instruction? Would you have to provide instruction for all the forms, or would instruction in only some of them serve to heighten learners' awareness sufficiently?
>
> Focus on just one form, say third-person, and develop an explanation for it as part of the "first day on past tense." How much would you really have to say before launching into some structured input activities? Can you keep your explanation short and concise—one minute or less?

learners identify the person to whom the propositional content of the sentence referred and by asking them to give an opinion. Read the following two activities that attempt to teach *-ing* complements with the English verb *enjoy*. Which of the two keeps meaning in focus? Which does not?

Activity E. Looking for Verb Endings. In the following paragraph circle all the uses of *-ing*. With what verb does it occur?

> Barnard Smith is an instructor who enjoys only certain aspects of his job. On the one hand, he enjoys teaching. He especially likes to teach Portuguese 101. He really enjoys preparing new and innovative tasks for learners to do in class. On the other hand, he does not enjoy correcting essays. He finds it tedious.

Activity F. Looking for Verb Endings. Check off the statements you think are true based on what you know about your instructor.

- ☐ He/She enjoys teaching.
- ☐ He/She enjoys watching the news at night.
- ☐ He/She enjoys preparing exams.
- ☐ He/She enjoys correcting exams.
- ☐ He/She does not enjoy reading student essays.

If you said that Activity E does not follow the principle of keeping meaning in focus but Activity F does, then you are correct. Note that in the first activity, the learner can perform the task of circling verb endings and noting that *enjoy* is the co-occurring verb without understanding the meaning of the sentences. If you need to prove this to yourself, then substitute the following nonsense words for the *-ing* verbs: *fract, croder, slarg.* The activity can still be performed, and it would be performed without making any form-meaning connections. In Activity F, on the other hand, the task cannot be performed without the learner making the form-meaning connections. In order to indicate whether or not the sentence is applicable to the instructor, the learner must know what the sentence means and how the grammar encodes meaning in each.

Move from Sentences to Connected Discourse

When we teach grammar via structured input activities, it is important to begin with sentences first, the shorter the better. Short, isolated sentences give learners processing time, whereas in longer stretches of speech, grammatical form can get lost if the demands to process meaning overwhelm the learner. The principle is exemplified in the following set of four activities (G–J) on the use of third-person singular verb forms. Note the progression of activities from isolated (but related) sentences to connected discourse (short narration).

Activity G. Alice and Ray. Look at the drawings of events from a typical day in the lives of Alice and Ray. Listen as your instructor reads a sentence. Say whether that activity is part of Alice's routine or Ray's.

> MODEL: (you hear) This person eats lunch with friends.
> (you say) That is Ray.

Activity H. In What Order? Without referring to the drawings about Ray's day, put the following activities in the correct order in which he does them.

_____ **a.** He goes to bed late.
_____ **b.** He sleeps in his math class.
_____ **c.** He works at the pizzeria.
_____ **d.** He goes to music class.
_____ **e.** He gets up late.
_____ **f.** He watches some TV.
_____ **g.** He eats lunch with friends.
_____ **h.** He tries to study.

Now compare with the drawings. Did you get them all in the right order?

Activity I. The Typical Student. Read the following sentences. Are they true for a typical student at your school?

The typical student . . .	TRUE	NOT TRUE
1. gets up at 6:30 a.m.	☐	☐
2. skips breakfast.	☐	☐
3. drives to school.	☐	☐
4. sleeps in at least one class.	☐	☐
5. studies in the library, not at home.	☐	☐
6. works part time.	☐	☐
7. eats a microwaved dinner.	☐	☐
8. watches David Letterman at night.	☐	☐
9. goes to bed after midnight.	☐	☐

Your instructor will now read each statement and then ask you to raise your hand if you marked it as true. Someone should keep track of the responses on the board. In the end, how did the class respond to each statement?

Activity J. John's Day.

Step 1. Break into groups of three and listen as your instructor reads a short narration.

Step 2. With your group members, give as many details as you can remember by completing the following sentences. The group with the most details wins. You have three minutes.

      1. John gets up at _____.
      2. He requires at least _____ to wake up fully.
      3. He prefers not to _____ in the morning.

      [*the list continues*]

Step 3. Look over the details that you have recalled. Read a sentence to the class and then say whether or not you do the same thing.

MODEL: John gets up at 8:00, and so do I.
           John gets up at 8:00, but I don't.

[*Part of narration read by instructor.* "John is a student at X university. On most days, he gets up at 8:00. But the mornings are very difficult for him since he just isn't a morning person. He needs to drink at least three cups of strong coffee to wake up. And more often than not he reads the newspaper in silence since he prefers not talking to anyone until he is fully awake . . ."]

Use Both Oral and Written Input

In activities, the learner should be provided opportunities to hear and see the input. In the progression of activities exemplified above, you saw both oral and written input. Note, however, that it is not just a matter of one activity being oral and one being written. In at least two activities, learners were exposed to both oral and written structured input. In Activity I, learners read sentences that they subsequently heard their instructor speak. In Activity J, learners heard structured input and then received structured written input on verb forms as they completed their sentences with other kinds of information. In short, any combination of oral and written input within a single activity is fine.

Suggesting that structured input be both oral and written is not just a matter of calling for variety in the activities. The issue here is individual variation. While all learners need oral input, some learners benefit from "seeing" the language and even claim they need to see it in order to learn it. Using oral input only would place these learners in uncomfortable—and ineffective—learning situations.

Have the Learner Do Something with the Input

Learners cannot be passive recipients of language. Instructors should not simply talk *at* the learners or ask learners to simply read something. The learner must be actively engaged in attending to the input to encourage the processing of grammar. In the examples that we have seen, the learner always responds to the input in some way: saying yes-no, agreeing-disagreeing, checking off things that apply, matching, ordering, and so on. Note that the learner *does not respond by producing the targeted structure.* In those cases where production does occur, it does not involve the structure contained in the input. For example, in Step 2 of Activity J (in which learners in groups of three attempted to recall details of the narration), the structured input contained third-person singular verb forms, but the information that learners produced did not require verb forms. Instead, they recalled time of day, food items, and other features. In order to provide the requested information, they needed to process the verb forms in each sentence in Step 2 (they had to know, for example, what *gets up* means in order to recall the requested information). Learners will certainly be given opportunities to produce the forms in subsequent activities, but at this point in the day's lesson we are concentrating on providing learners with structured input and having them actively process it.

Keep the Learner's Processing Strategies in Mind

Learners should focus attention during processing on the relevant grammatical items and not on other elements of the sentence. Return to Activity B on past tense. Do you recall that temporal adverbials such as *right now* and *later* were not used in the structured-input activities? This is because we were keeping in mind the processing strategies that learners use, and we wanted them to focus on the verb endings rather on the lexical items. Here are two additional examples: If one is teaching person-number endings, it does little good to have each and every input sentence contain an explicit subject noun or pronoun because the learner is more likely to attend to this for person number information than to the verb ending. Or, if one is teaching object pronouns in Spanish, it does little good to have each sentence begin with an explicit subject. Rather, "target" input sentences should begin with object pronouns, and subjects should be implied or positioned after the verb.

---

*P*ause to consider . . .

what to do if your language, like English, requires subject nouns and pronouns. French, for example, requires explicit subjects. One must say *Il se lève*; one cannot say *Se lève* (at least under standard and typical conditions!). How does the following input activity "keep in mind the processing strategy" of word order and lexical items vs. grammatical form? (The activity is part of a series that focuses on third-person object pronouns.)

Activité. Select a female relative or friend and then indicate which sentences apply to you.

Nom: _____   Relation: _____

Je …
☐ 1. la déteste.
☐ 2. la respète.
☐ 3. la connais (plus que les autres).
☐ 4. la visite les fins de semaine.
☐ 5. l'admire.

When we work with processing instruction and structured input, we should not lose sight of one of the critical tenets of communicative language teaching: *a focus on the learner.* Thus, processing instruction includes structured-input activities that are *affective* in nature: activities that ask for an opinion, require a personal response, or, in general, tap the student's own world. However, in the first few activities in a sequence, it is useful to begin not with learner-centered activities but with what can be called *referentially oriented activities.* These are activities that use an immediate concrete reference to ascertain the truth-value of a sentence. For example, a picture is shown and students are asked which of two sentences best describes the picture. The picture creates the immediate reference, and there is only one right or wrong answer. Referentially oriented activities enable instructors to ascertain whether or not students are actually focusing on the relevant grammatical items in the input before being led into affectively oriented activities. The use of referential and affective activities is exemplified in the sequence of activities presented earlier: Activities G and H are purely referential; Activities I and J are affective, and Step 3 of Activity J requires a purely personal response. All four activities, however, focus on third-person present-tense verbs.

TYPES OF ACTIVITIES FOR STRUCTURED INPUT

What learners do with input can be classified into various types of structured input activities, as depicted in Figure 5.3. Variations in content and technique within each of these activity types can help to create a variety of activities. For example, within the category of binary options (that is, giving learners two possible answers), one can answer "True" or "False," "Yes" or "No," "Agree" or "Disagree," "Mom" or "Dad," "instructor" or "student," "dog" or "cat," "Good" or "Bad," or any other two-option answer.

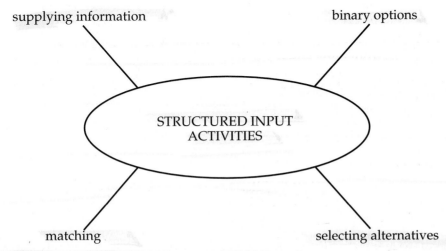

FIGURE 5.3. Major Types of Structured Input Activities

Binary Options

Let's take an activity based on a binary option and demonstrate how it can be altered using a different binary option. Recall that Activity I required learners to indicate what is true for the average learner at their school. This activity can be recast as (or even followed up by) a "Likely"-"Unlikely" selection task.

Activity K. The Typical Student. (alternative version of Activity I). Based on your experience, determine whether the following are likely or unlikely.

LIKELY	UNLIKELY	
☐	☐	**1.** A student who works part time takes more morning classes.
☐	☐	**2.** An engineering student studies more than an art student.
		(and so forth)

Matching

In matching activities, the learner indicates the correspondence between an input sentence and something else: matching a picture to an input sentence, matching a name to an input sentence, matching an event to its cause (both could be input sentences), matching an event to its logical consequence (both could be input sentences), matching a name to an action, matching days of the week to an activity. Returning to our example of the use of third-person present tense, in Activities G and H you saw how learners matched an input sentence to a person (Alice or Ray). In the following activity, learners match events to other events in order to make logical connections.

Activity L. Associations. For each sentence in Column A, indicate to which activity in Column B it is most logically connected.

Column A	Column B
Alice …	She …
1. works part time.	**a.** goes to the gym.
2. exercises five times a week.	**b.** studies every night.
3. gets good grades.	**c.** earns $5.00 an hour.

Supplying Information

In Activity J, learners supplied missing information. The input was structured around third-person verb forms used to talk about people's routines. The information that the learners supplied did not require them to produce the targeted verb forms; the verbs were already supplied. For example, "He prefers not to _____ in the morning." Thus, in information-supplying activities that provide structured input, learners don't produce the grammatical item that is being taught but something else.

For another example, read the following activity, in which learners are getting structured doses of a particular English modal in the input (but it could just as well be the morphological conditional tense in Romance languages). What kind of information are they supplying?

Activity M. Would He or Would He Not?

Step 1. Select someone from the class whom you all think you know well. That person should sit by himself during the first part of this activity.

Step 2. Write that person's name in the blank as indicated. Then complete each statement with information that you believe to be true.

Unless he had to, _____
(name)

1. would never eat _____.

2. would never watch _____.

3. would never go to _____.

4. would never spend money on _____.

5. would never _____.

On the other hand, _____
(name)

6. would probably eat _____ without reservation.

7. would go to _____ on vacation.

8. would study _____, time permitting.

9. would gladly spend money on _____.

10. would _____.

Step 3. Each group should give its completed statements to the instructor, who will read each statement aloud. If the selected person says "That's true," then the group will receive a point. Which group knows him the best?

Selecting Alternatives

In this category is included any type of activity in which learners are given a stimulus and are asked to select from three or more alternatives. Either the stimulus or the alternatives contain the targeted grammatical items that are being practiced in the activity. Selecting alternatives is illustrated in the following structured-input activity, which focuses learner attention on third-person present tense.

Activity N. How Well Do You Know Your Instructor? Select the phrase that best completes each statement about your instructor. Afterward, your instructor will tell you if you are correct or not.

1. As soon as he gets home, my instructor . . .
    a. reads the mail.   b. has a cocktail.
    c. plays with his children/dog/cat.   d. does something else.
2. When it's time for dinner, he . . .
    a. prepares the meal.   b. helps with the meal.
    c. waits for the meal.   d. orders a pizza.

[the activity continues in similar fashion]

Surveys

One of the more engaging activities providing structured input is the survey. The survey is interesting to learners because they interact with a variety of class-mates and the focus is, of course, on them. In a survey, one or both of the follow-ing can happen: (1) the learner responds to a survey item, (2) the learner elicits survey information from someone else. Surveys can use a variety of the response formats discussed above (binary options, supplying information, selecting from alternatives, and matching) with typical survey tasks including the following:

- indicating agreement with a statement
- indicating frequency of an activity
- answering "Yes" or "No" to particular questions
- finding a certain number of people who respond to an item in the same way

In the following survey, learners first indicate their own degree of agreement with each statement. The statements are structured to target the grammatical concept of object pronouns, concentrating on first-person plural.

Activity O. Attitudes toward the Government

Step 1. Indicate the extent to which you agree with each statement.

5: strongly agree
4: agree
3: somewhat in agreement
2: disagree
1: strongly disagree

The government . . .	5	4	3	2	1
1. understands us.	☐	☐	☐	☐	☐
2. helps us.	☐	☐	☐	☐	☐
3. controls us.	☐	☐	☐	☐	☐
4. ignores us.	☐	☐	☐	☐	☐
5. taxes us too much.	☐	☐	☐	☐	☐
6. doesn't represent us.	☐	☐	☐	☐	☐
7. guides us.	☐	☐	☐	☐	☐

Step 2. Share your responses with the class. Someone should tabulate the scores and calculate a class average for each item.

Step 3. Overall, does the class have a positive, negative, or mixed attitude toward the government?

> *P*ause to consider . . .
>
> the effect of converting Step 1 of Activity O to a paired activity with one learner interviewing the other. Does the underlying purpose of the activity change? Will both learners still be exposed to structured input if one interviews the other?

Signature searches are a type of survey activity in which learners mill around the room attempting to find people who can answer affirmatively to a particular statement. In the following signature search, learners gather information related to their classmates' moods and states of being. (In many Romance languages, as in this example from a Spanish class, the verbs all would require reflexive pronouns; the English version requires the verb *get* to indicate change of state.)

Activity P. State of Mind. Find people in the class who answer "Yes" to the questions below. Rules: (1) you may not use anything but Spanish; (2) you may not ask a person more than one question in a row; (3) if you find someone who answers "Yes" to a question, ask for that person's signature on the line next to the question; (4) when being asked a question, listen carefully and do not look at your paper; (5) do not sign your name unless you have been asked a complete question.

1. Do you get tense when speaking in Spanish?_____
2. Do you get nervous before taking a big exam?_____
3. Do you get angry easily?_____
4. Do you get depressed during the holidays?_____
5. Do you get bored when you're not in school?_____

As a follow up, the instructor can ask learners to report on their findings "Robert, who said that he gets angry easily? (David) Dave? Is this true? Do you get angry easily? At people or at things? When you get angry with a person, do you normally tell that person?").

Some might find it confusing that we classify signature searches as structured input. After all, aren't the learners talking? Aren't they producing the structure that you are trying to embed in the input? The answer is that they aren't. In Activity P, the learners are not creating structures or forms; they are reading aloud. Everything they need is right there on paper; in other words, output is not generated from the developing system. Learners who ask the questions get input because they must read the questions and know what they mean. The learner who responds "Yes" or "No" receives oral input from a classmate. No original language is created or produced during the task. Signature searches, as well as other surveys and activities in which students do not create language, serve another function: they place input in the hands of the learner. Note that, during the signature search (and a survey), the person asking the question or reading the statement provides input to the person listening. In this way, learners share in the work of providing input. This is why

it is important to tell learners to *listen* to the other person and not read from the page at the same time when being asked a question.

P*ause to consider . . .*

the nature of active and passive responses. Recall from the first section of Chapter 4 that the terms *active* and *productive* have in the past been used to refer to skills such as speaking or writing. Listening and reading skills, on the other hand, were described by the terms *passive* or *receptive.* Now reformulate the notion of "active" based on what you know about input processing. What new concept do you have for "active"? How would you characterize the differences between speaking/writing and listening/reading in your reformulation?

SUMMARY

In this chapter, we critically examined traditional grammar instruction in terms of second language acquisition theory and research. Specifically, we saw that traditional grammar instruction seeks to manipulate learners' output, whereas the developing system is dependent upon input for its growth. Because acquisition is "input dependent" and we want our classes to be communicatively rich, we outlined an alternative approach to grammar instruction. First, we examined strategies that learners use to process input and found that certain strategies can easily work *against* the perception and processing of grammatical form in the input. We then discussed how structured input activities could exploit these strategies to *ensure* that learners attend to grammatical items in the input. Finally, examples of certain types of structured input activities, as well as principles to guide their creation, were offered.

Missing from the present chapter is a discussion of output. We are not suggesting that learners should never produce the grammatical items and that they should only get structured input. Nothing could be further from the truth. In the next chapter, we explore meaning-based grammar activities, which we call "structured output." For now, we stress that getting grammar into learners' heads requires them to process meaning-bearing input first. Our contention is that input can be structured to highlight a particular grammatical feature and aid its acquisition.

KEY TERMS, CONCEPTS, AND ISSUES

traditional grammar instruction
behaviorism
historical inertia
grammar drills

mechanical
meaningful
communicative
relationship of instruction to language acquisition
input vs. intake
input processing
processing strategies
communicative value
, structured input guidelines for the construction of structured input activities ⌐
    present one thing at a time
    keep meaning in focus
    move from sentences to connected discourse
    use both oral and written input
    have the learner do something with the input
    keep the learner's processing strategies in mind ✓
- referential vs. affective activities
activity types for structured input
    binary option
    supplying information
    matching
    selecting alternatives
vocabulary and structured input

EXPLORING THE TOPICS FURTHER

1. *Efficacy of structured input.* Cadierno's dissertation (1992) is highly readable and provides considerable detail on the research she and VanPatten conducted. VanPatten and Cadierno's (1993) article is shorter reading than the dissertation and also quite informative. See also VanPatten (1993).
2. *The debate on the role of grammar in second language instruction.* In Chapter 2 of the same dissertation, Cadierno reviews the literature on the effects of form-focused instruction. VanPatten (1988) explains some of the problems with the evidence for the effects of instruction, not the least of which is how instruction is carried out. See also Garrett (1986), Krashen (1982), and Terrell (1991) for various perspectives on the role of grammar instruction.
3. *Effects of instruction.* In a quantitative fashion, Long's classic (1983) article addressed the question, Does instruction make a difference? Ellis (1986) addresses the same question in his book by examining the effects on rate, route, and ultimate attainment in the target language; see, especially, Chapter 9. A similar review is found in the book by Larsen-Freeman and Long (1991, Chapter 8). See *Studies in Second Language Acquisition* (June 1993), a special issue of that journal focusing on the role of grammar instruction in second language acquisition.
4. *Input processing.* For research and discussion on input processing, read VanPatten (1994) and Mangubhai (1991). Some of the child language acquisition literature is pertinent to the present discussion, most notably Peters (1985).
5. *Communicative value.* VanPatten's work (1985b, 1990) on the role of communicative value in input processing is fairly accessible reading. See Bransdorfer (1991) for a review of the work on communicative value.

Structured Output: A Focus on Form in Language Production

output *(out' poŏt')* n. *1. the act of producing; production. 2. the amount of something produced or manufactured in a given span of time.*
American Heritage Dictionary

INTRODUCTION

Every language learner has had the awkward experience of groping for words and forms when communicating in the second language. The following exchange is a good example.

SPEAKER: Vous connaissez les œuvres de Hugo?
LEARNER: Je-uh, je lis—*no that's not right*—je ... j'ai lit ... lu? J'ai lu? *No,* j'ai lit, *yeah,* j'ai lit «Les Miserables» uh, dans le lycée, *but in English. I mean,* en anglais.

Do you remember struggling with forms and producing halted and nonfluent speech when you were learning your second language? Do you still sometimes come to a verb form and tick off its conjugations in your head before actually producing the form? Or do you produce a form or a structure and think to yourself, That doesn't sound right? These questions are related to issues of access during production and how learners tap their linguistic systems to produce utterances in the second language.

In the previous chapter, we examined the use of structured input to help get form into the learner's developing system. Our theory was that, because the developing system uses intake derived from input, instruction might try to structure the input in particular ways and at particular times to facilitate the process of extracting form and structure from the input. The learner would get "concentrated" input that still met the fundamental requirements of input for acquisition: it would be meaning bearing and comprehensible. This input would result in richer grammatical intake for use by the developing system.

In the present chapter, we examine the parallel concept of *structured output*. In order to understand the rationale behind structured output, we introduce the concept of *access* as it relates to productive use of language. We then examine why certain traditional output-based activities are insufficient/ineffective in terms of developing fluency. This examination leads us to propose the use of structured output in language teaching.

WHY "OUTPUT"?

117

*CHAPTER 6
Structured Output:
A Focus on Form in
Language Production*

As you read the previous chapter and reviewed the activities that focus on structured input, you might have said to yourself that input is not enough, that learners must eventually use a form or structure in their output. We agree with this position. While input is *necessary* for creating a system, input is not *sufficient* for developing the ability to use language in a communicative context. Recall that the processes involved in producing language, or what might be called "making output," can be distinguished from those used in getting language into the developing system. Production of the foreign language (be it writing or speaking) involves those processes that operate at point III in Figure 6.1. These processes include *access* (retrieval of correct forms), *monitoring* (editing one's speech when one realizes "something is wrong"), and *production strategies* (stringing forms and words together to make sentences) and are affected by a variety of factors.

For the purposes of our discussion of output and a focus on form, we concentrate on the concept of *access* in this chapter. *Access* is a term coined by Terrell (1986 and 1991), the second major component of his *binding/access framework* (see Chapter 3 for a brief discussion of *binding*). According to Terrell, producing an utterance in a language minimally involves two processes or abilities: (1) being able to express a particular meaning via a particular form or structure; (2) being able to string forms and structures together in appropriate ways. The first ability Terrell calls "access," while he refers to the latter as "production strategies." An example of access would be coming up with the word *went* when attempting to express the concept of "having gone somewhere," as opposed to *will go* when talking about some projected or intended going.

As Terrell points out, access does not follow automatically from acquisition. Just because a learner has incorporated a particular form or structure in the developing system does not mean that it can be accessed easily (and thus produced automatically). In fact, learners can acquire a great deal of grammatical information but not be able to use it in communicative situations, as in the case of learners in courses such as "German for Reading Knowledge." In these kinds of reading-based courses, learners build up a system, but their experience with the language does not include opportunities to create output. In one informal experiment that he conducted, Terrell (personal communication) noted certain positive effects of providing opportunities for making output. In the first session of a German-as-a-foreign-language class, learners received a Total Physical Response lesson. All learners listened to and then carried out particular commands. During the second session, half the learners gave the same commands to the other half. The result was that half the learners received input only while the other half received input *and* were required

input ⟶ intake ⟶ developing system ⟶ output

FIGURE 6.1. An Outline of Processes in Second Language Acquisition

TABLE 6.1. Results of Terrell's Informal Experiment on Access

Learners	Average access time
Those who received commands (received input only)	2.23 seconds
Those who gave commands after receiving input	1.68 seconds

Source: Terrell (personal communication)

to access and make output. Each student in the class was subsequently tested on the ability to access the forms, that is, his ability to produce the correct command. The test revealed that all learners could access but that those who had to give the commands after listening to them and acting them out could access faster (see Table 6.1)

> ***P****ause to consider . . .*
>
> the factors that might influence the ability to access grammatical forms and structures from the developing system. Terrell mentions the "strength of binding," namely, the frequency of the form in the input so that its presence in the developing system is reinforced. Can you think of other factors? What about phonological (sound) shape? Relationship to other forms and structures? Number of functions attached to one form and vice versa (number of forms attached to one function)?

In short, while input processing is linked to acquiring form and structure, access is linked to *accuracy* (correctness) and *fluency* (ease and speed) in output. The implication for language instruction is that learners need not only input to build a developing system but also opportunities to create output in order to work on fluency and accuracy. Focusing on fluency and accuracy, however, does not necessarily entail a return to mechanical drills and meaningless practice. A focus on output in language instruction should make every attempt to have learners produce language that communicates something—has meaning—to someone else.

TRADITIONAL APPROACHES
TO FORM-FOCUSED OUTPUT

A survey of introductory language textbooks reveals an almost exclusive focus on production. As soon as vocabulary is presented, there are exercises for producing it. When pronunciation is taught, it is via production. And when grammar is presented, every textbook has hundreds of manipulative and controlled practices that have the learner "creating" output with particular forms or structures. In Chapter 5, we questioned the utility of these practices for getting linguistic information *into* the developing system. But one could also ask if these output-oriented drills actually have any utility for building accuracy and fluency in output. Before answering this question, we briefly review the nature of such exercises.

In the last chapter, we saw that traditional approaches to grammar instruction focusing on output very often involve what Paulston noted as a progression from mechanical to meaningful to communicative drills. These drills are distinguished according to two criteria: (1) focus on meaning and (2) range of possible student responses. Recall that a mechanical drill is an exercise in which learners do not have to understand the stimulus or even understand what they are saying in order to complete the exercise: there is no focus on meaning. The substitution of nonsense words was used to demonstrate this. In addition, there is always one—and only one—learner response possible in a mechanical drill. With meaningful drills, learners must understand the meaning of both the stimulus and their answer; it is not possible to substitute nonsense words in the practice and still reach the desired effect. As in mechanical drills, in meaningful drills there is only one response possible and that response is known by instructor and other learners alike. Communicative drills are also meaning focused, but, unlike mechanical drills and meaningful drills, the range of learner responses is open since there is no single correct response. In short, there is some kind of exchange of unknown information in communicative drills.

The original purpose of mechanical drills was to instill good habits in language learners and to internalize correct forms and structures. Yet, given the developments of second language acquisition research and the importance placed on input and input processing in developing an internal system, the original function of mechanical drills is lost. Do they serve some other purpose? Do they serve to increase fluency or accuracy? Following Lamendella's 1977 work, we can question the use of pattern practice and mechanical drills. According to him, mechanical drills do not make use of the same brain processes (or *neural networks*) involved in accessing language during communicative language use. Mechanical drills bypass deeper levels of processing where form-meaning connections are involved. Viewed in another way, the learner "switches off" the mechanisms and processes used in relating form to meaning and performs the drill without thinking very much. Recall that the definition of access is "being able to express a particular meaning via a particular form or structure." The learner generally performs mechanical drills in such a way that the processes needed to develop more fluent and accurate access are bypassed. Whatever has potential for being learned is not processed deeply enough to make a difference.

More recently, Schmidt has questioned the utility of mechanical drilling and practice based on his review of possible psychological mechanisms underlying the development of fluency. After reviewing five major models of skill development from the field of cognitive psychology, Schmidt concludes that there is no theoretical support for the belief that fluency is simply a matter of increasingly skillful application of rules: learning a rule and then practicing it until it becomes automatic.

As commonly practiced, the technique of pattern practice rests on the assumption that short training sessions with a small number of exemplars, each of which is typically practiced once, will lead to fluency based on automatic rule application. The theories reviewed in this paper suggest that unless such practice is very extensive (introducing the boredom factor), neither the specific examples practiced nor the general rule will be available subsequently for fluent use. (Schmidt 1992, p. 381)

Even if one were to accept the belief that practice makes perfect (or fluent, in this case), Schmidt rightfully points out that the psychological literature that *could* be used to support this position has nothing to do with language. Studies on practice and training effects involve such nonlinguistic issues as typing, target-letter detection, and alphabet arithmetic. It is difficult to conceive of the same psychological mechanisms responsible for rapid performance in those studies underlying the much more complex and cognitively challenging tasks of first or second language speaking as well.

In short, we do not see much utility in mechanical practice for the development of fluency and accuracy in production. Mechanical practice is obsolete, based on shaky theoretical constructs tied to habit-formation theory. In terms of communicative language teaching, mechanical practice is of dubious value. But isn't it nevertheless true that meaningful and communicative drills involve form-meaning connections, so aren't they consistent with the broader philosophies and aims of communicative language teaching? While this is indeed true in principle, in practice researchers have found that meaningful drills are not the best use of class or homework time. Given the limitations in both class and outside work, communicating already-known information has been shown to be a poor way to facilitate the development of the processes underlying access. The reasoning is simple: Why spend time creating messages that your listener or reader already knows?

Several researchers have investigated what learners do with communicative drills in class. (We give more detailed discussion of this research in Chapter 8, so we will touch upon only the major issues here.) Because learners understand quickly that the purpose of meaningful and communicative drills is to practice a grammar point, they very often abandon the informational message in the utterances and convert the practice into a mechanical drill (Brooks 1990; Kinginger 1990). That is, focus on meaning is minimal if not nonexistent, and learners instead concentrate on getting the form or structure correct. This is particularly true when the learners encounter such drills outside of any larger communicative purpose. Kinginger's findings point to learners focusing on the *drill* and not the *communicative* part of a communicative drill.

For example, in the following communicative drill (which does require the exchange of unknown information) the two learners must use the present perfect to communicate. The activity's grammatical focus does not escape either instructors or learners. Yet, as the practice unfolds, being accurate with the grammar becomes more important than exchanging information because the latter aspect of the activity is rather incomplete. Each sentence is disconnected from the others.

Use the following verbs to describe what you have or have not done this weekend.

MODEL: study → I have not studied chemistry this week.

1. open
2. write
3. leave
4. break
5. speak

In addition, in the materials from which this practice was taken, several mechanical drills precede it. Thus, the communicative practice is actually preceded by a series of activities in which informational exchange is either tenuous or nonexistent. The communicative drill does not form part of a cohesive series of activities based on information exchange. As a result, learners may very well perform this activity by simply "going through the motions." The crucial question that emerges from this discussion is the following: Can classroom output activities that focus on form also be activities that focus on information exchange? The answer is yes, and we turn our attention now to these types of activities.

STRUCTURED OUTPUT: FORM WITH MEANING

In this section we explore what we call "structured output activities." *Structured output activities* have two major characteristics.

1. They involve the exchange of previously unknown information.
2. They require learners to access a particular form or structure in order to express meaning.

Structured output activities share most of the same guidelines for construction that we developed in Chapter 5 for structured-input activities. The obvious exception is that the guidelines refer to production, not input. These guidelines for developing structured output activities are listed in Table 6.2. We will review these guidelines by examining three different activities.

Applying the Guidelines to Create Structured Output Activities

Presenting "one thing at a time" once again refers to focusing on only one form and one function of a particular grammatical device or structure. Re-

TABLE 6.2 Guidelines for the Development of Structured Output Activities

a. Present one thing at a time.
b. Keep meaning in focus.
c. Move from sentences to connected discourse.
d. Use both written and oral output.
e. Others must respond to the content of the output.
f. The learner must have some knowledge of the form or structure.

member that most traditional output drills have learners manipulate a variety of forms in one activity; they also generally attempt to cover all functions of a form or structure within several activities. With structured output, the focus is on one form and/or one function at a time. In the following French-language activity, "Present one thing at a time" means the following: (1) only the second-person singular of (2) the past tense (imperfective aspect) within the context of talking about (3) habitual actions. In other words, the activity does not include all person-number manipulations mixing imperfective and perfective aspect.

Activity A. What You Used to Do.

   Step 1. You are attempting to find out if a fellow classmate was a model student in high school. Think of questions that you can ask about what he or she used to do or about events that used to happen involving your partner that would help you gather the information. You should probably come up with about eight good questions.

   MODÈLE: Est-ce que tu faisais des questions quand tu ne comprenais pas quelque chose? *(Did you usually ask questions when you didn't understand something?)*

   Step 2. Now, interview the person of your choice. Be sure to jot down your partner's responses because you will need them later.

Activity A satisfies the requirement "Present one thing at a time" because the learner focuses on producing *tu* (second-person singular) forms and each question formulated concerns a past habitual action or event. In addition, the activity follows the second guideline, "Keep meaning in focus." Each and every question created by the learner is for the purpose of obtaining information from someone else. Thus, both questioner and respondent must attend to meaning.

Pause to consider . . .

the nature of the communication in Activity A. Would the interviewee have to respond with complete sentences? Keep in mind the purpose of the activity as you respond. Is the purpose for the interviewer to practice making output or for the interviewee to practice making output?

The guideline "Sentence-level output should precede discourse-level output" points to the importance of allowing learners to access forms and structure at the sentence level before proceeding to connected sentences. This does not mean that output for beginners should be restricted to sentences only and that discourse-level output should be reserved for more advanced learners. It merely suggests that, within a given lesson or series of activities, learners should not be forced to string utterances together at the outset. In the following sequence of activities focusing on first-person object pronouns (*me* in Italian), notice how the learner moves from output with simple sentences to output involving connected sentences.

Activity B. My Friends.

Step 1. Write at least five statements about what your friends do for you—or to you—that makes you appreciate them.

ESEMPIO: Me ascoltano. *(They listen to me.)*

Step 2. Now write at least five statements about what your friends do to or for you that sometimes gets on your nerves.

ESEMPIO: Non me renderono di soldi. *(They don't return money to me.)*

Step 3. Now present your sentences to a partner. Your partner will subsequently present his/her sentences to you. How much similarity is there?   *— connected discourse*

Activity C. My Parents.

Step 1. Now think about your parents. What do they do to or for you? Repeat Steps 1 and 2 from Activity B, this time substituting your parents for your friends.

Step 2. Compare and contrast your friends and parents by sharing your statements with the class. Use connectors like *anche* and *ma* as well as topic starters like *Per cominciare* to make your presentation flow.

[Instructor notes: Tell students to jot down things they hear. Afterward, class explores the question, Is there a pattern to our relationships with friends and parents that we can see based on this information?]

You may also notice that the string of Activities B and C, as well as the steps within the activities, demonstrates another guideline for structured output: "Use both written and oral output." The actual roles of written and oral output in activities depend on purpose and topic. Overall, however, structured output activities should not favor one of these modalities over the other. One might include both written and oral output within the same activity, or some activities might be oral and others written. Again, choice depends on purpose and topic.

The guideline "Others must respond to the content of the output" indicates that the output created by the learner is purposeful: because it contains a message, someone in some way must respond to the content of the message. As exemplified in the activities above, a response can be a number of things including:

- comparing with something else
- taking notes, then writing a paragraph about what was said
- making a list of follow-up questions and interviewing a partner to get the new information
- filling out a grid or chart based on what was said
- signing something
- indicating agreement or disagreement
- determining veracity of the statement
- responding using any of several scales
- drawing something
- answering a question

(You might wish to review the types of responses to structured input given in Chapter 5, since many overlap.) The point here is that the respondent must indicate in some way that he or she has attended to the meaning of the other's output.

Pause to consider . . .

why it is important to ensure that the meaning of a learner's output is attended to. What might happen if it were not?

The final guideline, that "The learner must have some knowledge of the form or structure," simply means that structured output activities flow from previous work. They are not starting points but part of a continuum of work with a particular grammatical feature. This brings us to a question: What is the relationship of structured output to structured input? In the communicative approach we favor, structured output follows structured input. Structured input encourages form-meaning connections during input processing so that intake is created for the developing system. Because structured output activities work at accessing existing or developing linguistic knowledge, they should thus follow structured input activities rather than precede them when both types of activities focus on the same grammatical form or structure.

Pause to consider . . .

activities A, B, and C above. In what way do these particular structured output activities serve also as structured input activities? (Hint: Think about not what the output maker is doing but what the other person is doing.) Would you say that this is probably the case for most structured output activities? Why, or why not?

PARADIGMS AND RELATED ISSUES

125

CHAPTER 6
*Structured Output:
A Focus on Form in
Language Production*

The guideline "Present one thing at a time" might prompt some instructors to ask, "Since learners get exposure to pieces and parts of grammar via structured input and output, when do they get to see the "big picture"? When do they see the actual paradigm or the list of rules?" Before answering the question, it is important to review what a paradigm is as well as what motivates the question.

In linguistics, a *paradigm* is a representation that displays the various forms of a given grammatical structure. While we often think of paradigms as verb paradigms, the concept of a paradigm is readily applied to nouns, articles, relative pronouns, and other grammatical features. Following are sample paradigms from Spanish, French, and German, respectively, that illustrate the various uses of paradigms.

Spanish Verbs that Take -g

hacer *(to do; to make)*		poner *(to put; to place)*		salir *(to leave; to go out)*	
hago	hacemos	pongo	ponemos	salgo	salimos
haces	hacéis	pones	ponéis	sales	salís
hace	hacen	pone	ponen	sale	salen

French Contractions of à *and* de *with the Definite Articles* le *and* les

à + le = **au** à + les = **aux**	de + le = **du** de + les = **des**

German Personal Pronouns in the Accusative

Singular		*Plural*	
mich	*me*	uns	*us*
Sie	*you*	Sie	*you*
dich	*you*	ihr	*you*
ihn	*him, it*		
sie	*her, it*	sie	*them*
es	*it*		

Paradigms, it should be noted, are abstractions and generalizations. They are tools to organize information and present data, but they do not correspond to the way knowledge is structured in the brain. What is especially important is that paradigms represent neither the way morphological forms are acquired nor the order in which they are acquired. As argued by a number of linguists and psycholinguists (see, for example, Bybee 1991), paradigms do not exist in native speakers' heads unless put there by teachers or books. The child who enters elementary school in Argentina is perfectly capable of using most verb forms in Spanish and does not have a grid in her head explicitly marked with categories such as "singular/plural" and "first/second/third person." That child already possesses a complex network of form-meaning connections in which the form *pienso* (I think) is connected not only to the concept of "present tense" but also to *pensé* (preterit tense, "I thought"), *pensamiento* (the noun, "thought") and so on.

Likewise, the second language learner develops an equally complex, albeit in most cases incomplete, network that does not resemble any paradigm in a textbook. Bybee, for example, uses the following type of figure to illustrate how morphological information can be connected in the mind. (Note: *saber* = to know, *cantar* = to sing, and *comer* = to eat, *sabio* = wise, *canción* = song, *comida* = meal; food.)

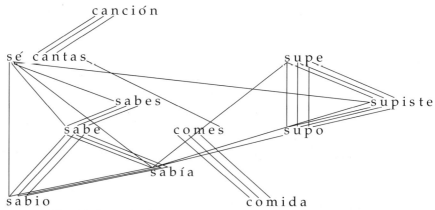

FIGURE 6.2. Mental Network of Verb Associations in Spanish.
Source: adapted from Bybee 1991, pp. 82–83

What Bybee suggests is that the psychological status of inflections and forms might come about only as learners *internalize whole words that contain those inflections.* Thus, a learner might internalize the verb *sé* first and then *sabe.* The *restructuring process* (the process that accommodates new linguistic data into the developing system) makes a connection between their common verb roots since their meanings are obviously connected (both involve the process of "knowing"). The learner might then internalize *sabes, cantas,* and *comes,* and still other connections begin to form in the mind (again, due to unconscious *restructuring*), this time related to verb endings. Learners might then get input data about the preterit (simple past) tense, and other connections begin to be made. The process continues, the connections becoming more and more complex and intertwined. Note that as learners acquire nouns and other words, these will also become connected to verbs if they share a root representing overlapping meanings *(comes, comida).* A paradigm, then, is actually a shorthand for a particular set of connections; paradigms have no psycholinguistic validity for acquisition.

Yet some learners report a need or desire for paradigms and many instructors feel a need to provide them. Our interpretation of this situation is that paradigms can serve an *affective* function: although lacking any immediate psycholinguistic usefulness, paradigms may satisfy some psychological or emotional need to summarize or keep track of the grammar. A learner might feel anxious or mystified without the "big picture" that a paradigm can provide. As suggested in Chapter 5, paradigms and lists can be used to show learners where they are headed, with the particular feature that is under immediate attention highlighted. In our experience, however, paradigms can thwart the acquisition of grammar if used to preview what is being learned. Instructors and learners alike might become so preoccupied with "mastering" the paradigm that they lose sight of the importance of developing form-meaning connections and the need to communicate real information in the classroom. They lose sight of the value of "one thing at a time" as learners struggle to cope with all the forms of a verb. In such cases, the presentation or use of the paradigm at the outset has lost its function as a previewing device and has become, instead, the goal.

This will become even more likely if the lesson goal is a formal test on the grammar feature. After all, if learners know or believe that a good grade depends on success in conjugating verbs and displaying knowledge of rules, then they will use a paradigm to help themselves memorize the material to be tested. Although this is probably a fine strategy for particular kinds of test preparation, the issue under discussion here is learning to speak and gaining fluency. Remember the example from the introductory section of this chapter and how the student halted and searched for the correct verb as he spoke? If learners memorize from paradigms, then they will generally grope for verb forms and even tick off verb conjugations in their mind as they attempt to speak: "Ellos no … *uh* … no voy … *I mean* … *uh* … voy, vas, va, vamos, van … van! Ellos no van." In cases such as this one, learners vocalize their thoughts and actually run through the paradigm orally. The result is halting and disfluent speech.

Another possibility, of course, is to present paradigms *after* some success with a set of forms or structures, to let students know what they have been learning. In this way, a paradigm can serve as a review, summarizing what has been learned or practiced.

Teaching one thing at a time and use or non-use of paradigms is related to another issue, namely, the purpose of grammar instruction. When grammar instruction serves the need of communication, then teaching one thing at a time makes special sense. Suppose, for example, that we have a lesson on "Talking about Your Weekend." The grammar item implied in this topic is the need for past tense to talk about what happened. However, "Talking about Your Weekend" is a broad topic. What aspects of the weekend are we talking about? What activities do we want to discuss? Is there some cognitive-informational purpose (for example, comparing what we did last weekend to what some other group did)? And, most importantly, *whom* do we want to talk about? We explore the nature of lesson goals and lesson structure in a later chapter, but it is important to point out here that a lesson on "Talking about Your Weekend" may require that only certain verb forms be used (not comprehended) by students. For example, the lesson may require only first-person singular (for talking about yourself), second-person singular (for asking a classmate questions), and/or third-person singular (to report on a fellow classmate). Thus, particular parts of a paradigm may be more important in one lesson than in another. Or, parts of a paradigm may be more important in one part of a lesson than in another part of that same lesson.

Here is one illustrative example. Returning to the topic "Talking about Your Weekend," we can imagine a scenario in which the lesson begins with talking about a typical student. Appropriate structured input and output activities would explore what the student probably did over the weekend, and so the learners would practice third-person singular past tense. The final structured output activity in the sequence might be the following.

Activity D. A Description. Based on all the activities and discussion that have taken place so far, create a short (seven or eight sentences) description of what the typical student on your campus did over the weekend. Remember to use such connectors as *also, but, on Saturday,* and any others you think of to give your description some flow and to connect the ideas smoothly.

Next, learners could work on first-person singular, again with appropriate structured input and output activities, with the final activity possibly the following.

Activity E. Last Weekend, I . . . With a partner, make statements about what you did over the weekend. Each time you make a statement your partner will respond with "I did, too" or "I didn't." When you and your partner have five activities in common, raise your hands. You will then share them with the class. (Note: Do not make simple statements like "I slept" or "I got up." Everyone sleeps and everyone gets up! Make statements such as "I slept ten hours Saturday night" or "I got up really late on Sunday—at noon.")

Finally learners could work on second-person singular using structured input and output activities, with the final activity being some sort of interview.

Looking again at the above sequence of activities for teaching past-tense verb forms, we see that if grammar is at the service of topics and communication, then the relevance of paradigms decreases. Because the immediate communicative goal of each part of the lesson is specifically delineated (talking about someone else's weekend, talking about your own weekend, asking questions of another person), only one piece of the paradigm is needed at each point of the lesson. One reason, then, that some instructors might question the guideline "Present one thing at a time" is that they do not see grammar at the service of communication. Indeed, they see communication at the service of grammar and look for ways to "practice the preterit in a communicative context." In this case, it is understandable why certain instructors are eager to have their students learn the "big picture."

VOCABULARY AND OUTPUT

The focus of this chapter has been grammar, namely, linguistic form and structure. However, Terrell's concept of access applies just as well to lexical items as it does to grammar; learners must develop fluency in vocabulary and must learn to access it easily and accurately during communicative interchanges. Thus, "structured output" is a concept that can be applied to the development of activities that encourage learners to use newly learned vocabulary in a productive manner. (Note: vocabulary and input were discussed in Chapter 3.)

Because the very nature of vocabulary encompasses meaning (words represent concepts), it is difficult to imagine vocabulary activities that are mechanical in nature. Although textbook materials generally use meaningful vocabulary practices before learners move on to communicative practices, many textbooks also follow another sequence in vocabulary learning and practice: from producing isolated words to producing phrases to producing utterances. While this sequence is not always observed rigidly, textbooks and instructional materials nevertheless tend to have students work first with single words and then with those words used in sentences. In one textbook, for example, the following activity is the first used to practice vocabulary useful for describing student rooms. Note how the learner need only respond with one word from the vocabulary list that precedes the activity. (The vocabulary list is embedded within a visual display contrasting two students' rooms. This is the visual that the activity refers to.)

Activity F. Two Rooms. Describe the two rooms. What is there . . .

1. on Mary's desk? on Jacqueline's desk?
2. next to Mary's bed? next to Jacqueline's bed?
3. under Mary's table? under Jacqueline's table?

Pause to consider . . .

how Activity F is meaningful but neither mechanical nor communicative. In what way do the criteria of (1) meaningfulness and (2) freedom of response determine that this is a "meaningful" practice? Next, reflect on the topic of this activity and the kind of speaking the learners produce. How meaningful is this meaningful practice?

Later, in the fourth activity in vocabulary used to describe rooms, the learner must string together utterances. Thus, the learner has moved from isolated words to connected sentences (discourse) with the new vocabulary.

Activity G. Rooms and Personalities. A room reveals an occupant's personality. Describe the room in the photo. What is in the room? What adjectives and words describe the room the best? Give as many details as you can.

Moving from isolated words to words used in sentences does not seem unreasonable to us during structured output activities. However, as we recommended in the previous section, work with vocabulary does not have to be a series of unconnected activities. Nor should the work be divorced from the student's own world. Instead, the activities can form a series of connected pieces that build toward something: the learning of vocabulary has a purpose. In the following, note how we reconceptualize the activities described above so that they form part of some connected train of thought.

Activity H. On the Floor.

Step 1. Name the items that are on the floor in Mary's room.

Step 2. Now name the items that are on the floor in Jacqueline's room.

Step 3. Who leaves more items on the floor? Who would you say is neater?

Activity I. Compared to Your Room . . .

Step 1. Look at the photo below. Describe the room and tell where the objects can be found.

Step 2. Now compare the room in the photo to your own room. Are they similar or different? Who is neater? You or the occupant of the room in the photo?

Step 3. Present your case to the class to see if they agree. You might need phrases such as "I never leave . . . " or "I always put _____ away." Feel free to ask your instructor how you say other related phrases.

---

*P*ause to consider . . .

the teaching and learning of vocabulary in communicative language teaching. Do you see any need to introduce and work with vocabulary any differently from grammar? In what ways is the acquisition of grammar similar to the acquisition of vocabulary?

SUMMARY

In this chapter, we advocated the development and use of the output analog to structured input. Structured output activities enable learners to access forms and structures in their developing system to communicate an idea. (The actual development of the linguistic system was the focus of Chapter 5.) As with structured input activities, the creation of one's own structured output activities follows a series of guidelines. In terms of sequencing, structured-output activities should *follow* structured input activities. Thus, a coherent grammar lesson is one that takes the student from processing a grammatical feature in the input to accessing the feature from her developing system to create output. As with structured input activities, structured output activities are never divorced from meaning. During these kinds of activities learners make output that encodes a message.

We also discussed in some detail the nature of paradigms. Prompted by the guideline "Present one thing at a time," we explored the debate about when—and whether—learners should see the whole paradigm. We saw that paradigms lack psycholinguistic validity and are inventions of linguists and instructors for describing and talking *about* language. The suggestion that paradigms could be used as preview devices was accompanied by a note of caution, for they can undermine grammar instruction in the communicative classroom by becoming a list of things to master.

We ended the chapter with a brief discussion of vocabulary and output. It is clear that, as with grammar, learners need opportunities to use vocabulary to communicate information. Only in this way can they work on those processes responsible for the development of fluency and accuracy in second language speech.

KEY TERMS, CONCEPTS, AND ISSUES

input is necessary but not sufficient
output
access
  accuracy
  fluency
monitoring
production strategies
sequence of drills
  mechanical
  meaningful
  communicative
structured output
guidelines for creating structured output activities
  present one thing at a time
  keep meaning in focus
  move from sentences to connected discourse
  use both written and oral output
  others must respond to the content of the output
  learner must have some knowledge of the form or structure
restructuring
paradigms
  psycholinguistic validity
  instructional uses
    affective considerations
    preview
    summary
vocabulary and structured output
  words → sentences → discourse

EXPLORING THE TOPICS FURTHER

1. *The need for structured output.* For some arguments for the necessity of having learners work on production, see Terrell's (1986, 1991) discussions of binding (learning
from input) and access (production). A more challenging reading is by Swain (1985),
who argues for "comprehensible output": having learners produce, thus making
them better processors of input. Swain's perspective is based on immersion-pro-
gram data and complements work on language classrooms nicely.

2. *Traditional approaches to output.* Paulston (1972) presents the most succinct treatment
on output drills and practices. You might also want to look at the output activities
in such books as *Puntos de partida* (first through fourth editions), *Rendez-vous* (first
through third editions), and others. Rivers (1983, Chapters 2 and 3) describes some
of the limitations of drills, as does Krashen (1982).

CHAPTER 7

Suggestions for Testing Grammar

test (tĕst) n. 1. a means of examination, trial, or proof. 2. a series of questions or problems designed to determine knowledge or intelligence. 3. criterion; standard.

American Heritage Dictionary

INTRODUCTION

Why do learners always want to know if what is being taught is also going to be on the test? Have you ever asked an instructor, "Is this going to be on the test?" Why would a learner ask such a question? Some instructors feel that this question shows that the learners are not really interested in learning, or that the learners are too lazy to try to learn all the material. Perhaps, for some learners, the question might reflect laziness, but for others it reflects a concern with efficiency. One interpretation of the question, "Is this going to be on the test?" is that it signals how learners use tests to organize their time and interaction with the course content.

As we have seen, traditional grammar instruction is biased toward the manipulation of output. Consequently, so is traditional grammar testing. Traditional grammar tests all too often require learners to produce the grammar in mechanical and less-than-meaningful ways ("Fill in the blank with the correct form of . . ."). As we saw in Chapters 5 and 6, grammar instruction can and should focus on meaning. To do so, learners should first be given the opportunity to process grammatical forms in the input and to make form-meaning connections; this aids the development of the internal linguistic system (Chapter 5). Output practice, as we have argued, should dispense with mechanical manipulations and should always engage the learner in creating utterances that carry messages (Chapter 6). Given this orientation in grammar *instruction*, what are the implications for *testing* grammar?

Because the primary goal of communicative language teaching is to promote learners' ability to interpret, express, and negotiate messages, grammar is taught and learned within the context of that goal. And because grammar is taught, most instructors (*all* instructors?) will test it. In this chapter, we offer some suggestions for testing grammar in what can be called "meaningful" or "communicative" ways. That is, we will present test sections in which the testing of grammar is consonant with the teaching of grammar. (In subsequent chapters, we offer suggestions for testing other aspects of the language.)

133

WASHBACK EFFECT

Krashen and Terrell made the following statement. It captures, for us, the essence of good classroom testing.

> [Testing] can be done in a way that will have a positive effect on the student's progress. The key to effective testing is the realization that testing has a profound effect on what goes on in the classroom. Teachers are motivated to teach and students are motivated to study material which will be covered on tests. Quite simply, if we want students to acquire a second language, we should give tests that promote the use of acquisition activities [in and out of the classroom]. In other words, our tests should motivate students to prepare for the tests by obtaining more comprehensible input and motivate teachers to supply it. Using an approach in the classroom which emphasizes the ability to exchange messages, and at the same time testing only the ability to apply grammar rules correctly, is an invitation to disaster. (Krashen and Terrell 1983, p. 165)

Krashen and Terrell point out what is generally referred to as a *washback effect*. What and how you test has ramifications for what instructors do in the classroom, what learners *expect* instructors to do in the classroom, and what learners do *outside* the classroom. In other words, testing cannot be viewed as an isolated event; it must be an integral part of the teaching/learning enterprise.

FOUR CRITERIA FOR A GOOD TEST

Carroll (1980) identifies four general criteria in foreign language testing: economy, relevance, acceptability, and comparability. By *economy*, Carroll means obtaining the greatest amount of information about the learners' language in as little time as possible and with a minimum of energy expended by either the instructor or learners. For a test to be economic, we suggest that it merely sample the material covered, not exhaust it. Sampling is part of everyday life. For example, we often read opinion polls about what America thinks. The pollsters do not ask every single American what he or she thinks; rather, they sample a group of Americans and infer or project from the sample to all Americans. So it can be with testing language in general and grammar in particular. An instructor can select from among the many items covered and infer or project something about the learner's overall knowledge or ability.

Relevance refers to the match between the course and curriculum goals and the tests. For example, if you teach a course called "Reading German for Graduate Students," you would not give an oral exam at the end of the course. If you teach a course in conversational use of Italian, you would not want to give a formal composition as the final exam. Creating formal written discourse is not relevant to a course emphasizing informal oral discourse. For a test to be relevant, we suggest that it reflect not simply what is taught but, more importantly, how it is taught. And of course, how we teach influences the types of tests we should give.

Acceptability is a concept that takes the learners' point of view into consideration. It implies learners' willingness to participate in the testing and their satisfaction that the test evaluates their progress. Learners should not perceive themselves as the victims of the test. For many learners, acceptability is tied to familiarity. If they are not familiar with a testing format or procedure, they may view it as unacceptable. For example, if free spontaneous recall ("Write down everything that you remember reading without looking back at the passage") was not an activity type used in class, then the learners might not accept it as a valid way to test their reading comprehension. Likewise, if an instructor uses the target language only fifty percent of the time in class, the learners might not accept a test of listening comprehension.

Comparability is a concept that takes the institution's point of view into consideration. It means that we should obtain similar test scores across different groups of learners taking the test at the same time, as well as similar scores across different tests at different times for the same group of learners. In other words, test scores for learners who are taught the same material by the same method should be similar. Also, different tests—whether they examine the same material or examine different material—should yield similar results. For example, those enrolled in the 9 a.m. section of Portuguese 102 should have test scores similar to the scores of learners enrolled in the 2 p.m. section if the two sections have common goals, materials, syllabi, and methods. The same test should also yield similar results if it is offered a year later. Finally, two different tests examining the same content should yield similar results. If one is harder or easier than the other, the results will not be comparable.

STRUCTURED INPUT FORMATS FOR TESTS

In Chapters 5 and 6 on grammar instruction, we presented guidelines for developing structured input and structured output activities. These guidelines, repeated below, help make grammar instruction consistent with the overall goals of communicative language teaching. In addition, they are informed by some general tenets of second language acquisition research. The principles are:

a. Present one thing at a time.
b. Keep meaning in focus.
c. Move from sentences to connected discourse.
d. Use both oral and written input/output.
e. Have the learner 'do something' with the input, or have other learners respond to the content of the output.

These same guidelines can be utilized in the construction of test sections. The sample test section below (Section A) uses an input-based testing procedure. Learners first must attend to the verb ending in order to determine which person is being described. They then agree or disagree and state their reasons. Note that meaning is kept in focus and that learners do something with the input. The guideline "Present one thing at a time" is observed because the items are restricted to the third-person singular. But the test section covers more than just this one verb form: two tenses are being tested as well (past and present). The items can be read to learners or by them, as both oral and written language are desirable.

Section A. John F. Kennedy or Bill Clinton? First match the sentence you hear with the man. Then indicate whether or not you think it is a true statement.

1. □ Kennedy   □ Clinton
    □ agree   □ disagree
2. □ Kennedy   □ Clinton
    □ agree   □ disagree
3. □ Kennedy   □ Clinton
    □ agree   □ disagree
4. □ Kennedy   □ Clinton
    □ agree   □ disagree

[Test takers hear the following items.]

1. He was a great man.   **2.** He keeps strange hours.   **3.** His brother wanted to be president, too.   **4.** He hopes to change America.

If an instructor employed both structured input and output activities in classroom lessons, then Section A will be consistent with the way the forms were taught and should therefore be both relevant and acceptable to the learners. It tests the learners' ability to attach meaning through the grammar. Section A is also an economical way of sampling learners' knowledge of present and past-tense verb forms. You do not need to test everything in one section!

Whereas Section A tests third-person singular, Section B tests the first-person plural. If both sections were part of an exam, the criterion of "relevance" would be met because learners would be tested on more than just the third-person forms. In the following test section, learners must again attend to verbal distinctions in order to determine the time frame of the sentence. Meaning is kept in focus in two ways: first, in the global context of having learners identify the frame of reference, and then by having the learners do something with the input (they indicate whether the item applies to them).

Section B. Indicate whether the speaker is relating information from his childhood or information about the present. Then decide if the information applies to you.

MODEL: (you hear) We would go to the beach for a week after school let out.
           (you choose):   childhood
           (you indicate): This does not apply to me.

1. □ childhood   □ present
    □ This applies to me.   □ This does not apply to me
2. □ childhood   □ present
    □ This applies to me.   □ This does not apply to me
3. □ childhood   □ present
    □ This applies to me.   □ This does not apply to me

[Test takers hear the following sentences.]

1. We moved around a lot.   **2.** We have two dogs.   **3.** We ate dinner promptly at 5.   **4.** We had many opportunities.   **5.** We speak when spoken to.   **6.** We read a little every night before going to bed.

Activity B from Chapter 5 (p. 100) could be used exactly as it was formulated for classroom use as a section on the test. The targeted items require learners to process the verb forms for past, present, or future markings. In the testing version (Section C), you would still want to keep one thing in focus at a time and therefore limit the items to third-person plural, for example. The choice of third-person plural is a deliberate one because Sections A and B utilize other forms. By relating the sections in this way, an instructor addresses not only Carroll's recommendation for economy and our guideline for "one thing at a time," but also a concern for *completeness*. The test should sample a bit of everything the learners were taught and not be overly limited in scope.

Section C. Listen to each sentence. Then select one of the time-related adverbials that can be added to the sentence you hear.

MODEL: (you hear) Terry and Pat deposited money in the bank.

(you select from)

a. last Monday
b. right now
c. next week

[Test takers hear the following items.]

1. Terry and Pat vacationed in Hawaii.   **2.** Terry and Pat will buy a house together.   **3.** Terry and Pat are preparing their taxes.   **4.** Terry and Pat adopted a baby.   **5.** Terry and Pat will face many problems.

You might question why a test would need to include input-based formats when you have already moved to output in the classroom. In other words, since instruction always moves to output in the end, why can't you simply test via output-based formats? The question is a good one. A method that emphasizes comprehensible input and structured input in the instruction cannot then ignore these in the testing. To do so runs the risk of making these instructional elements irrelevant as classroom practices, in the minds of the learners. In short, the test can reinforce classroom practice or it can undermine it.

STRUCTURED OUTPUT FORMATS FOR TESTS

Output-based testing formats that follow the guidelines for structured output activities can be combined with input-based sections. An example of an output-based test format combined with input would be to add some structured output to Section B above. When learners explain their selections, they need to use the very structures that are being processed in the input. And, depending on the level of the learners, they could be asked to comment on the item. Here is an example.

Section E. Indicate whether the speaker is relating information from his childhood or information about the present. Then decide if the information applies to you. Finally, explain how it does or doesn't apply and comment on it. A model is provided.

MODEL: (you hear). We would go to the beach for a week after school let out.

(you choose): childhood

(you indicate): This does not apply to me.

(you explain): When we were kids, we went to the mountains for vacations.

(you comment): As we got older, my brothers and sisters and I did not like the mountains because they were so isolated.

1. □ childhood   □ present
  □ This applies to me.   □ This does not apply to me

_____
_____
_____

2. □ childhood   □ present
  □ This applies to me.   □ This does not apply to me

_____
_____
_____

3. □ childhood   □ present
  □ This applies to me.   □ This does not apply to me

_____
_____
_____

[Test takers hear the following sentences.]

1. We moved around a lot.   **2.** We have two dogs.   **3.** We ate dinner promptly at 5.   **4.** We had many opportunities.   **5.** We speak when spoken to.   **6.** We read a little every night before going to bed.

As a test section, Section E meets the guidelines for developing structured input/output activities: one thing at a time (past versus present verb forms; first person plural); meaning is kept in focus (each individual will respond differently to the output portion); a combination of sentences and connected discourse; a combination of oral input and written output; the learners 'do something' with the input. This test section also incorporates Carroll's testing criteria: it is relevant (it follows the structured instructional pattern), economical (it samples knowledge), and acceptable (because the same activity types were used in classroom activities, learners will perceive the test as valid and reasonable).

Almost any structured output activity can be developed into a testing section. In Chapter 6 we saw the following activity, which focused on using the first-person singular object pronoun in Italian, *me*.

Activity B (from Chapter 6). **My Friends.**

> **Step 1.** Write at least five statements about what your friends do for you—
> or to you—that makes you appreciate them.

> ESEMPIO: Me ascoltano.

> **Step 2.** Now write at least five statements about what your friends do to
> or for you that sometimes gets on your nerves.

> ESEMPIO: Non me renderono di soldi.

With a different focus (for example, professors, pets, or roommates) this activity can become a test section. The example, Section F, focuses on family.

Section F.

> **Step 1.** Using *me,* write at least three statements about what parents (or
> brothers, sisters) do for you—or to you—that makes you
> appreciate them.

> **Step 2.** Again using *me,* write at least three statements about what your
> parents (or brothers, sisters) do to or for you that sometimes gets
> on your nerves.

Note how, in the test section, the instructions are reduced from "Write five sentences" to "Write three sentences," reflecting Carroll's criterion of economy in testing. Many instructors feel that the number of items in a test section must be a multiple of five. Although this is the convention, there is no rule that states a test section can not have three items. We suggest that the number of items in a section reflect how "important" that grammatical feature is. (We place the word *important* in quotes because it is a relative term. Great debates rage over which grammar features are important and which are not.)

Pause to consider . . .

how to score the output test Sections E and F. What would you give points for? What would you take points off for? If the purpose in Section F, for example, is correct use of *me,* would you score for anything else?

BEING RESPONSIBLE FOR WHAT HAPPENS IN CLASS

In both Chapters 5 and 6, we advocated an approach to grammar instruction that is meaning based. Grammar activities should lead students to exchange information with each other and with the instructor. In this section, we encourage "washback effects" by suggesting that the information exchanged in class is appropriate for a test. Just as comprehension checks (see Chapter 3) are ways of ensuring that learners are attending to the input, using the results of in-class activities as the basis for test sections reinforces the importance of interaction with classmates and paying attention in the classroom. Moreover, using the content of classroom interactions on tests can be viewed as an extension of one of the guidelines for creating structured output activities: "Others must respond to the content of the output."

Recall from Chapter 5 the following structured input activity.

Activity O (from Chapter 5). **Attitudes Toward the Government.**

Step 1. Indicate the extent to which you agree with each statement.

> 5: strongly agree
> 4: agree
> 3: somewhat in agreement
> 2: disagree
> 1: strongly disagree

The government . . .	5	4	3	2	1
1. understands us.	☐	☐	☐	☐	☐
2. helps us.	☐	☐	☐	☐	☐
3. controls us.	☐	☐	☐	☐	☐
4. ignores us.	☐	☐	☐	☐	☐
5. taxes us too much.	☐	☐	☐	☐	☐
6. doesn't represent us.	☐	☐	☐	☐	☐
7. guides us.	☐	☐	☐	☐	☐

Step 2. Share your responses with the class. Someone should tabulate the scores and calculate a class average for each item.

Step 3. Overall, does the class have a positive, negative, or mixed attitude toward the government?

We now propose to adapt this activity in two different ways as a test section. As the quoted excerpt by Krashen and Terrell (see p. 134) suggested, we should give tests that encourage learners to engage in acquisition activities. In other words, tests should "teach" learners that paying attention to input and meaning-based activities are not just for fun but are critical for acquisition. Creating test sections that depend on information exchanged in class should clearly demonstrate to the learners just how important classroom interactions are. In order to complete the test section, the learners must have participated in and attended to the interaction that leads to it. Section G encourages individual expression while Section H focuses more specifically on the interaction itself. The class interaction supplies the content for both sections.

Section G. Compare and/or contrast your classmates' attitude toward the government with your own by writing at least a five sentence paragraph using *us*. You can use the seven verbs below to help stimulate your thinking.

> MODEL: The class believes that the government understands us but I do not agree.

understand	control	help	tax
represent	guide	ignore	

Section H. We responded to the following statements in class. Select three of the statements to which the class had strong reactions (both agreement and disagreement) and recount the information used to support the argument.

The government . . .
1. understands us.
2. helps us.
3. controls us.
4. ignores us.
5. taxes us too much.
6. doesn't represent us.
7. guides us.

MODEL: The class strongly agreed that the government helps us. The examples we gave were student loans, social security, and Medicare.

---

*P*ause to consider . . .

how you would score Sections G and H. Would you count the accuracy of the statements about the class opinion? Why or why not, and what are the consequences of either position? Would use of the pronoun figure into your scoring criteria; would it be the *sole* criterion for getting the item correct?

Activity P was also included in Chapter 5 as an example of a structured input activity. It, too, can be adapted for a test to hold learners accountable for the interactions they have had in the classroom.

Activity P (from Chapter 5). **State of Mind.** Find people in the class who answer "Yes" to the questions below. Rules: (1) you may not use anything but Spanish; (2) you may not ask a person more than one question in a row; (3) if you find someone who answers "Yes" to a question, ask for that person's signature on the line next to the question; (4) when being asked a question, listen carefully; (5) do not sign your name unless you have been asked a complete question.

1. Do you get tense when speaking in Spanish? _____
2. Do you get nervous before taking a big exam? _____
3. Do you get angry easily? _____
4. Do you get depressed during the holidays? _____
5. Do you get bored when you're not in school? _____

Note how Section I adapts Activity P for testing purposes. The learners are focused on a specific element of the grammar at the same time they are responsible for what happened in class.

Section I. Write a sentence for each of the following that describes how you feel in that situation. Then indicate who else in the class feels the same way you do.

1. When speaking Spanish, I _____
_____. _____ also feels
this way.

.

.

.

5. When I'm not in school, I _____
_____. _____ also feels
this way.

Similarly, if Activity M from Chapter 5 were carried out in class with a student named "Tom," then Section J would be the natural follow-up for a test.

Activity M (from Chapter 5). **Would He or Would He Not?**

Step 1. Select someone from the class whom you all think you know well. That person should sit by himself during the first part of this activity.

Step 2. Write that person's name in the blank as indicated. Then complete each statement with information that you believe to be true.

Unless he had to, _____
(name)

1. would never eat _____.
2. would never watch _____.
3. would never go to _____.
4. would never spend money on _____.
5. would never _____.

On the other hand, _____
(name)

6. would probably eat _____ without reservation.
7. would go to _____ on vacation.
8. would study _____, time permitting.
9. would gladly spend money on _____.
10. would _____.

Section J. Identify three things that you and *(name of class member)* both would do and three things neither of you would do. Write in complete sentences.

*P*ause to consider . . .

how to write a test section for multisection courses. How would the directions lines for Section J have to be different if the test were given to 20 sections of French 101, which are taught by twelve different instructors?

So far, all of our examples of testing the content of classroom interactions have been output-based testing sections. But there is no reason why an input-based testing section could not also test information exchanged in class. For example, Activity M (from Chapter 5) was an input-based task in class. The following could be used as an input-based testing section.

Section K. We have seen in class what Harriet does, doesn't do, would do, and would never do. For each pair of sentences you hear (or read), indicate which one is true for Harriet.

1. **a.** Harriet would never watch a soap opera.
   b. Harriet watches soap operas.
2. **a.** Harriet would never eat snails.
   b. Harriet eats snails.
3. **a.** Harriet would never go to Iowa.
   b. Harriet goes to Iowa.

As you examine Section K, note how the learner must attend to the verb form as part of paying attention to the meaning. That is, the grammatical difference between *would never eat* and *eats* determines the truth-value of each sentence. There is no better way of keeping meaning in focus than by working with the truth-value of information!

Pause to consider . . .
_____

how learners might react to test sections that examined information exchanged in class. In other words, would they find test sections of this nature acceptable? Why or why not? What would the instructor have to do to make such sections acceptable to the test takers?

SUMMARY

Entire books have been written on language testing—both theory and practice—and we have not attempted to survey all the issues in this chapter. We focused very specifically on testing grammar so that teaching is not viewed as somehow divorced from testing. On the one hand, we adapted the kinds of activities done in class to test sections. On the other, we took certain interactive classroom activities and created test sections based on those interactions. In this approach, the learners are consistently given the opportunity to apply the content to themselves, to state their own opinions and beliefs. Instructors accomplish several things by doing this: (1) we keep meaning in focus; (2) we provide a context for using the grammar (not merely contextualizing the grammar); (3) we connect processing the language with producing it. Grammar becomes the *means* to an end; knowing the grammar rules and memorizing the forms is *not* the goal. Learners, therefore, should not view grammar only as an object of study and manipulation. Rather, they should view grammar as a way to express meaning, interact, and communicate. Because learners are motivated by tests, we can use tests to underscore what grammar is supposed to do for them.

KEY TERMS, CONCEPTS, AND ISSUES

test
washback effect
economy
   sampling
relevance
   test what and how you teach
acceptability
   test takers' perspective
comparability
   similar results
   institutional perspective
relationship of structured input activities to test sections
   one thing at a time
   keep meaning in focus
   move from sentences to connected discourse
   use both written and oral input/output
   the learner must do something with the input
   others must respond to the learner's output
attending to form-meaning relationship
completeness
learner responsibilities
   attending to input in class
   attending to interactions in class
   applying content to self

EXPLORING THE TOPICS FURTHER

1. *General considerations.* Krashen and Terrell (1983, Chapter 7) rely on Carroll's general criteria for language testing (1980) for the basis of their discussion of testing. Both works are worth reading. Bachman's (1990) book on testing is both comprehensive and readable.

2. *Testing grammar.* Omaggio Hadley (1993, Chapter 9) offers various examples of classroom test items. Although she organizes them into the categories listening, reading, writing, and speaking, you will find that many items have a grammatical focus that can be adapted to an approach based on structured input and output.

3. *Washback effects.* Shohamy's (1993) monograph on the power of tests recounts the washback effects that national standard testing produced in Israel. She presents pros and cons and warns of some unexpected effects of tests.

Spoken Language

In Part I, we defined communication as the expression, interpretation, and negotiation of meaning. The chapters in Part III explore further how communication can and does take place in classrooms. Chapter 8 is an overview of issues related to how language is used in classrooms—the purposes of communication, communicative drills, and teacher-fronted and paired interaction. We provide suggestions for developing learners' communicative language ability by focusing on classroom communication as the exchange of information.

Chapter 9 is the second of our chapters on testing. Through an examination of the ACTFL Oral Proficiency Interview and the Israeli National Oral Proficiency Test, we explore several issues related to testing oral language: elicitation procedures, evaluation, rating scales, bias, and interrater reliability. We include suggestions for adapting classroom activities to testing situations and explore the communicative burden that different testing formats place on the test taker.

CHAPTER 8

Spoken Language and Information-Exchange Tasks

com-mu-ni-ca-tion (*kə-myoo'-n̄ə-kā'- shən*)
n. 1. the act of communicating; transmission.
2. the exchange of thoughts, messages, or the like,
as by speech, signals, or writing.

American Heritage Dictionary

INTRODUCTION

When you first started taking language classes, how much communicating did you do in the target language? Was communication a daily part of instruction? Weekly? Did your instructor warm up the class with a few questions at the beginning of the hour? Was this communication? At what level did group discussions become a part of the class routine? What was your first conversation class like? Was it combined with composition? What did you talk about? Did you really learn to converse? Do you remember the first time you had to use the target language in a nonclassroom setting? How did you do? Were you scared? Did your classroom experiences prepare you for that exchange outside the classroom? How did the classroom prepare or not prepare you?

In Chapters 5, 6, and 7, we explored the teaching of grammar, with an emphasis on moving from structured input to structured output activities in helping the learner acquire particular properties of language. Our approach focused on getting the learners to comprehend and process grammatical form in structured input; in this way, they can make the form-meaning connections that seem to be necessary for the derivation of intake. It is well worth remembering, however, that the teaching of grammar—regardless of approach—does not guarantee that learners will acquire all the properties of language that we would like them to. Nor does the teaching of grammar guarantee that what is taught will appear in the more "spontaneous" output of learners. Recall that Chapter 6 focused on structured output activities, in which learners were given opportunities to use a particular grammatical feature in a very focused and structured (but nonetheless communicative) manner. The goal of these activities is twofold. First, the learner receives practice in accessing grammatical forms from the developing system, thereby developing fluency (in other words, building up the networks in the brain responsible for accessing grammar when making output). Second, by being guided to produce correct, meaningful utterances designed to communicate messages, the learner provides more input for

147

fellow learners. Structured input and structured output activities therefore assist learners in their acquisition of grammar. These activities are thus consistent with the more general tenets of communicative language teaching.

Language classrooms need not be limited to manipulations of forms, no matter how meaningful or purposeful those exercises are. We must move from structured input and output practices to more open-ended types of communicative activities. In this chapter, we explore the ways activities can move beyond forms in order to foster the use of language in communicative exchanges. To do this, we examine a variety of concepts: communication, purpose of communication, communication in the classroom, information-exchange tasks, and the development of strategic competence.

COMMUNICATION AND COMMUNICATIVE LANGUAGE ABILITY

The act of communication in most settings involves the expression, interpretation, and negotiation of meaning (Savignon 1983). That is, a person wishes to express an idea (opinion, wish, request, demand) to someone else and does so. The other person must understand both the message and the intent of the message. Sometimes interpretation is partial, and some negotiation is needed. How many times have you heard the following expressions?

I'm sorry. Did you say . . . ?

I'm not sure what you mean.

I don't get what you're telling me.

What are you getting at?

Say what?

Are you kidding?

It's hard for me to put in words, but . . .

What I mean is . . .

No way!

Do you know what I'm saying?

As you will see throughout this chapter, communication always happens in some sort of context. In many second language contexts, communication breakdowns are likely to happen. With underdeveloped second language knowledge and ability, learners might not have the resources to express themselves easily or to interpret a speaker of the second language. This could be due to either underdeveloped cultural knowledge or underdeveloped linguistic knowledge. In the latter case, learners simply cannot express themselves easily because of missing vocabulary ("Geez, how do you say 'screwdriver' in this language?") or missing grammar ("How do you say 'If it hadn't have been for John' in Italian?"), or because pronunciation is a problem (the Asian early-stage ESL speaker in the supermarket who asks for lettuce and is shown where the radishes are).

Leeman Guthrie (1984) provides an excellent example of an exchange between a classroom learner and his instructor in which a problem in communicating an idea leads to negotiating the meaning. One of the important points to glean from this example is that *both* the instructor and the learner are negotiating meaning. The instructor needs to understand Roger's message just as much as Roger needs to express his intent in a comprehensible manner. The instructor has been discussing the idea of "the typical French person" with the class, and Roger has just met a French person.

INSTRUCTOR: Roger, vous venez de faire la connaissance d'un Français. Quelles sont vos impressions?

ROGER: Ah ... c'est ... c'est ne Français typique.

INSTRUCTOR: Il n'était pas typique?

ROGER: Ne personne est typique.

INSTRUCTOR: Personne n'est typique? C'est à dire qu'il n'est pas possible de généraliser, c'est ça?

ROGER: Oui.

[Translation]

INSTRUCTOR: *Roger, you have just met a French person. What are your impressions?*

ROGER: *Ah ... it is ... it is no typical French.*

INSTRUCTOR: *He wasn't typical?*

ROGER: *No person is typical.*

INSTRUCTOR: *Nobody is typical? That is to say that it isn't possible to generalize, is that so?*

ROGER: *Yes.*

(adapted from Leeman Guthrie 1984, p. 49)

In this exchange, Roger attempts to say "There is no such thing as a typical French person" and does so by translating, in part, from English. The instructor interprets his utterance as meaning the person that Roger just met was not

---

*P*ause to consider . . .

what *communicative competence* is. Savignon (1983) says that communicative competence consists of four underlying competences: *grammatical competence* (knowledge of the structure and form of language), *discourse competence* (knowledge of the rules of cohesion and coherence across sentences and utterances), *sociolinguistic competence* (knowledge of the rules of interaction: turn taking, appropriate use of first names, appropriate formulae for apologizing, appropriate greetings), and *strategic competence* (knowing how to make the most of the language that you have, especially when it is "deficient"). Do you think that one underlying competence is more important than another? Do they interact in some way, balancing each other out? Which competences are more important than others to the beginning, intermediate, or advanced language learner?

typical. Roger realizes from the instructor's response that he must reformulate his utterance, say it in another way, and eventually the *two* work out what Roger means to say. Both Roger and the instructor demonstrate a certain *strategic competence:* instead of abandoning the idea, they attempt to get it across in another way. We will return to the issue of strategic competence at the end of this chapter when we examine activities that help foster its development.

PURPOSES OF COMMUNICATION

In the nonclassroom world, people engage in oral communication for a variety of reasons. However, the two most common purposes of communication can be described as *psycho-social* and *informational-cognitive*. The psycho-social purpose of language involves using language to bond socially or psychologically with someone or some group or to engage in social behavior in some way. Thus, asking someone "How's it going?" might be less a desire to know the actual details of someone's life than a means of exchanging pleasantries or letting someone know that "you care." The informational-cognitive use of language involves communication for the purpose of obtaining information, generally for some other task. Stopping and asking someone "Do you have the time?" if we think we are running late is generally an informational activity rather than a psycho-social behavior; we ask because we really want to know the time so that we can decide if we need to walk faster, run, or catch a cab. In a different context, the very same question ("Do you have the time?") could have a psycho-social function as a pickup line. Telling someone that you will not be in the office tomorrow but working at home and can be reached there is not a psycho-social behavior: its purpose is to inform that person of your whereabouts because the information is necessary.

To be sure, psycho-social and informational-cognitive uses of language can and often do co-occur. A director of a movie might tell actors where to stand, whether or not they should underplay or play up a line, and so on. Information is exchanged: the actor needs the information to perform the job. At the same time, the director might use language in a particular way to let the actors know his feelings: "I trust you. You will do well" or "Don't screw this up. We're behind schedule and it's your fault." In this way, the director not only instructs/informs but also reminds all participants of their relationship to the project.

---

*P*ause to consider . . .
_____

the two broad categories of purposes for language use. Observe some daily interactions between native speakers. What psycho-social uses of language do you see? Informational-cognitive uses? For the average person traveling abroad, which language purpose do you think is more important? For the business person abroad? For the learner spending a year in France, Germany, or Japan?

What of the language classroom? While the instructor may use language for both psycho-social and informational-cognitive purposes, it is doubtful that the learner, especially in the beginning and intermediate stages, would use language for many psycho-social purposes. The classroom context typically does not promote the kind of interaction that requires language to be used psycho-socially. However, the classroom does lend itself exceptionally well to the use of communicative language for informational-cognitive purposes. The classroom is ideally suited to the development and implementation of activities in which learners exchange information for a common purpose. Before we examine these kinds of activities, let's review some very typical interactional patterns between instructors and learners.

CLASSROOM DISCOURSE

Communicative Drills

In Chapter 5, we discussed Paulston's traditional hierarchy of mechanical, meaningful, and communicative drills or practices. The drills differ in terms of who controls the response and what types of messages it contains. For communicative drills, the learner controls the response and provides new information; the differences are summarized in Figure 8.1. So, in response to the question "What did you eat last night?" during a communicative drill or practice, the learner gives new and real information unknown to the listener ("I ate a tuna sandwich"). Although communicative drills might have the semblance of real communication, they fall short of providing learners with opportunities that allow them to work at expressing, interpreting, and negotiating meaning with another person. Such drills fall short of providing an extended exchange between two or more people.

To examine how short drills fall, let's return to Leeman-Guthrie's research. In the following example, the instructor is leading the class through a question-and-answer communicative drill in which learners practice the interrogative pronoun *lequel* ("which one") and its variants. The exercise calls for

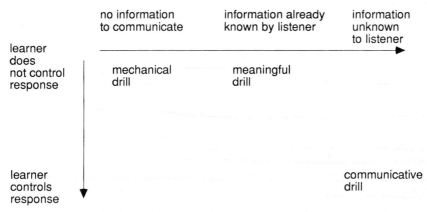

FIGURE 8.1. Factors Determining Practice or Drill Type

two learners to interact, but they do so without the kind of success the instructor hopes for. The learners continually circumvent the obvious linguistic intent of the activity because they are conforming to the rules of everyday conversation. That is, they attempt to exchange real information, but the instructor, who has a different purpose in mind, constantly brings the learners back to the linguistic point of the exercise. There is thus very little negotiation happening in the exchanges.

INSTRUCTOR: Okay, bon.
Demandez à ... Carol ... si elle connaît des chanteurs et lesquels.
Ask her if she knows any singers and which ones.
LEARNER A: Uh ... connas-tu des chanteurs?
LEARNER B: Je connais ... Mick Jagger.
(laughter)
LEARNER A: xxx
INSTRUCTOR: Elle connaît Mick Jagger.
INSTRUCTOR: Susan, est-ce que tu connais des acteurs?
LEARNER C: Oui, je connais ...
INSTRUCTOR: *(interrupting)* Lesquelles?
Oui, lesquelles?
LEARNER C: Oh, je connais ... um ... Shirley MacLaine, Jane Fonda ...

[Translation]

INSTRUCTOR: *Okay, good.*
Ask . . . Carol ... if she knows any singers, and which ones she knows.
LEARNER A: *Uh . . . do you know any singers?*
LEARNER B: *I know . . . Mick Jagger.*
(laughter)
LEARNER A: xxx
INSTRUCTOR: *She knows Mick Jagger.*
INSTRUCTOR: *Susan, do you know any actors?*
LEARNER C: *Yes, I know . . .*
INSTRUCTOR: (interrupting) *Which ones? Yes, which ones?*
LEARNER C: *Oh, I know . . . um . . . Shirley MacLaine, Jane Fonda . . .*

(adapted from Leeman Guthrie 1984, p. 47)

In another revealing study, Brooks (1990) found that learners reproduce in pairs those behaviors that the instructor uses at the whole-class level. He states that

rather than use the exercise to participate in a communication simulation activity, as originally intended by the teacher, the students seem to have turned the activity into another chance to reinforce the rules of Spanish grammar, thereby getting ready for the subsequent quiz. . . . It appears as though the two students have learned through imitation and inference, rather than explicit instruction, an acceptable manner for doing this type of activity. (Brooks 1990, p. 162)

The following two exchanges (adapted from Brooks's study) demonstrate his point. Note the pattern of interaction between instructor and learner in A that is subsequently played out between two learners in B.

A. Teacher-Fronted Activity

INSTRUCTOR: ¿Es antipática?
LEARNERS: *(several together)* No.
INSTRUCTOR: No es antipática.
LEARNER: Es muy simpático.
INSTRUCTOR: ¿Simpático? *(said loudly with rising intonation)*
LEARNER: Simpática.
INSTRUCTOR: Sí, es muy simpática.

[Translation]

INSTRUCTOR: *Is she mean?*
LEARNERS: (several together) *No.*
INSTRUCTOR: *She isn't mean.*
LEARNER: *He is nice.*
INSTRUCTOR: *Nice?**
LEARNER: *She is nice.*
INSTRUCTOR: *Yes, she is very nice.*

B. Paired-Student Activity

A: Ah, ¿cómo son Carolina y Luz?
B: Carolina y Luz es
   no
   son rubiøs *(final vowel inaudible)*
A: Son *(voice in holding tone)*
   rubi . . .
   a. . .
   rubias
B: ¿«a» o «as»?
A: «as»
B: «as», sí. Rubias *(prosodic stress on "as")*

[Translation]

A: *Ah, what are Carolina and Luz like?*
B: *Carolina and Luz is*
   no
   are blonde.
A: *are . . .*
   blo . . .
   n . . .
   d
B: «a» or «as»?
A: «as»
B: «as», *yes. Blonde.*

*Translator's note: The Spanish adjective is inflected for gender. The instructor is vocally drawing attention to the inflection, which cannot be rendered in the translation.

Leeman Guthrie and Brooks provide just two examples of what is often the typical discourse pattern in language classrooms. They demonstrate that as far as communicative drills go, whether led by an instructor or carried out by pairs of learners, communication and negotiation of meaning may well not be taking place.

> ### *Pause to consider* . . .
>
> what message the instructor sends the learners about communicating in the target language. Reexamine the exchange between instructor and learners that focuses on *lequel*, noting that the instructor translated her directions to the class. What effect does translating one's utterances have on the classroom dynamic? On the type of interactions one can expect? On creating a classroom environment conducive to communication?

Teacher-Fronted and Paired Interaction

In addition to the kinds of discourse and observational research noted above, there is also quantitative research on interactional patterns and communication in the language classroom. Like the research conducted by Leeman Guthrie and Brooks, this research reveals that teacher-fronted activities provide few opportunities for the expression and negotiation of meaning among participants (perhaps because there are too many potential participants). Rulon and McCreary report on the findings of one investigation in which they compared small-group activities and teacher-fronted activities. Their conclusion was that small-group work produced twice the number of content confirmation checks (indications that a person has understood, such as "I got it. Then what?") and thirty-six times the number of content clarification requests ("Right?" "Do you follow?" "So, you mean . . . ?") as did the teacher-fronted tasks. Learners did much more of the talking when given the opportunity to work in groups. In the words of the researchers, "Very little negotiation of either content or meaning was actually taking place in these [teacher-fronted] classes" (Rulon and McCreary 1986, p. 194). At the same, these researchers found no statistical difference between group and teacher-fronted activities in terms of the amount of informational content covered. So there seems to be more communication occurring in paired work than in teacher-fronted activities, with just as much content covered.

Porter (1986) also found that learner-to-learner interactions in the classroom resulted in increased opportunities for self-expression for the learner. But she also found that uneven proficiency resulted in yet more interactions. In other words, advanced-intermediate pairings resulted in increased negotiation for both learners compared to intermediate-intermediate and advanced-advanced pairings. In terms of quality of interaction, Porter reports only one "negative" finding: that sociolinguistic competence is not something that can be developed in the absence of native-speaking interlocutors.

<table>
<tr><td>

***P**ause to consider . . .*

Porter's "negative" finding. Why would sociolinguistic competence not develop in most classroom situations? On what does the development of sociolinguistic competence depend? Is sociolinguistic competence linked to psycho-social or informational-cognitive uses of language? Is it linked to both?

</td></tr>
</table>

To compare teacher-fronted and learner-interactive work in the classroom, let's examine the following two versions of the same activity called "What Did You Do Last Week?" One is teacher-fronted and the other is group-work oriented. Activity A is a fairly typical question-and-answer approach to getting learners to talk: the instructor asks questions and the class answers (this is an example of communication-as-question-and-answer, which we explored in Chapter 1). Activity B demonstrates what Porter as well as McCreary and Rulon claim about paired interactions. That is, the same content can be covered even though the learners are the ones talking.

Activity A. What Did You Do Last Week? (Teacher-fronted) Ask your class the following questions. Ask the questions of a number of students and try to get a variety of responses.

1. What did you do last week? (*Call on two or three students.*)
2. Who did something different? (*Offer examples such as* "go to the beach," "play a sport," "walk in the park.")
3. Who would say that last week was a very active week for them? (*Have students raise hands and then call on two or three of them.*)
4. What did you do that was active?
5. Who would say that last week was a sedentary week for them? (*Have students raise hands and then call on two or three of them.*)
6. What did you do that was sedentary?
7. Overall, how many of you say that last week was an active one? A sedentary one?

Activity B. What Did You Do Last Week? (Paired interaction)

Step 1. Working with a partner, indicate if each activity is sedentary or not.

		SEDENTARY	ACTIVE
1.	dancing at a party	☐	☐
2.	running five miles	☐	☐
3.	playing video games	☐	☐
4.	playing a sport	☐	☐
5.	reading a book	☐	☐
6.	watching TV	☐	☐
7.	writing a letter	☐	☐
8.	making dinner	☐	☐

Add three activities to the list and indicate whether or not they are sedentary.

------------ ☐ ☐

------------ ☐ ☐

------------ ☐ ☐

Step 2. Interview your partner about what he or she did last week. Comparing the responses to the choices you made in Step 1, use the following scale to rate your partner's week.

Very sedentary	As sedentary as active	Very active

1	2	3	4	5

Step 3. Compare your evaluations with the rest of the class. Overall, to what degree was everyone's week sedentary or active?

As you compare the activities above, ask yourself, Who does most of the talking in each activity? In the first version, the instructor talks just as much as (if not more than) the entire class does. At least fifty percent of any language use will come from the instructor; the other fifty percent will come from the twenty-five or so learners. However, because not all the learners can participate in a teacher-fronted activity, it is also quite possible that several learners might never produce any language in the first version of the activity. In contrast, the second version requires that all learners participate as they ask questions of each other and share the information with the whole class. While completing the task, the learners are actively engaged in constructing the discourse about the topic.

We can conclude that teacher-fronted activities might not be optimum for providing opportunities for communicative interchange. Pair and group work, on the other hand, do provide such opportunities; however, they do so only if there is a perceived need or desire in the learners to communicate and if learners do not recapitulate the role of the instructor in teacher-fronted, form-focused activities (as exemplified in the exchange cited earlier from Brooks 1990). The implication here seems clear: in order to bring communication (expression, interpretation, and negotiation of meaning) into the classroom, instructors will have to look to something other than form-focused activities. Instructors need to go beyond drills to provide the opportunities learners need to develop communicative language proficiency.

CLASSROOM COMMUNICATION AS INFORMATION EXCHANGE

As we have seen, communication involves the expression, interpretation, and negotiation of meaning in a given context. The context most relevant to instructors and learners is, of course, the classroom. We focus now on creating classroom activities that allow for communication within the context of the language classroom. We call these activities "information-based" tasks or "information-exchange" tasks. These activities require learners to obtain information from each other that is then put to use in some way. The schematic display in Figure 8.2 shows what is involved in developing activities that foster communication in the classroom.

Identify the topic or sub-topic to be addressed.

↓   ↑

Design an appropriate immediate purpose.

↓   ↑

Identify the information source(s).

FIGURE 8.2 The Construction of Information-Exchange Tasks

Identifying the Topic

We see in Figure 8.2 that information-exchange tasks do not occur in a vacuum. They are generally part of some larger informational unit or are relevant to current events surrounding the learners. Many language courses, for example, build syllabi around vocabulary groups or themes. Thus, courses (and textbooks) have a food chapter, a family chapter, a jobs and professions chapter, among others. Identifying a topic or subtopic for a task is best achieved when a concrete question can be asked. In other words, the topic can be explored by questions that learners will eventually answer with the information they obtain.

Taking the example of food, we can immediately generate a list of questions that explore various topics and subtopics:

1. What are a typical student's eating habits?
   a. What does a student eat for breakfast? Lunch? Dinner?
   b. What does a student eat for snacks?
   c. Where do students eat?
   d. When do students eat?
   e. How do student eating habits compare with those of nonstudents?
2. What is the nutritional content of the foods we eat?
   a. Is meat good for you?
   b. Do you need fat in your diet? How much?
   c. What is the difference between carbohydrates and proteins?
   d. Why does everyone talk about cholesterol levels?
3. What do people from other cultures eat?
   a. How are nutritional needs met in the various diets?
   b. How does our diet compare with theirs?
4. How do you prepare certain foods?
   a. What ingredients do you need?
   b. How much time is involved?
   c. Who is responsible for food preparation in your household?
5. Does what you eat affect your frame of mind?
   a. Can you be addicted to food?
   b. Is chocolate an aphrodisiac?

Needless to the say, this list of questions is far from exhaustive; we could generate a great number of other questions. A glance at the list reveals that some questions are broader than others; some have a much more narrow focus. Certain questions rely on personal experience while others involve the world outside our own. Some are concrete and others more abstract. Some can be explored using the learners' own experiences and knowledge while others require consulting an outside information source. What needs to be kept in mind is lesson planning, that is, time and material management. When moving their classes toward communication through information exchange, instructors need to ask themselves such questions as "What topics can be treated in a 50-minute class period?" and "What topics can be treated in a 10–15-minute activity?"

Designing an Appropriate Purpose

Once a topic or subtopic is selected and a question is developed, an appropriate immediate purpose needs to be designed. The immediate purpose can take the form of a task that learners must complete. Such tasks include:

- filling in a grid, chart, or table
- writing a paragraph
- making an oral report
- answering questions
- sharing information with others for comparative purposes
- creating an outline
- creating a list of questions
- creating a survey
- drawing something (a picture, a graph, a diagram)
- creating a photo montage

In constructing an information-exchange task, it is important *not* to mistake "getting or exchanging information" as the purpose of the task. Getting and exchanging information are the *means* to some other *end* or *purpose*. Learners will not only get and exchange information—they will *do something with it*. What they *do* with the information is, in essence, the true purpose of the task. Instructors must be able to identify the purpose, not only for themselves but for the learners as well. We can see the importance of this by comparing the following two versions of the same activity. In the first version, even though learners exchange information, the activity lacks an end: the learner is not given a purpose for obtaining and exchanging the information. In the second version of the activity, the learner is asked to fill in a chart and make a comparison. The learner now has a reason for getting information and knows what to do with it.

Activity C. Compare Your Birthday Experiences. Working with a classmate, compare how you have celebrated your birthdays by asking and answering the following questions.

How did you celebrate your birthday two years ago? Five years ago? Ten years ago? Where did you spend the day and with whom did you spend it? Was it fun? Were a lot of people present? What kind of food was served?

Activity D. Compare Your Birthday Experiences

Step 1. Fill in the following chart as you interview a classmate.

Birthday	Where?	With whom?	Food?	Fun?
2 years ago				
5 years ago				
10 years ago				

Step 2. Now write a paragraph in which you compare and contrast your own
birthdays with the three birthdays your classmate just described.

The information-exchange task structures the interaction between the
learners, accomplishing several things. First, if two learners were given the list
of questions in Activity C to ask and answer, they might fall into perpetuating
the teacher-fronted dynamic described by Brooks. Would the learners conceive
of the activity as an opportunity for information exchange? Would they simply
try to get through the list of questions? Would they imitate their instructor?
Second, if we restructure the interaction as in Activity D, the learners become
task oriented; they must work together to fill in the chart. Filling in the chart
gives each learner an information base to work from, either to write the paragraph, as suggested in Step 2, or to keep for testing purposes (as suggested in
Chapter 7). Activity D is more "free form," with the learners more likely to
move on to topics other than birthday celebrations and to use their native language to discuss these other topics.

*P*ause to consider . . .

the classroom dynamic Activities C and D generate. How will pairs of
learners know when they have completed the activity? What happens when
they do?

Identifying Information Sources

Whatever the task selected, it must fit with the topic and guide the learners'
oral interaction. Task selection is tied to the information source necessary to
carry out the interaction; the nature of the topic will indicate what the information source should be. There is no need to limit information exchanges to

personal information or information generated from personal experiences such as the class's sleeping habits or their likes and dislikes. The learners' experiences are a rich source and certainly ought to be exploited, but learners also know things about the world beyond their own experience. They know, for example, such things as who certain famous people are, what these people did, what many principles of science are, and how to add and subtract. What they know beyond their own personal experience, therefore, is also a rich source to be exploited for information-exchange activities. A reading or listening text is another source of information for classroom communication. Learners can consult either an oral or written text that provides information related to the task. (We explore the use of readings and texts in Chapter 10.) Thus, rather than ask and answer questions of each other, learners can get information from a text for the purpose of completing a task.

The purpose of the task will often clarify if not dictate the information source required. If the purpose is to fill in a chart *about a classmate's eating habits,* it will be clear that the information source is the learners' personal experience. If the purpose is to create a list of questions they would like to ask *a Brazilian about the disappearing rain forests,* then the information source could very well be outside the learners' personal experiences and might be provided by a reading or by a guest speaker to the class. In the following example, learners' world knowledge is the source of information needed to complete the activity.

Activity E. What Else Was Going On Then?

Step 1. Complete the following with accurate information.

> **1.** When John F. Kennedy was assassinated . . .
>   **a.**
>   **b.**
>   **c.**
> **2.** When Nixon resigned the presidency . . .
>   **a.**
>   **b.**
>   **c.**
> **3.** When Columbus landed in the Caribbean . . .
>   **a.**
>   **b.**
>   **c.**

Step 2. Compare your answers to a classmate's. Is your information correct? What information did your classmate think of that you did not?
Step 3. Compare your items to those of the rest of the class, adding any new items to your list.
Step 4. Select one of the episodes above and prepare a brief oral presentation. Remember to use connectors (such as *also, but, at the same time*) to make your presentation flow.

> ## *P*ause to consider . . .
>
> the options for using texts as information sources. In order for authentic information exchange based on written texts to occur, the learners should not all have read the same texts. Why would Learner A ask Learner B questions about a text that A herself has just read? Pairs of learners can instead be given two different texts to read. Together, they then must fill out a chart, complete an outline, or write a paragraph based on the information they provide each other. Can you think of other options? What about having only one person read a text?

LANGUAGE DEMANDS IN INFORMATION-EXCHANGE TASKS

In designing oral communication tasks for a class, two considerations must be addressed: the level of the learner and the linguistic demands of the task. The level of the learner influences the degree of structure required in the task. For example, beginning-level learners might not respond well to the lack of structure in the direction, "Discuss with a classmate why the Mediterranean diet is good for the cholesterol conscious." Beginning-level learners find it easier to *respond* to a series of statements (true/false, agree/disagree, probable/improbable) than to make those statements or to discuss them. Whereas advanced-level learners might easily interact with each other after being told, "Find five other people in the class who share your views on the reunification of Germany," beginning-level learners would need a more structured task. This might involve a series of steps: 1. "Indicate which of the following statements about the reunification of Germany you agree with." 2. "Find three classmates who share at least three of your views." Not only do these steps structure the interaction, but Step 1 offers beginning learners the linguistic support they may need to be successful.

No matter what the oral communication task might be, the learners will need certain linguistic forms and structures in order to carry out the task. For Activity D on birthday celebrations, learners need past tenses; for Activity E

> ## *P*ause to consider . . .
>
> the grammar required by an information-exchange task. Select one of the tasks presented in this chapter and make a list of the grammar necessary. Be sure to be specific. Do not just list "past tense"; list "past tense to express single events, 1st person singular forms only." Do you see that grammar instruction might not need to be as complex as in traditional approaches if you are preparing learners for a particular task?

("What Else Was Going On Then?") they need to be able to express habitual actions (imperfective aspect) in the past. Thus, if an oral communication task works best if learners have some facility with past-tense forms, these should be taught before the communication task is presented and could be reviewed, albeit quickly, before starting the communication task. However, it is important to remember that learners might not need all forms of a verb paradigm or all rules of a structure or semantic distinction in order to carry out a task. In the example with the birthday activity, learners do not need *all* past-tense forms and functions, only several.

DEVELOPING STRATEGIC COMPETENCE

As we saw at the outset of this chapter, negotiating meaning during an interaction is one of the hallmarks of communication; this is particularly true for second language learners. We saw an example of such negotiation on page 149 as Roger attempted to reformulate his utterance about whether or not there was such a thing as a typical French person. The tasks we have examined so far tended to be fairly structured: what learners had to do was very clear, and learners were assisted by a preparation in grammar and vocabulary before starting the task. Whereas these information-exchange tasks certainly encourage the expression and interpretation of meaning, they do not *necessarily* encourage the kind of negotiation important in developing the strategic competence that Roger demonstrated. Consider the following description of strategic competence:

> "[strategic competence] is analogous to the need for *coping* or *survival strategies*. What do you do when you cannot think of a word? What are the ways of keeping the channels of communication open while you pause to collect your thoughts? How do you let your interlocutor know you did not understand a particular word? Or that he or she was speaking too fast? How do you, in turn, adapt when your message is misunderstood?" (Savignon 1983, p. 40)

Tarone (1984) lists and discusses a variety of communication strategies that contribute to strategic competence. Of those, two seem to be appropriate for discussion here: *paraphrase* and *mime*. Mime is quite simply acting out a word or thought or using a gesture to support what one is saying. For example, a learner doesn't know or can't remember how to say "inches," so he says "It's like this" and then moves his hands apart to show the relative length of the object he's describing. Or perhaps he doesn't know how to say "shave," so he mimes the act of shaving to communicate his idea.

Paraphrase Activities

Paraphrase is a more complex type of strategy, and Tarone lists at least three subtypes. The first is *approximation*, using a related word or term when one doesn't know the specific term; the related term functions for the purpose of the communication at hand (use of the superordinate term *nose* for *trunk* when talking about an elephant; use of analogy: *like an octopus*). Another type of paraphrase is *word coinage*, a process of making up a new word to communicate a concept (*ballhitter* for *bat* or *racquet*). The third type of paraphrase, and perhaps the most widely used, is *circumlocution*. This strategy involves describing the properties of an object or action or "talking around" a concept ("I bought this thing. What do you call it? It's long and skinny, for cleaning the floor." Or, "Last night I had a—a—you know, when you're asleep and you see things in your mind. . . .")

In short, these two strategies help the learner keep the flow of conversation moving and invite the listener to help negotiate the exchange. In so doing, they help keep the learner from relying on two other strategies that Tarone rightfully describes as negative strategies: avoidance (of a topic) and message abandonment.

Encouraging learners to use such strategies is the aim of various activity types. The first actually focuses on developing strategic competence itself by requiring learners to talk around something they can't say. Activity F, adapted from a recurring activity in *Pasajes: Actividades* (Bretz, Dvorak, and Kirschner 1983), gets learners to use the language they already possess to talk about concepts for which they most likely do not have the exact target-language forms, if indeed the concepts exist in the target language at all.

Activity F. Explain, Please.

Your friend Luisa, who is an exchange student from Costa Rica, has heard the following English words and phrases used in conversation. She didn't quite understand what they meant. Explain to her, in Spanish, what they mean. [The person could just as well be Yoshi from Japan, Marcel from France, Antonietta from Italy.]

1. funny bone	**3.** laughing stock	**5.** dead to the world
2. punchline	**4.** deadbeat	**6.** bed head

The next activity, Activity G, also gets learners to interact by using what language they have to describe objects for which they probably do not have the target-language word.

Activity G. Characteristics

Step 1. Students work in groups of three or four. Each group is given one picture of a familiar object. Groups do not see other groups' pictures. (Examples: windshield wipers, blender or other food processor, ceiling fan, rawhide bones for dogs)

Step 2. Each group first brainstorms a list of five characteristics of the object. They do *not* write a paragraph or definition; they simply make a list.

Step 3. Using the list, each group has three minutes to describe the object for the members of the other groups. After three minutes, the other groups may ask clarification questions but may not make guesses about the object. They then write down what they think the object is.

Another type of activity that promotes the development of strategic competence is the *information-gap* task. The *gap* refers to information that one person possesses but others do not. Gaps, therefore, create the absolute need to communicate as well as the need to cooperate. Information-gap tasks were briefly described with reference to the use of texts as information sources in communication activities (see the **Pause to consider . . .** on p. 161). The example described two learners working cooperatively to fill out a chart, each learner contributing information from a text the other has not read. Activity H is a fully developed version of such a task.

Activity H. Compare Provinces.

Step 1. Each person in the group reads a different short text produced by the national travel bureau. Each text describes the desirable features of a particular province in order to generate tourism to that region. As you read your own text, think about how you might describe or explain the content of the reading to the other members of your group.

Step 2. Working together, the group completes the following chart. Remember to try not to use English if you must use a new word from your text that the others might not know.

Province:	A	B	C
Terrain			
Festivals			
Sporting			
Climate			

Step 3. Weighing all the information, as a group decide which province you would prefer to visit. Is it the same province the other groups in the class chose?

Information-gap activities may be based on sources of information other than texts. For example, the following activity is based on a visual.

Activity I. The Garden

Step 1. Each person in the group, except one, will receive part of a picture of a garden. No one is to show his or her picture to anyone else.

Step 2. Each person in the group then describes his or her picture to the others using only the target language.

Step 3. As a group, decide what the original garden looked like and describe it so that the person who did not receive a picture can draw the garden.

(In the drawings would be some familiar objects for which the learners would not have the vocabulary: birdbath, bird feeder, pond, flower pot.)

Group Decision Activities

Other kinds of negotiative activity that encourage learners to collaborate include solving a problem, reaching a consensus, or otherwise making some sort of decision. Perhaps the best-known set of such materials is the *Non-Stop Discussion Book* (Rooks 1981), which also is available in several languages other than English. The following activity has been developed from one originated by Rooks, Scholberg, and Scholberg (1982). Note as you examine it that learners must negotiate the contents of the time capsule and that strategic competence comes into play when learners have to talk about things for which they don't have vocabulary or terms. The activity is structured so that each person in the group, and then the class as a whole, will have a particular point of view to express and defend. However, consensus marks the conclusion of the two phases of the activity.

Activity J. The Time Capsule

Step 1. Your university wants to place a time capsule in the new library being constructed. The capsule will be opened in the year 2200, and in it will be ten items that represent the last part of the 20th century. What will those ten items be?

Step 2. The capsule is only two cubic feet in size, so anything you choose must be small. Also, the items selected should reflect not only the achievements of our society but also our values.

Step 3. Work in groups of five or six to come to a consensus about the contents of the time capsule. You can use the following list to guide

---

Pause to consider . . .

the teaching and learning of negotiation devices such as clarification checks, indications of lack of comprehension, and so on. For example, negotiation devices include expressions such as:

"Sorry. What did you say?"
"Pardon me? I didn't catch that."
"Could you say that again, please?"
"Say what?"

What examples of such devices can you think of for the language you (will) teach? Can you think of how these might be taught in class? What kinds of activities could you develop for them?

your discussion, but you must choose at least three of the ten from items not on this list.

a particular book	TV listings
a particular movie	a particular credit card
a gun	a VCR
running shoes	a miniature TV
the telephone directory	a pair of jeans
a brochure for Disney World	a baseball

Step 4. Present and explain your list to the rest of the class. Listen and take notes as the other groups present and explain their lists. Finally, as a class, come to a consensus on what to include in the capsule.

Structured Output versus Information-based Communication Tasks

One of the issues arising from the discussion in this chapter is the difference between structured output activities (Chapter 6) and information-based communication tasks. On the surface the two do look alike, since information is exchanged in each. But a closer inspection reveals that information-based communication tasks do not necessarily focus on a particular form or structure; structured output activities always do. If we compare the information-based communication tasks in this chapter with any of the structured output tasks in Chapter 6, it is apparent that information-based tasks require various forms, vocabulary, and discourse devices whereas the structured output activities are quite focused in terms of what the learner needs in order to create a message. Whereas structured output tasks are explicitly grammar practices (albeit communicative grammar practices), information-exchange tasks are explicitly communication practices. In a certain sense, structured output activi-

---

*P*ause to consider . . .

feedback that instructors provide on learners' output. How would you treat errors when learners are engaged in communicative language tasks? Here are some possibilities:

1. direct correction (pointing out the error)
2. indirect correction (rephrasing the learner's utterance to look like a confirmation check and, thus, to model correct grammar)
3. delayed feedback (noting learners' common errors and then pointing them out at the end of class or on a special "review" day)
4. no special feedback

As you ponder these possibilities, keep in mind the following: What kind of errors would you give feedback on (if at all)? Do all errors need some kind of treatment?

ties form a specialized category of information-based communication tasks. However, the reverse is not the case: communication tasks are not a special type of structured output.

SUMMARY

Oral communication occurs when a person says something to which the other person should attend for meaning. People communicate with each other for a variety of purposes, but underlying all communication is some exchange of meaning or information. In the classroom, information-exchange tasks work best at giving learners a purpose for using their developing language abilities. As non-teacher-fronted (but, certainly, teacher-assisted) tasks, there must be some clear communicative or informational end in information-exchange tasks. Although free conversation between instructor and learners can often serve as an interesting and useful oral communication activity, we have seen that pair and group tasks that involve the sharing of information provide many more opportunities for learners to develop communicative skills such as strategic competence. These tasks need to be carefully constructed, with attention paid to the level of the learners and the linguistic demands that can be placed on them. As they engage in these kinds of tasks, learners come to understand that activity in language classrooms can be much more than the practicing of subcomponents of communicative ability. Classrooms can become places where learners talk about real things and learn about each other.

KEY TERMS, CONCEPTS, AND ISSUES

communication
   expression, interpretation, and negotiation of meaning
      breakdowns
purposes of communication
   psycho-social
   informational-cognitive
contexts of communication
communicative language ability
communicative competence
1 grammatical competence
2 discourse competence
3 sociolinguistic competence
4 strategic competence
classroom discourse
   teacher fronted
   paired or group interactions
information-exchange tasks
   steps for construction
      identify topic or subtopic

design immediate purpose
    identify information source(s)
language demands of tasks
    level of learner
    linguistic demands
information-gap tasks
information-exchange tasks versus structured output activities

EXPLORING THE TOPICS FURTHER

1. *Communicative language ability.* The classic works on relating communicative competence to language teaching are by Canale and Swain (1980) and Savignon (1983). Proficiency, as measured by the Proficiency Guidelines of the American Council on the Teaching of Foreign Languages, is discussed by Omaggio (1986, 1993).
2. *Negotiative language use.* An accessible account of research on information-gap tasks is Doughty and Pica (1986). See also Crookes and Gass (1993a), (1993b) and Breen (1985) for research, theory, and suggestions for classroom practice.
3. *Feedback/error correction.* This topic is somewhat controversial in language teaching and learning. Much like the debate on grammar instruction, the debate on error correction once centered on whether or not to correct learners' errors rather than on how or when to do so. Larsen-Freeman and Long examine error correction from an input perspective (1991, Chapter 5). Hendrickson's (1978) review of the literature is still a frequently cited work examining error correction from an output perspective.

CHAPTER 9

Suggestions for Evaluating Spoken Language

e-val-u-a-tion (ĭ-văl'-yōō-ā'-shən) n. *the systematic gathering of information for the purpose of making decisions.*
Weiss (Weiss 1972, cited in Bachman 1990)

INTRODUCTION

Have you ever stopped to consider how many tests you have taken in your life? Of course, we are tested in the academic context: chapter tests, unit tests, midterm exams, final exams, Master's exams, Ph.D. comprehensive exams, oral defense of a thesis. We are also tested outside the academic context: driver's test, employment test, aptitude test, personality test. Popular magazines are full of tests: How well do you and your partner fit? Are you obsessive/compulsive? Do you have what it takes to be an executive? Different decisions are associated with each of these tests. In the academic context, these decisions range from receiving a grade to receiving a degree. In nonacademic contexts, they include whether or not we obtain a driver's license, get a job, or have our aptitudes and personality categorized. Our society validates the use of tests—ostensibly objective measures—to make decisions. Testing and evaluation are simply a part of our everyday lives.

Whereas decision making is part of the testing enterprise, many instructors use test scores to make decisions other than what grade to assign to a learner. When asked the question "Why do you give tests?" instructors are very likely to give any of the following answers: to motivate learners to study, to assess progress, to validate classroom practices, to fulfill the grading requirement of the school/college/university. Regardless of the motivation, the outcome is that a decision is made, either implicitly or explicitly. Based on a test score, for example, an instructor could decide if the learners had studied, if they were making progress, and if they will pass the course.

In this chapter, we examine a variety of issues important to a discussion of evaluation in classroom language instruction. We focus, however, on oral testing and describe two tests of oral proficiency as well as various evaluation criteria. Finally, we make some practical suggestions for developing test sections based on the information-exchange tasks presented in Chapter 8.

TWO TESTS FOR EVALUATING
SPOKEN LANGUAGE

In this section, we review two oral proficiency tests. The first is the Oral Proficiency Interview (often called the "OPI"), which was developed by the American Council on the Teaching of Foreign Languages (ACTFL) in conjunction with the Educational Testing Service and several government agencies. The other test is the Israeli National Oral Proficiency Test developed by Elana Shohamy and her colleagues for the purpose of determining the ability of Israeli secondary students to use English prior to admission to university.

Elicitation Procedures

The Oral Proficiency Interview

The ACTFL Oral Proficiency Interview has been likened to a face-to-face conversation because an interviewer "converses" with an interviewee. But like many other oral testing situations in which one of the participants in the conversation evaluates the other's language abilities and purposefully elicits certain kinds of language, the interaction can be said to be only "conversation-like." The goal of the OPI is to obtain a sample of speech that can be rated using the ACTFL Proficiency Guidelines as the measure. These Guidelines comprise level-by-level (from Novice to Superior) descriptions of learner performance specifying the *content* that a learner at a particular level might dominate (such as simple greetings, health matters, family, daily routines, work, and politics), the *functions* the learner dominates (such as expressing agreement/disagreement, narrating in the past, present, and future, and hypothesizing and supporting opinions), and the *accuracy* present in the learner's speech (such as systematic errors that interfere with communication and sporadic errors that do not interfere with communication). The levels from Novice to Superior will be described in the next section when we examine evaluation criteria. For now, we would like to concentrate on the OPI itself.

The procedures used to elicit learner language during the OPI are termed phases—Phase 1: Warm-up; Phase 2: Level Check; Phase 3: Probes; and Phase 4: Wind-down. Omaggio Hadley (1993, pp. 456-58) describes each phase as follows:

> *Phase 1: Warm-up.* The warm-up portion of the interview is very brief and consists of greeting the interviewee, making him or her feel comfortable, and exchanging the social amenities that are normally

used in everyday conversations. Typically, the warm-up lasts less than three minutes, but it serves a variety of purposes. First, on the psychological plane, it allows the interviewee to begin thinking in the language and sets him or her at ease. On the linguistic plane, it reorients the person being tested to hearing and using the language while giving the tester an opportunity to determine where the next phase of the interview should begin. This relates to the evaluative function of the warm-up, which is to allow the tester to get a preliminary idea of the rating that will eventually be assigned. Once the warm-up is completed, the tester moves on to Phase 2.

Phase 2: Level Check. This phase consists of establishing the highest level of proficiency at which the interviewee can sustain speaking performance—that is, the level at which he or she can perform the functions and speak about the content areas designated by the ACTFL Guidelines with the greatest degree of accuracy. On the psychological plane, this phase of the interview allows the person being tested to demonstrate his or her strengths and converse at the level that is most comfortable for him or her. Linguistically, the level check is designed to elicit a speech sample that is adequate to prove that the person can indeed function accurately at the level hypothesized by the interviewer during the warm-up phase. If during the level check, the interviewer can see that his or her hypothesis was incorrect, the level of questions is adjusted upward or downward accordingly. On the evaluative plane, the level check allows the interviewer to get a better idea of the actual proficiency level of the interviewee, establishing the floor of his or her performance beyond a reasonable doubt. This phase of the interview is repeated several times throughout the entire testing process and alternates with the probe phase, described next.

Phase 3: Probes. Probes are questions or tasks designed to elicit a language sample at one level of proficiency higher than the hypothesized level in order to establish a ceiling on the interviewee's performance. Psychologically, this allows the tester to show the person being tested what he or she is not yet able to do with the language, verifying the rating that will eventually be assigned to the speech sample. On the linguistic plane, the probes may result in *linguistic breakdown*—the point at which the interviewee ceases to function accurately or cogently because the task is too difficult. If a probe is successfully carried out, the interviewer may begin level checking at this higher level to see if his or her hypothesis about the true proficiency level is wrong. If the interviewee does demonstrate during the probe phase that he or she does not have the language to carry out the task, then the probe can be considered a valid indicator that the hypothesized level is correct. Several probes should be used during the interview, alternated with level checks, to establish beyond any question the appropriate rating.

Phase 4: Wind-down. When a ratable sample has been obtained, the tester brings the interviewee back to the level at which he or she functions most comfortably for the last few minutes of the interview. This serves to make individuals feel successful and allows them to leave the test with the echo of their own voice still in their ears, reminding them that they functioned well in the language. Linguistically, the wind-down portion of the interview represents the most accurate use of the language of which the person is capable. On the evaluative plane, this last phase gives the tester one more opportunity to verify that his or her rating is indeed correct. The tester may end the interview by thanking the person who was interviewed, saying what a pleasure it has been talking with him or her, and wishing the person a pleasant day. Again, the termination of the conversation should resemble as much as possible the way in which conversations normally end in authentic language-use situations.

An OPI can take anywhere from fifteen to thirty minutes depending on the level of the learner and the experience of the interviewer. From the perspective of an elicitation procedure, the OPI is well described. Each test giver follows the standard, prescribed phases. OPI training insures that raters carry out the interview uniformly and apply the ratings consistently: OPI testers can be certified by ACTFL only after a rigorous training session with follow-up practice interviews. The OPI is referred to as a "single-format test," for it consists of only one task (an interview) and there are no other components to the test. On the basis of this one format, a holistic rating such as Novice-High, Intermediate-Mid, or Advanced is assigned.

There are two important concepts that emerge from a consideration of testing, namely, bias and interrater reliability. *Bias* refers to situations in which elicitation and evaluation procedures are not the same for all test takers. The test giver is the variable in this scenario. He or she might ask harder (or easier) questions of certain test takers or might evaluate one person differently from the way another is evaluated. *Interrater reliability* refers to the desire to have all raters evaluate a test the same way. An OPI evaluation, for example, should not vary depending on who the tester was; given a set of criteria, all raters should apply them the same way. If they do, there is interrater reliability. (See Carroll's consideration for comparability described in Chapter 7.) ACTFL training serves the purpose of working toward bias-free and reliable testing.

Although useful for a variety of reasons, the OPI has been questioned because of its single-format nature. Shohamy, for example, has questioned to what extent an oral interview can provide a representative sample of language proficiency. She states that " . . . viewing oral language as constituting a multiple of different speech styles and functions (e.g., discussing, arguing, apologizing, interviewing, conversing, being interviewed, reporting, etc.) means that being interviewed, the speech style and function tapped in an oral interview, represents only a single type of oral interaction. No doubt that it is an important speech style, but clearly, there are also other oral interactions which are equally important in real life situations" (Shohamy 1987, p. 52).

The Israeli National Oral Proficiency Test

In a series of studies, Shohamy and her colleagues (1982, 1986) found that a learner's performance on an oral interview was not a valid predictor of that learner's performance on other oral tasks. Given those findings, Shohamy has recommended a multiple-format approach to testing oral proficiency. This test was introduced in Israel in 1986 as the national examination for students at the end of the twelfth grade. The decision to accept students into university is made based on this test. The Israeli National Oral Proficiency Test in English as a Foreign Language (INOPT), in contrast to the OPI, is multicomponential by design and, therefore, more comprehensive. In addition to the oral interview, three other tasks are also used to evaluate test takers' oral proficiency: role play, a reporting task, and group discussion.

Shohamy, Reves, and Bejerano (1986) justify the four formats on several grounds. First, each format elicits a different speech style, so that the test as a whole comprises a range of speech styles that reflect communicative language use in authentic situations. Second, their research demonstrated that the test did discriminate well among various levels of oral proficiency. Third, their statistical analyses on the test (i.e., correlations of performance across each format and an analysis of shared variance) allowed them to conclude that each section of the test was indeed different from the other sections. Finally, they concluded that if the goal was to test various speech styles, then each would need to be tested via separate oral tests, for no one format could be used as a valid measure of overall oral proficiency and performance on no single format reliably predicted performance on another.

Shohamy and her fellow researchers offer the following descriptions of the four formats used in the INOPT. Each lasted about ten minutes, and different testers were assigned to administer the separate test formats. You will undoubtedly notice that their Oral Interview and the ACTFL OPI are quite similar.

Test 1: Oral Interview. The rationale underlying this test was to guide the test-taker into a dialogue with the tester. The test elicits answers to questions asked by the tester on different topics at different levels of proficiency. The test followed the model of the Foreign Service Institute Oral Interview (Lowe 1982). It included the following four phases.

1. *Warm-up:* In this phase the test-taker was put at ease and the tester derived a preliminary indication of the test-taker's level of proficiency in speech and understanding.
2. *Level-check:* During this phase the tester checked the functions and content where the test-taker's performance was most accurate.
3. *Probing:* In this phase the tester assessed the highest level at which the candidate could function.
4. *Wind-up:* In this phase the test-taker was returned to the level at which he or she could function most comfortably, and thus was left with a feeling of accomplishment. The scoring of the test-taker's performance on the oral interview was done on the basis of the rating scale used for all tests . . . [included in the following section on evaluation criteria]

Test 2: Role Play. The rationale behind this test was to stimulate the test-taker to produce spontaneous speech-behavior within given roles eliciting specific speech functions. In it the test-taker had to play one role, with the tester playing another, both partners in a dialogue. The test-taker was given a card describing a situation and his or her expected role in it . . . The card was written in the test-taker's mother tongue (Hebrew), so that the interference of reading comprehension in the foreign language could be avoided. The tester then engaged in a simulated conversation derived from the situation described on the card. A score was assigned by an assessor who was not involved in the [role play], on the basis of the same rating-scale used for the other tests.

Test 3: Reporting Test. The rationale underlying this test was to stimulate the test-taker into a monologue in the foreign language, based on authentic input in Hebrew. The student was given a newspaper article in Hebrew. He or she was asked to read it silently and report its general content to the tester in his or her own words, in English. The test-taker was specifically asked not to translate the text, but rather to report freely, referring back to the text only if necessary. This test was also scored on the basis of the rating scale used to rate oral proficiency for all the other experimental tests.

Test 4: Group Discussion. The rationale underlying this test was to stimulate the test-takers into a spontaneous discussion of a controversial issue, in which they could express views about topical matters, debate and argue about them, defend their opinions and try to persuade the other participants to accept them. Four students were asked to discuss a topical subject or issue controversial enough to lead to a lively discussion. Members of the group picked a card at random from among the twenty cards on the table. The card provided information regarding the topic of discussion they were about to hold, and some cues for discussion, such as guiding questions with relevant lexical items . . . They were given a few minutes to read the card and plan the procedure for their discussion among themselves in the mother tongue, before they were to start the actual discussion in English (Reves 1982). The tester listened to the discussion without participating in it or interfering with it, and scored the performance of each of the four participant test-takers on the basis of the rating scale used for all the other tests in this study. (Shohamy, Reves, and Bejerano 1986, pp. 215–16)

*P*ause to consider . . .

the relative economy of the OPI and INOPT. For the OPI we have a fifteen-to-thirty minute single-format test. For the INOPT we have a four-format test, each format lasting ten minutes. Carroll's suggestion for economy in testing encourages us to test only a sample of the test taker's abilities. How are both the OPI and INOPT economical approaches to testing oral language?

Evaluation Criteria for Tests of Spoken Language

The speech sample elicited via the OPI is judged against the ACTFL Proficiency Guidelines. Four basic proficiency levels are identified (Novice, Intermediate, Advanced, and Superior), with three ratings (Low, Mid, and High) for Novice and Intermediate levels and only two ratings within Advanced (Advanced and Advanced-High). The following level descriptions are taken from Omaggio Hadley (1993, pp. 502–4). Because of space constraints, we include only one within-level rating, Intermediate-Mid, as an illustrative example.

Novice   The Novice level is characterized by the ability to communicate minimally with learned material.

Intermediate   The Intermediate level is characterized by the speaker's ability to:
—create with the language by combining and recombining learned elements, though primarily in a reactive mode;
—initiate, minimally sustain, and close in a simple way basic communicative tasks; and
—ask and answer questions.

Intermediate-Mid   Able to handle successfully a variety of uncomplicated, basic and communicative tasks and social situations. Can talk simply about self and family members. Can ask and answer questions and participate in simple conversations on topics beyond the most immediate needs; e.g., personal history and leisure time activities. Utterance length increases slightly, but speech may continue to be characterized by frequent long pauses, since the smooth incorporation of even basic conversational strategies is often hindered as the speaker struggles to create appropriate language forms. Pronunciation may continue to be strongly influenced by first language and fluency may still be strained. Although misunderstandings still arise, the Intermediate-Mid speaker can generally be understood by sympathetic interlocutors.

Advanced   The Advanced level is characterized by the speaker's ability to:
—converse in a clearly participatory fashion;
—initiate, sustain, and bring to closure a wide variety of communicative tasks, including those that require an increased ability to convey meaning with diverse language strategies due to a complication or an unforeseen turn of events;
—satisfy the requirements of school and work situations; and
—narrate and describe with paragraph-length connected discourse.

Superior   The Superior level is characterized by the speaker's ability to:
—participate effectively in most formal and informal conversations on practical, social, professional, and abstract topics; and
—support opinions and hypothesize using native-like discourse strategies.

The four speech samples elicited by the INOPT are each judged separately according to the following scale (Shohamy et al. 1986, p. 219). Scores from each section are added together to yield a final score.

4: Unintelligible
   No language produced
   No interaction possible
5: Hardly intelligible
   Very poor language produced
   Only simplest, fragmentary interaction possible
6: Clearly intelligible
   Simple language produced
   Interaction possible
   Not articulate
7: Responsive in interaction
   Slightly more sophisticated language produced
   Consistent errors: but do not interfere with fluency
   Strong MT [mother tongue] interference (translated patterns, etc.)
8: Almost effortless in expression
   Adequate in interaction
   Errors: not consistent
9: Facility of expression
   Comfortable, initiating in interaction
   Sporadic mistakes
10: No limitation whatsoever
   Near-native

As indicated earlier, the OPI and the INOPT are similar because each contains some type of interview. Here we would like to point out that the two tests overlap in another significant way: each uses holistic ratings (that is, a single final "score" for the entire test). As Bachman (1990, p. 328) points out, using holistic scores implies that "language proficiency is viewed as a unitary ability, with scores 'expressed in a single global rating of general language ability' (Lowe 1988, p. 12)." Bachman goes on to argue that proficiency is *not* a unitary ability but, rather, a componential one because we can identify the pieces and constituent parts of oral proficiency. (See, for example the four underlying competences discussed in Savignon 1983 that were briefly mentioned on p. 149) The distinction between unitary and componential is not only an important theoretical distinction but also a practical one. On the practical level, instructors must decide how to score a test of spoken language and what kind of feedback they wish to give to learners about their performance.

> ### *Pause to consider . . .*
>
> the diagnostic uses of classroom tests. One of the important functions of classroom testing is its diagnostic function: by examining learners' performance on a test, we can provide them feedback on their strengths and weaknesses. Does a global, holistic score provide an instructor the capability of giving diagnostic feedback? Think about what you would want to know about your own oral proficiency in the second language. Would a high score on an oral proficiency test mean that you did not have weaknesses you could work on? Would a low score indicate what specific things you could do to improve?

COMPONENTIAL RATING SCALES

If oral proficiency is not a unitary ability then it should not be tested as such (Shohamy et al. 1986) and, just as importantly, it should not be scored as such (Bachman 1990). Bachman proposes, therefore, that tests of oral proficiency be evaluated using componential scoring criteria and provides the following criteria used in a test of oral proficiency he developed with a colleague (Bachman and Palmer 1983). The three scales assess grammatical, pragmatic, and sociolinguistic competence, as shown in Table 9.1. (Pragmatic competence is similar to discourse competence and refers to cohesion across utterances.) It is important to note that each component contributes a different amount to the total final score; thus, the points listed under "Rating" vary from component to component with differing ranges (for example, 0–6 for Grammatical Competence but 0–4 for Pragmatic Competence). The more important component is weighted more heavily.

Because the Bachman-Palmer criteria are designed to separate a language learner's communicative language ability into its component parts, the criteria can be adapted according to several principles. In adapting such rating scales for classroom use, an instructor might alter the weight of a scale (adding or subtracting how many points it is worth) or vary the components according to the elicitation procedures. Even though Shohamy's group used the same criteria to evaluate the speech samples in each of the four test formats, it is possible to vary the criteria depending on the type of elicitation procedure. (You will work with this concept in the Workbook.)

> ### *Pause to consider . . .*
>
> whether the grade assigned at the end of a language course is unitary or componential. What would it mean to you, to the instructor, and/or to your parents that you earned a B in Russian 101?

TABLE 9.1. Scales for Evaluating Grammatical Competence, Pragmatic Competence, and Sociolinguistic Competence

	Grammatical Competence	
Rating	Range	Accuracy
0	No systematic evidence of morphologic and syntactic structures	Control of few or no structures; errors of all or most possible types
1	Limited range of both morphologic and syntactic structures, but with some systematic evidence	Control of few or no structures; errors of all or most possible types
2	Limited range of both morphologic and syntactic structures, but with some systematic evidence	Control of some structures used, but with many error types
3	Large, but not complete, range of both morphologic and syntactic structures	Control of some structures used, but with many error types
4	Large, but not complete, range of both morphologic and syntactic structures	Control of most structures used, with few error types
5	Complete range of morphologic and syntactic structures	Control of most structures used, with few error types
6	Complete range of morphologic and syntactic structures	No systematic errors

	Pragmatic Competence		
Rating	Vocabulary	Rating	Cohesion
0	*Extremely limited vocabulary* (A few words and formulaic phrases. Not possible to discuss any topic, due to limited vocabulary.)	0	*No cohesion* (Utterances completely disjointed, or discourse too short to judge.)
1	*Small vocabulary* (Difficulty in talking with examinee because of vocabulary limitations.)	1	*Very little cohesion* (Relationships between utterances not adequately marked; frequent confusing relationships among ideas.)
2	*Vocabulary of moderate size* (Frequently misses or searches for words.)	2	*Moderate cohesion* (Relationships between utterances generally marked; sometimes confusing relationships among ideas.)

3	*Large vocabulary* (Seldom misses or searches for words.)	3	*Good cohesion* (Relationships between utterances well-marked.)
4	*Extensive vocabulary* (Rarely, if ever, misses or searches for words. Almost always uses appropriate word.)	4	*Excellent cohesion* (Uses a variety of appropriate devices; hardly ever confusing relationships among ideas.)

Sociolinguistic Competence

R	Distinguishing of registers	R	Nativeness	R	Use of cultural references
0	Evidence of only one register	1	*Frequent* non-native but grammatical structures or impossible to judge because of interference from other factors	0.5	No evidence of ability to use cultural references
1	Evidence of two registers			2.5	Some evidence of ability to use cultural references
2	Evidence of two registers *and* control of either formal or informal register	3	*Rare* non-native but grammatical structures	4	Full control of appropriate cultural references
3.5	Control of *both* formal and informal registers	4	*No* non-native but grammatical structures		

Source: Bachman and Palmer (1983)

11.5

ORAL TESTING IN CLASSROOMS: ADAPTING INFORMATION-EXCHANGE TASKS AS ORAL TESTS/QUIZZES

The INOPT includes four formats to elicit a variety of speech styles and functions. We can indeed classify the formats along those lines, but we can also classify them according to the degree of *communicative burden,* which we define as the responsibility of an individual test taker to initiate, respond, manage, and negotiate an oral event. The communicative burden of a group discussion is less than the communicative burden of an oral interview. In a discussion, multiple participants share the communicative burden, each one assuming the responsibilities of initiating, responding, managing, and negotiating the event. In contrast, most of these responsibilities are the test taker's during a one-on-one interview. The test taker alone must respond to the interviewer and manage the interaction. During classroom testing, an instructor must consider the communicative burden of a test format and decide if it is an appropriate burden based on the level of the learner and on the classroom practices leading up to the test.

The communicative burden of a test format becomes an issue when considering whether to give an oral quiz or an oral test. Most people distinguish quizzes from tests in terms of length and comprehensiveness. Quizzes are shorter and less comprehensive than tests (daily quizzes, pop quizzes, and lesson quizzes vs. unit tests, and end of semester tests, for example). In practical terms, a quiz might incorporate only one or perhaps two formats whereas an oral test might incorporate the four used in the INOPT. One might decide that an oral quiz at the end of a lesson in the first semester should have a low communicative burden whereas a quiz at the end of a lesson in the fourth semester should have a greater one. Moreover, one might decide to quiz spoken language in the first year of language instruction but to test it only in the second year. In short, there are a number of instructional decisions to make regarding oral testing, and these decisions depend on a variety of factors (including experience of the instructor, time available, and the goals of the curriculum).

These decisions may well have a washback effect on instruction. By knowing and being familiar with the characteristics of the test (any kind of test, not just one of spoken language), instructors might incorporate activities into the classroom that they feel will lead to success on the test. That is, the type of test can influence both *what* instructors emphasize and the *way* in which they emphasize it. For example, if learners must take a test of communicative language ability at the end of a course, then the instructor would probably carry out activities that allow learners to develop their communicative language ability. Most, if not all, instructors would make a concerted effort to speak the target language in class and to do listening comprehension activities throughout the course if twenty-five percent of the points on the final exam were determined by learners' performance on listening comprehension exercises.

The content of the oral test or quiz can have another kind of washback effect on instruction. If the content of the oral test is overtly tied to classroom activities, then learners are provided a stronger motivation for participating in the activities. The following examples of test sections illustrate this point. We once again recommend that instructors adhere to the principle that they *test what and how they teach.* Testing and teaching should be interrelated so that learners are responsible for what happens in class.

In Chapter 7 we converted structured input and output activities to test sections. We do the same here, converting four of the information-exchange tasks presented in Chapter 8 into test sections. Recall the following activity from Chapter 8.

Activity D. Compare Your Birthday Experiences

Step 1. Fill in the following chart as you interview a classmate.
Step 2. In a paragraph, compare how the two of you have celebrated your birthdays.

Birthday	Where?	With whom?	Food?	Fun?
2 years ago				
5 years ago				
10 years ago				

Here is a test section based on Activity D:

Section A

Phase 1. *Warm-up.* Make the test taker feel comfortable.

Phase 2. *Initial questioning.* Who was your partner? When is that person's birthday? When is your birthday?

Phase 3. *Activity-related questions.* Referring to the chart, tell me whether you and [name of partner] have celebrated your birthdays in similar or different ways.

[*Procedural note to tester:* Let the test taker talk from the chart but do not look at it yourself. If you read the chart, then the test taker will not be exchanging real information with you; he or she will be telling you what you already know. Be sure to ask for clarification when you don't understand. Be conscious of whatever time limits there are on the test so that you move the interaction along with probe questions such as, *What about five years ago?* and *What about ten years ago?*]

Here is an information-gap task from another activity in Chapter 8.

Activity H. Compare Provinces

Step 1. Each person in the group reads a different short text produced by the national travel bureau. Each text describes the desirable features of a particular province in order to generate tourism to that region.

Step 2. Working together, the group completes the following chart.

Province:	A	B	C
Terrain			
Festivals			
Sporting			
Climate			

Step 3. Decide which province you, as a group, would prefer to visit.

The following test section proceeds logically from Activity H:

Section B

Phase 1. *Make the test taker feel comfortable.*

Phase 2. *Initial questioning.* [*Test taker should not need to refer to the chart.*] What province did you read about? Tell me what you remember about it. Who else did you work with? What provinces did they read about?

Phase 3. *Activity-related questions.* [*Allow the test taker to use the chart.*] Where did you as a group decide to go? Why did you pick that one? Province B is also very beautiful; why didn't the group choose it? Did you agree with the group choice or did you prefer another location?

Phase 4. *Beyond the activity.* Have you ever been anywhere like the provinces described? Where was that? *or* Did these descriptions remind you of any place in the United States? *or* If you had to describe your hometown [*or some other place such as where the school is located*], what would you say?

Recall that consensus building was the focus of Activity J.

Activity J. The Time Capsule

Step 1. Your university wants to place a time capsule in the new library being constructed. The capsule will be opened in the year 2200, and in it will be ten items that represent the last part of the 20th century. What will those ten items be?

Step 2. The capsule is only two cubic feet in size, so anything you choose must be small. Also, the items selected should reflect not only the achievements of our society but also our values.

Step 3. Work in groups of five or six to come to a consensus about the contents of the time capsule. You can use the following list to guide your discussion, but you must choose at least three of the ten from items not on this list.

a particular book	TV listings
a particular movie	a particular credit card
a gun	a VCR
running shoes	a miniature TV
the telephone directory	a pair of jeans
a brochure for Disney World	a baseball

Step 4. Present and explain your list to the rest of the class. Listen and take notes as the other groups present and explain their lists. Finally, as a class, come to a consensus on what to include in the capsule.

Two test sections could be based on Activity J:

Section C

Phase 1. *Make the learner feel comfortable.*

Phase 2. *Initial questioning.* Whom did you work with? What items did you and your group select? Was it easy to reach a consensus?

Phase 3. *Activity-related questions.* Compare and contrast the list of items your group chose and those the class chose. Why did your group choose something that is not on the final list?

Phase 4. *Beyond the activity.* Our class selected ten items for the time capsule. Of these ten items, which is the one that you think is most representative of our times. Why do you think that?

Section D. If you did not do the Time Capsule as an in-class activity, then you could have a pair or group of learners do it as a quiz or part of a test. In order to reduce the amount of time required to carry out the activity, you could (a) reduce the number of items they have to decide on and (b) eliminate Step 4, the presentation of the list.

Pause to consider . . .

a nontraditional alternative. We have cautioned against the simple question-and-answer approach to communicative language teaching and have promoted the communication-as-information-exchange paradigm. Even though the test versions suggested for Activities D, H, and J promote information exchange, they still have the flavor of a question-and-answer exercise. Can any oral test be a truly communicative exchange? What would happen if the test giver were truly a participant in the communicative event? Consider the possibility of *doing* a communicative activity *with* the test taker instead of having the test taker report on a previous experience with the activity. How different would the interaction between test taker and test giver be in those circumstances? What would you, the test giver, learn about the test taker's communicative language ability that the traditional format would not reveal?

Let's turn now to the following activity from Chapter 8 and its corresponding test sections.

Activity F. Explain, Please.

Your friend Luisa, who is an exchange student from Costa Rica, has heard the following English words and phrases used in conversation. She didn't quite understand what they meant. Explain to her, in Spanish, what they mean. [The person could just as well be Yoshi from Japan, Marcel from France, Antonietta from Italy.]

1. funny bone
2. punchline
3. laughing stock
4. deadbeat
5. dead to the world
6. bed head

Section E

Preparation: Write approximately twenty words or phrases on separate index cards.

Phase 1. Make the learner feel comfortable.

Phase 2. Have the learner randomly select two index cards (face down so the item cannot be seen) and choose one to explain to you. Repeat the procedure two more times (for a total of three).

Section F. Have two learners take the test together. Each selects two index cards but does not show them to the other learner. Their task is to explain to the other what is written on the card. The person listening can ask questions. Limit the interaction to two or three minutes per index card.

Pause to consider . . .

the appropriate evaluation criteria for each of the test sections presented. Can you use the same evaluation criteria for all of them? How would the criteria vary? Which test sections would make better quizzes than tests? Which would make better tests than quizzes?

SUMMARY

In this chapter we explored oral testing, beginning with a look at two tests for evaluating spoken language, the ACTFL Oral Proficiency Interview and the Israeli National Oral Proficiency Test. Both tests prescribe very specific elicitation procedures and utilize specific evaluation criteria, thereby addressing two important issues in testing: bias and interrater reliability. We suggested the use of tests that examine a variety of speech styles and functions via multiple formats.

Test taker performance on both the OPI and INOPT is measured using holistic (single-score) ratings. Following Bachman (1990), we advocated instead the use of analytic criteria in recognition of the componential nature of language proficiency. We presented several componential rating scales, which allow a more precise evaluation of the speech sample as well as a more detailed diagnosis of the learner's language. We suggested that the choice of rating scales should depend on the types of oral interactions elicited and whether the interaction involves just a test giver or other learners.

As in Chapter 7, we adapted classroom activities for testing situations. Some formats place a greater communicative burden on the test taker than do others; the degree of communicative burden should guide an instructor's testing procedures, especially with early-stage learners. Testing learners' communicative language ability can have a positive washback effect on instruction. If there is to be an oral test with content related to classroom activities, learners will have additional motivation not only to participate in the class but to strive to improve their communicative language ability.

KEY TERMS, CONCEPTS, AND ISSUES

elicitation procedures
  Oral Proficiency Interview
    phases
  Israeli National Oral Proficiency Test
    components
evaluation criteria
training of test givers
  absence of bias
  interrater reliability
speech styles and functions (discussing, arguing, apologizing, interviewing, being interviewed, conversing, reporting, and so forth)
unitary ability versus componential ability
single holistic score versus component weighting scales
diagnostic feedback
communicative burden
  level of learner
  classroom practices
quiz versus test
washback effects on instruction

EXPLORING THE TOPICS FURTHER

1. *ACTFL OPI.* A widely read book is by Omaggio Hadley (1993), who describes the use of the OPI for evaluation and the use of the ACTFL Guidelines in curriculum development. See also the OPI familiarization kit written by Liskin-Gasparro (1982) and published by Education Testing Service. For debate on the ACTFL OPI and the ACTFL Proficiency Guidelines, see Valdman (1987), which assumes some familiarity with the Guidelines and the OPI.
2. *INOPT.* See Shohamy, Reves, and Bejerano (1986).
3. *Language testing in general.* Bachman (1990) is a thorough book but not necessarily for novices. For a better introduction, read Madsen (1983). Chapter 1 of Henning's (1987) book provides a very good description of the types and purposes of language tests.

PART IV

Reading and Writing

The focus of this unit is literacy in a second language, namely, reading and writing. Chapter 10 begins with a survey of some of the research on second language reading that provides a critical point of departure for rethinking traditional approaches to instruction. We challenge in Chapter 10 the traditional approach to reading that places a list of comprehension questions at the end of a passage; in its place, we explore an alternative framework for the presentation of reading materials. In Chapter 11 we distinguish between writing (simply putting pen to paper) and composing (thoughtfully creating coherent language). We begin with a model of the thought processes involved in composing and apply that model to traditional second language writing activities. We then propose an approach to second language composing that utilizes these thought processes. In Chapter 12, our final chapter on testing, we provide suggestions for testing reading and writing consistent with the instructional approaches introduced in Chapters 10 and 11.

CHAPTER 10

Comprehending Written Language

read (rēd) v. 1. to comprehend or take in the meaning of (something written or printed). 2. to learn or get knowledge from (something written or printed). 3. to perceive, receive or comprehend (a signal, message or the like).

American Heritage Dictionary

INTRODUCTION

What does the typical language learner do with the set of comprehension questions at the end of a reading passage? Do learners use them to check comprehension, or do they use them to somehow limit interaction with the text? The meaning those learners try to construct from the passage is based not on the original language but on their (often faulty) translation of it. How do learners who write the native-language equivalent over every word in a passage conceptualize what it means to read in another language? How do learners who see second-language words on a page but say native-language words in their heads conceptualize what it means to read in another language? Whether they write the translation or think it, such readers are not learning to read in another language. Native readers of Italian see Italian words on the page and think Italian words in their heads!

Did you ever use a *look-back strategy* to answer comprehension questions about a passage? That is, did you use the words and wording of the comprehension question and then look back to the passage to make a match? You would then *lift off* the answer to the question from the similarly worded part of the passage. This *look-back-and-lift-off approach* to reading is problematic for two reasons. First, the readers rarely end up reading the entire passage; as a result, their comprehension consists of unconnected fragments of information. Second, some readers are so proficient at looking back and lifting off that they can do it without understanding what they have read!

In this chapter, we present an instructional framework that views reading in another language as just that—*reading in another language*—rather than as an exercise in translation. This framework encourages readers to construct meaning from the language of the passage and discourages their use of the native language to intervene in the process. Before describing the instructional framework, we first present some research findings that support such an orientation to reading instruction. The research focuses on two areas: readers and texts. Readers' characteristics were for a long time not entered into the comprehension equation. Instead, texts and their characteristics were considered the sole determining factors in comprehension. However, more recent studies have shown how much readers contribute to comprehension. We now review some current theories about reading, and we will use the results to rethink the nature of texts and readers' interactions with them.

AN INTERACTIVE MODEL OF READING

You might often hear readers say, "That passage was really hard" or "The passage was too difficult." You've probably said something similar yourself. We know now that it is not just the nature of the passage that makes a particular reading difficult or easy. Beginning in the late sixties and early seventies, research emerged that demonstrated the roles that readers themselves play in the comprehension process. Such research was conducted under the rubric of *schema theory*.

> According to schema theories, all knowledge is packaged into units. These units are the schemata [plural of *schema*]. Embedded in these packages of knowledge is, in addition to the knowledge itself, information about how this knowledge is to be used. A schema, then, is a data structure for representing the generic concepts stored in memory. (Rumelhart 1980, p. 34)

Therefore, the readers' contributions to comprehension are their "schemata"—their personal knowledge and experience that they rely on to represent and understand concepts. For example, two learners of Italian with the same language proficiency might each read an article on Italian politics with different results. The reader who has a political science background will most likely comprehend more of the article than the reader who has a music background because they possess different kinds of knowledge and different ways of applying that knowledge—their different schemata.

Schema-theoretic research led to new, *interactive* models for the reading process. Rumelhart (1977) proposed an interactive model of processing consisting of several knowledge sources representing different levels of linguistic representation (feature, letter, letter cluster, lexical, syntactic, and semantic knowledges). Interactive models of reading posit that the components of the model, namely, the knowledge sources, all act simultaneously and in parallel on the incoming written input. For example, semantic knowledge can be used to decide which letters comprise a word at the same time that letters in words may trigger semantic knowledge to be used. In a passage on medical care, you would expect certain words such as *doctor* and *nurse* to appear. When you arrive at these words in the passage, your brain does not necessarily need to analyze each letter and letter cluster to determine their meanings. In a certain sense, the brain is "ready" for these words and might need only the *d-o* of *doctor* or the *n-u-r* of *nurse* to access their meanings.

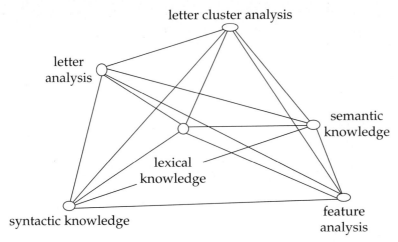

FIGURE 10.1. An Interactive Model of Reading

Interactive models fundamentally redefined the relationship among knowledge sources. Figure 10.1 is a graphic representation of a prototypical interactive model for reading. Note that in the interactive model, each knowledge source is connected to each of the others. Each can influence the others, singly or in combination, so that semantic knowledge can aid feature analysis or syntactic knowledge can aid letter analysis.

What follows is a very brief description of the elements of this model. *Feature analysis* refers to the act of recognizing a loop in a letter and the direction of that loop (*p*), whereas *letter analysis* is recognizing that the loops make a specific letter (*p* versus *d* versus *b*). Certain letters do and do not cluster in particular languages, and the clusters syllabify in particular ways. *Letter cluster analysis* thus tells us that the letters *th* cluster in English as in *the* and *ar-thri-tis*. *Syntactic knowledge* identifies the order of words in a language (for example, knowing that subjects often precede verbs so that the agent of an action is correctly identified: 'John hit Charlie' is not the same as 'Charlie hit John'). The same words ordered in different ways can produce different meanings, as in 'plan to fail' versus 'fail to plan.' It is our syntactic knowledge that identifies the meaning in the order of the words. *Lexical knowledge* concerns individual word properties and meanings, so that the word *work* is identified rather than similar words such as *word* and *fork*. *Semantic knowledge* governs meaning at all levels: words, phrases, clauses, sentences, paragraphs. For example, our semantic knowledge tells us that the differences between the following two sentences are probably minimal if the attraction is mutual, or maximal if the attraction is undirectional. 'Pat loves Chris' versus 'Chris loves Pat.'

According to interactive models of reading, comprehension is built up or constructed from knowledge sources interacting with each other on the input from the written page. *Comprehension*, by definition, is the process of relating new or incoming information to information already stored in memory. Readers make connections between the new information on the printed page and

Pause to consider . . .

how automatic the processes of reading are for fluent readers. As a fluent adult reader of your native language, feature and letter cluster analyses are automatic processes for you; you exert no mental effort in carrying them out. These processes become quite effortful for second language readers, particularly if the second language uses a different orthography than does their native language. What differences can you detect between the following pairs of symbols: (Θ θ) (Φ φ) (σ ϖ) (φ ψ)? Now imagine encountering these symbols in words along with other symbols whose features you must detect. How much effort are you expending on feature recognition? How much mental energy will you have left to uncover the meaning of the sentence or paragraph you are reading? Have you ever learned a language whose orthography was different from that of your native language?

their existing knowledge. They must allow the new information to enter and become a part of their knowledge store. "To say that one has comprehended a text is to say that she has found a mental 'home' for the information in the text, or else that she has modified an existing mental home in order to accommodate that new information" (Anderson and Pearson, 1984 p. 255).

Once interactive models of mental processes began to guide research and the interpretation of experimental results, reading was referred to as an *interactive process.* Educators quickly adopted the terminology to refer to readers and texts, who were the people and objects of reading. Educators began to refer to reading as the *interaction* between a reader and a text, so that we now talk about *interactive* approaches to teaching reading. McNeil provides a useful example of such an approach: the process of reading involves "actively constructing meaning among the parts of the text and between the text and personal experience. The text itself is [but] a blueprint for meaning" (McNeil 1984, p. 5). The blueprint metaphor is quite appropriate, for it originated in the construction field. Someone must take a blueprint and use it to make a building. In a sense, the blueprint guides the construction of the building but it is not the building. Similarly, the text guides comprehension but it is not comprehension. The reader takes the text and gives it meaning.

Pause to consider . . .

how the mind works—and when it doesn't work. Have you ever found yourself at the bottom of the page of what you have been reading but are unable to remember how you got there? What does that say to you about what comprehension is and isn't?

HOW READERS CONTRIBUTE TO COMPREHENSION

As we have seen, the readers' contribution to comprehension is their schemata, their personal "data structures" for representing concepts. For comprehension to take place, a reader's schemata must be activated. That is, conditions must be favorable for readers to bring their knowledge and experiences to the task of reading. Otherwise, the eyes may go horizontally and vertically across the page without the mind being engaged. How do schemata function? What do they do? They function to constrain the interpretation of incoming information (and *constrain* is used here in a positive sense) in several ways: to disambiguate, elaborate, filter, and compensate. Examples of each follow.

To Disambiguate. One way in which schemata constrain our interpretations is to disambiguate passage information: we tend to screen out certain possibilities in a passage consistent with our background knowledge. To demonstrate, Anderson and colleagues (1976) gave two ambiguous passages to two groups of readers, physical education majors and musicians. The first passage could have been interpreted as either a prison break or a wrestling match, the second passage as either a card-playing session or a musical practice session. Segments of each passage are given below to illustrate their ambiguous qualities.

1. Prison/Wrestling
   Rocky slowly got up from the mat, planning his escape . . . What bothered him most was being held, especially since the charge against him had been weak. He considered his present situation. The lock that held him was strong, but he thought he could break it.
2. Cards/Music
   When Jerry, Mike and Pat arrived, Karen was sitting in her living room writing some notes. She quickly gathered the cards and stood up to greet her friends at the door. They followed her into the living room but as usual they couldn't agree on exactly what to play.

Anderson et al. showed that physical education majors consistently interpreted the Prison/Wrestling passage as a wrestling match, whereas the music majors interpreted it as a prison break. On the other hand, the music majors consistently interpreted the Cards/Music passage as being about playing music, whereas the physical education majors interpreted it as playing cards.

To Elaborate. Schemata also play an elaborative function in comprehension when we use our knowledge to make inferences; we fill in gaps either in things we did not comprehend or in things that were not in the passage. The elaborative function of schemata, for example, leads readers to indicate that information was actually present in a text when it was not, if such information could be logically inferred from the content of the text (Perkins 1983).

Research on narrative texts has shown a definite structural pattern to elaborations. Fairy tales, for example, are organized around a highly predictable structure, a structure readily used by readers to organize and recall information. Riley (1990) found that her L2 readers were sensitive to the kinds of information present in fairy tales. In her study, subjects tended to provide endings to the various episodes in the story whether or not such endings appeared in the original. "For example, many subjects stated that the wife divorced her husband, the werewolf, in order to end the episode before recounting the [next] episode that contained the wife's marriage to the second knight" (p. 130). In the minds of the readers, a divorce from one husband logically preceded a marriage to another.

To Filter. Schemata also have a filtering function. Once a schema is activated, all incoming information is filtered through it. This function is not the same as disambiguating a text; rather, a schematic filter provides an evaluative perspective on unambiguous incoming information. This function of schemata was demonstrated in first language reading by Pichert and Anderson (1977, cited in Bransford 1979). Two groups of readers were given the same passage about two boys and the house in which they were playing. One group was to imagine themselves as potential house buyers, the other group as thieves. The information recalled by the two groups was different, reflecting their different perspectives on the information presented in the text. For example, the house buyers recalled that the house had a leaky roof while the thieves recalled that there was a color television set. The house buyers recalled the spaciousness of the dining room whereas the thieves recalled the open drawer of sterling silver. In a certain sense, what readers get out of a passage depends on what they bring to it.

Readers need not be provided with an external perspective in order to filter information. Steffensen, Joag-Dev, and Anderson (1979) demonstrated how Indians and Americans, reading letters describing marriage ceremonies in the two cultures, interpreted information about the two ceremonies through a culturally generated schematic filter. As Steffensen and colleagues point out, "Wearing an heirloom wedding dress is a completely acceptable aspect of the pageantry of the American marriage ceremony and reflects interest in tradition that surfaces on this occasion. [A subject from India] appears to have completely missed this and, on the basis of the Indian emphasis on the relative financial power of the two families (which can be shown by even such a small detail as wearing an up-to-date, fashionable sari), has inferred that the dress was out of fashion" (p. 21). An unambiguous sentence about wearing Grandma's wedding dress was filtered through the Indian reader's cultural perspective on weddings.

To Compensate. The final function that schemata can play in comprehension is to compensate for other knowledge sources such as underdeveloped orthographic knowledge, lexical knowledge, and syntactic knowedge. Just as the word constrain was not used with negative connotations earlier, the word compensate is not used here in a negative sense. For example, a non-native speaker of English would not have to know anything about the morphology of the past tense to determine correctly that each of the following sentences refers to a past event. These sentences demonstrate that certain knowledge sources can compensate for linguistic knowledge. What contextual cues are available in the following three sentences indicating a past time?

a. The Louisiana Purchase in 1804 dramatically increased the size of the United States.

b. The last time I saw him, he was getting better.

c. Armstrong and Aldrin walked on the moon before anyone else.

By utilizing such contextual cues as dates, adverbials, and historical knowledge, readers could construct meaning from these sentences. The intent of the example is not, however, to discount the role of linguistic knowledge in comprehension. To rely on a small set of knowledge sources without complete recourse to linguistic knowledge may lead a reader to construct inaccurate meanings. The following example demonstrates the point. Lee (1990) showed how one reader interpreted a passage on feudalism, a sociopolitical structure, as a feud between two individuals. Note that elements of the original are clearly the basis of the reader's reconstruction. (Subjects read the passage in Spanish but recalled it in English.)

Printed text (translated from Spanish)
Feudalism was based on an agreement of honor between two men. One, called a "lord or "don," controlled a lot of land. The other, called a "vassal," promised to serve and protect the lord so that the latter would permit him to use part of his land. While the agreement was in place, the vassal could use the land, including the buildings and peons, to make himself richer. In exchange for these rights, he gave part of his earnings to the lord and served him faithfully in time of war.

Reader's reconstruction
. . . there were two people who feuded over land. One was rich and already had a lot of land. His name was Mr. Don. The other was a simple farmer who owned just a little land. Mr. Don wanted this other man's land because it would make him more rich. . .

This subject's knowledge of the target language was not sufficient to correct his (mis)interpretation of the passage. Rather, he fed the incoming information through his knowledge of (or schema for) feuds in order to construct the meaning he did. Clearly, his background knowledge was compensating for his other knowledge sources. Yet if not for his background knowledge, the reader would not have been able to interpret any information from the text. This reader's reconstruction demonstrates that not only must a schema be activated for comprehension to take place, but the appropriate schema must be activated for accurate comprehension to result. This reader instantiated a schema for feuds, not feudalism. A prereading instructional practice that activated a feudalism schema would have gone a long way in helping this reader comprehend accurately.

We have seen in this section that comprehension is the process of relating new or incoming information to information already stored in memory. We then examined the comprehension process in terms of how schemata constrain the interpretation of incoming information; these schemata are the readers' contributions to comprehension. We saw that schemata operate in the following ways: (1) to disambiguate textual elements; (2) to elaborate on textual elements; (3) to filter textual elements through a perspective; and (4) to compensate (with positive and negative results) for other types of knowledge. Later in this chapter, we present an instructional framework that seeks to activate readers' background knowledge—knowledge appropriate to the text—in order to facilitate second language readers' comprehension. Before presenting this instructional framework, we examine how features of texts influence comprehension.

Pause to consider . . .

the negative connotations associated with the word *compensate*. Stanovich (1980) demonstrated that the knowledge sources in the interactive processing model for reading clearly compensate for each other during native language reading. In foreign language instruction, the compensation of topic knowledge and background knowledge for underdeveloped linguistic knowledge came to be viewed by some as negative and by others as positive. On the negative side, educators feared readers would be too successful with their comprehension and ignore developing their linguistic knowledge. On the positive side, educators took advantage of topic and background knowledge to encourage language learners to read early in their learning experience. Do you understand the two sides of the issue? Where do you stand? Do you see one knowledge source compensating for another as a negative or a positive dimension of reading in a second language?

THE EFFECTS OF TEXT FEATURES ON READING COMPREHENSION

Instructional materials for reading in a second language were once tied to the grammatical structures and vocabulary being taught. It was assumed (incorrectly) that learners could not understand language they had not been taught. Research has challenged these assumptions. For example, Lee (1987b) showed that learners who had never been taught the Spanish subjunctive (either forms or functions) could understand the information being conveyed by the subjunctive forms just as well as could learners who had been taught the subjunctive. Johnson (1981) gave original and simplified versions of a passage to learners of English as a second language. The passages had been simplified by reducing the number of relative clauses and the figurative language, using higher frequency vocabulary, and simplifying the sentence structure. She showed that the learners' comprehension was simply not affected one way or another by these simplifications. Strother and Ulijn (1987) also presented ESL learners with an original and simplified version of a passage. They simplified passive structures, nominalizations, and particles. They, too, found no difference in comprehension across the simplified and unsimplified versions of the passage.

Although the results of the three studies converge, you should not conclude that language plays no role in second language reading comprehension. Language does have a role in reading comprehension, but instructors should not view the language of the text as the only criterion for judging a text's appropriateness. Text characteristics need to be judged and evaluated in light of the readers' characteristics. In fact, whereas many researchers have found that simplification does not affect comprehension, others have found evidence that it does; we know that the language of the text *can* make a difference. Let's look at some examples where differences in comprehension have resulted from differences in the language learners read.

How specific the words are in a text can make a difference. First and second language readers comprehend the passage better when the lexical items are transparent and specific rather than opaque and general (Bransford and Johnson 1972; Carrell 1983; Lee 1986b). *Transparent* words explicitly refer to the topic; *opaque* ones do so indirectly. Note, for example, the use of *things* for *clothes* and *facilities* for *washing machines* in the following sets of sentences.

Transparent version
The procedure is actually quite simple. First you arrange the clothes into different groups. Of course, one pile may be enough depending on how much wash there is to do. If you have to do it somewhere else due to lack of washing machines, that is the next step; otherwise, you are ready to begin.

Opaque version
The procedure is actually quite simple. First you arrange things into different groups. Of course, one pile may be enough depending on how much there is to do. If you have to do it somewhere else due to lack of facilities, that is the next step; otherwise, you are ready to begin.

Not only does choice of lexical item affect comprehension; the way information is organized does, too. Carrell (1984) presented the same information to learners of English as a second language but organized it in four ways: (1) as a comparison/contrast; (2) as a problem with a solution; (3) as a collection or series of descriptions; and (4) as a cause-and-effect relationship. Both comprehension and retention of information were best for more highly organized information (comparison/contrast, problem/solution, and cause/effect) than for more loosely organized information (collection of descriptions). Lee and Riley (1990) found similar results on text organization with learners of French. They also found that providing learners with information about text organization prior to reading improved their comprehension.

Discourse can be organized differently not just at the text level but also at more local levels within the text. Flick and Anderson (1980) gave first and second language readers short passages that contained explicit and implicit definitions; examples of each type of definition follow:

Explicit: Negative pressure is that type of pressure whose value is below atmospheric.

Implicit: From fluid mechanics it can be shown that as a fluid or gas passes through a venturi, its velocity increases; but its pressure decreases to some value below atmospheric. This negative pressure is greatest at the point in the throat where the fuel pick-up is located.

(Flick and Anderson 1980, pp. 345-46)

They found that both first and second language readers comprehended explicit definitions better than they did implicit ones.

The research studies outlined above are only examples of the many investigations into the effects of text characteristics on comprehension. Even from this small sample of research, you can see that no facile conclusion can be reached. The language of the text might or might not affect comprehension. There really are no rules that account for when text characteristics will prevent readers from making their contributions to the construction of meaning. The research on reader contributions and language demonstrates that comprehension involves both reader-based and text-based factors. The two sets of factors are not easily isolated because they tend to interact. Perhaps the clearest demonstration of how the two interact is an experiment conducted by Mohammed and Swales (1984). They asked four groups of subjects to read an instruction booklet for an alarm clock and then use the instructions to set the alarm. Their subjects were native and non-native readers of English who had either a science or humanities background. They found that those with a science background, whether they were native or non-native readers,

---

*P**ause to consider . . .***

text selection for non-native readers. After reviewing a considerable amount of research, Swaffar, Arens, and Byrnes (1991, pp. 137–139) proposed the following as key considerations in selecting materials for L2 readers:

select topics familiar to students

select topics of interest to students

select texts with overt development of ideas

select texts with greater structural organization

select texts with a recognizable agent or concrete subject

select texts that have little extraneous prose

select texts that have unambiguous intents

select texts of appropriate length

Given what you have just read about both reader contributions to comprehension and the language of texts, how would you implement these recommendations? Are these recommendations absolutes, or are they related to other factors? When would text length be an issue? How would you determine "interest"?

completed the two tasks more quickly than did the others. Among the slowest to finish were two native readers with humanities backgrounds. There were two subjects who were unable to complete the tasks: both were non-native readers, one with a science background, the other in humanities with a low-level second language proficiency. Mohammed and Swales concluded that a particular level of language proficiency was required to comprehend the technical instructions; yet once that level was attained, background knowledge was a better predictor of success than language proficiency. You cannot read in a second language without some knowledge of that language. By the same token, you cannot comprehend much, in either a first or second language, unless you can bring more to the task of reading than just linguistic knowledge.

A FRAMEWORK FOR ASSISTING L2 LEARNERS TO COMPREHEND WRITTEN LANGUAGE

Because language learners do not have the verbal virtuosity of native readers, instructors need strategies to facilitate the reading comprehension process. The purpose for providing reading instruction is to build bridges between the reader and the information contained in the text. The framework presented in this chapter guides learners' interactions with a text in order to maximize their comprehension. There are three essential phases to the instructional framework: Preparation (prereading), Guided Interaction (during reading), and Assimilation (postreading). While we do present each phase separately, they should be conceived as a whole. Each phase of a lesson is interdependent on the other phases because they build on one another.

Preparation: Activating Appropriate Schemata

The linguistic demands on reading in a second language can inhibit learners' background knowledge from being activated to its fullest extent (Carrell 1983; Hudson 1982). Second language learners need help bringing their knowledge to bear on the process of comprehension. The initial phase of the instructional framework, therefore, must be to activate learners' background knowledge and direct it toward the information in the passage. In other words, schemata must be *activated* and must be *appropriate* to the passage being read. Activating the reader's knowledge of feudalism, for example, would have steered him toward an appropriate interpretation of the passage on page 195.

What knowledge needs to be activated so that readers will comprehend the information? The answer to this question quite simply depends on the text and what it says, as well as on the readers and what they know. As the research of Mohammed and Swales indicated, the needs of a group of engineering majors reading technical instructions are different from those of a group of humanities majors reading the very same text.

Many techniques serve to activate knowledge relevant to a particular text. We now describe a few of them.

Brainstorming

Brainstorming is synonymous with idea generation, or putting ideas "out on the table" but not criticizing or commenting on them in any way. The technique allows for the maximum of perspectives on a topic to emerge; it provides the instructor and readers a broad information base to begin bridging the gap between the readers and a text. Brainstorming takes place before readers are given a text. You ask them what they know about the topic of the text, recording everything they tell you (on the board or an overhead transparency) whether or not the information supplied is relevant to the particular text. Note the following examples, designed to precede a reading about weddings.

Activity A. Brainstorming with the Whole Class

Step 1. As a class, generate a list of all the ideas you associate with weddings. Come up with as many different ideas as possible in five minutes.

Brainstorming can also be carried out in groups or pairs. If groups are given the specific task of listing five things they know about a particular topic, then the potential for more diverse responses is there. Also, such task-oriented group work provides a mechanism for maximizing the participation of each individual.

Activity B. Brainstorming in Pairs

Step 1. Working with a partner, write five things you associate with weddings. Try to come up with five very different things. You have two minutes.

    1.
    2.
    3.
    4.
    5.

Step 2. Share your list with the rest of class and listen as they share theirs. Write down any ideas you did not think of. *(Option for Step 2: The instructor creates a master list of ideas on the board or overhead transparency.)*

Pause to consider . . .

why time limits should be imposed on brainstorming. What kind of classroom dynamic is generated when time limits are imposed and adhered to during activities? What might the interaction between instructor and learners, and learner and learner, be like if there were no stated time limit?

Once ideas have been generated, the readers need to verify whether or not the information is relevant to the text at hand. Brainstorming must be followed up by a task that has readers focusing on a particular text since *appropri-*

ate knowledge must be activated. They must examine what they collectively know in order to decide what is relevant (and thus appropriate) to the text at hand. The common follow-up to brainstorming is having readers quickly skim a text for the sole purpose of noting whether or not the ideas they generated are present in the text. They either confirm an idea's presence or reject the idea as being irrelevant. While this task might seem to be guided interaction, skimming the text with this very limited purpose is not really reading the text. The readers are not extracting what the author *has said* about that information; they only learn if the information is *present.*

Activity A. Continuation. . .

Step 2. As rapidly as possible, skim the text to determine whether or not the ideas on the board *(or overhead)* are actually in the reading. All you have to do is say whether or not the information is there; you do not have to know (not yet anyway) what the author says about that information. You have five minutes.

Step 3. Share what you found with the rest of the class. As you do, erase from the board all those ideas that are *not* in the text. Do you all agree?

Titles, Headings, and Illustrations

Most texts carry a title and subtitle that are sometimes, although not always, indicative of the content. Sometimes, headings mark the different ideas included in a text and informative illustrations and photographs describe some of its contents. You can exploit each of these sources of information as a means to activate appropriate schema, as in Activity C.

Activity C. Titles, Subtitles, and Headings

Step 1. Read the title and subtitle of the passage. Based only on this information, write three ideas you would expect to find in this reading.

    1.
    2.
    3.

Step 2. Share your ideas with two or three classmates. Did you come up with similar information? Did your classmates think of something you would like to add to your list?

Step 3. Now read the section headings. In which section(s) do you think you will find the ideas you and your classmates thought of?

Step 4. Quickly skim those sections to determine whether or not the information is there. Report back to the class what you found (or didn't find).

You can work with illustrations and photographs in a variety of ways. They can be the basis of an initial brainstorming task, or they can be used to confirm or reject ideas generated from a brainstorming task. In the following activity, the illustrations are used as the very first device to activate appropriate schema.

Activity D. Illustrations and Photographs

Step 1. Working with a partner, describe what you see in each of the photographs that accompany the article. Be as detailed in your description as possible.

Step 2. Based on these photographs, list at least three pieces of information you would expect to find in the article.

    1.

    2.

    3.

Step 3. Share your list with your classmates. Did they think of something you would like to add to your list?

Step 4. Quickly skim the article to determine whether or not these ideas are going to be treated by the author. Report back to the class what you find.

*P*ause to consider . . .

the purpose of reporting back to the class. Why is reporting back to the class an appropriate way to bring closure to brainstorming-oriented activities? What would the activities be like without such a task?

World Knowledge

Topic knowledge is but one type of schema; other schemata come into play that we can classify as *world knowledge.* For example, an article about liposuction that appeared in the *New England Journal of Medicine, Newsweek, Cosmopolitan,* or *Seventeen* would be approached and interpreted differently because we have a different set of expectations based on the type of magazine we are reading. The magazines are directed at different audiences; the tone of the authors, as well as their credentials, would be very different. The source of the text directly affects how readers should interpret the content; it determines which schema is appropriate. Whereas language learners probably have little knowledge of the various magazines and newspapers from the target culture, they can be guided to make associations with magazines and newspapers from their own culture. The following example illustrates this point.

Activity E. World Knowledge

Step 1. Read the title and subtitle. Then look at the pictures and read the captions. Based solely on this information, if this article were to be published in an American magazine or newspaper, which would it be?

    a. *Time*

    b. *Ladies' Home Journal*

    c. *The National Enquirer*

    d. *The New Republic*

    e. _____(some other one?)

Step 2. Working with a partner, compare the reasons for your choices. Were you thinking along the same lines?

World knowledge can be exploited in other ways as well. We are all probably very experienced at filling out forms in our native language. With this experience, we have certain expectations for the types of information requested on forms. That knowledge can facilitate second language readers' comprehension of forms in the target language. For example, we know we have to sign most forms we fill out. That knowledge would lead us to search for the place to sign whether or not we knew the target language words for "Signature" or "Sign here."

Pause to consider . . .

some common types of documents and forms that language learners could easily figure out on the basis of world knowledge. Do you have personal experiences you can relate?

Pretest/Posttest

In research settings, a common technique for measuring how much a subject has learned from an experimental treatment is to administer a test both prior to and after the treatment. In an instructional setting, the same pretest/posttest technique can be used to activate appropriate schemata. You could write a ten-item quiz on the content of the reading, administer the quiz, and then discuss it as a prereading activity. Critically, you would *not* correct the learners' answers since the point of reading the article is to learn the answers. The instructor would simply find out who believed what about the topic. The quiz serves to activate appropriate knowledge that readers subsequently apply to the text.

Activity F. Quiz

Step 1. To the best of your ability, answer each of the following questions. Leave no question unanswered. If you are uncertain, then make as good a guess as you can.

Step 2. Compare your answers with a partner [or *group* or *whole class*]. Did you have the same answers? Which answers are you sure of? Which ones are you unsure of?

Scanning for Specific Information

Passages vary so much from one to another that you might decide a particular passage does not need an extensive preparation. It might be appropriate simply to have readers scan the text for specific information that will activate an appropriate schema. For example, a certain text might contain a series of numbers that will clue the learners about the content. You could then direct them to find the numbers and determine what they refer to. Also, there might be two or three concepts that are crucial to understand in order to comprehend the text as a whole. Learners could be directed to find these terms in the text and then define them, thereby activating appropriate schemata.

Activity G. Scanning

Step 1. Find the following three words in the text and underline the sentences in which you find them.
   a. *feudalism*
   b. *stewardship*
   c. *tithes*

Step 2. Working with two or three classmates, either write a definition of the words or list as many things as you can think of that you associate with each.

Step 3. Share your work with the rest of the class. Are you all sure what these words mean?

Although learners can be taught to deduce the meanings of words from context, identify cognates, or simply skip over words they do not know, their comprehension of a text may depend on such an unknown word. When an unknown word is a key to understanding, we would encourage instructors to preview that word in an activity such as Activity G. The consequences for the learner are as obvious as misinterpreting *feudalism* as *feud*.

---

*P***ause to consider . . .**

reading as both a private and a social act. We have included paired and group work as part of the prereading activities because we believe reading need not be a solitary, private act but can and should also be a social, public one. Before reading further, do you think that the "Guided Interaction" phase of a reading lesson should be private or social?

Guided Interaction

If activating appropriate schema can be thought of as building a bridge between a reader and a text, then *guided interaction* is making a plan for crossing the bridge—and then crossing it. Second language readers, who tend to read word for word when left to their own devices, need to be directed in how to read in another language. The instructor's function is to provide that direction. You can think of the Guided Interaction phase of the lesson framework as the readers' *exploration* of the content. But these explorers are not going into uncharted waters or virgin territory. You will provide them a map or a route to follow. What is the best way to divide a long passage into manageable segments? On what information should the reader focus within those segments? The passage might be short but dense. Where are the appropriate points to stop the readers to make sure they have understood before they continue?

The Guided Interaction phase of the reading lesson consists of a combination of two types of tasks, namely, *management strategies* and *comprehension checks*. Management strategies suggest to the readers ways in which to divide a passage, to break it into sensible parts. Comprehension checks during the guided interaction phase of the lesson allow readers to monitor their comprehension in an ongoing way rather than read from start to finish only to find they did not understand. It is better to know immediately that you have not understood something than to arrive at the end of a reading and realize you missed something, if not everything, along the way. Management strategies and comprehension checks can be paired in the following ways.

Management strategies	*Comprehension checks*
1. read one section at a time of a passage with headings	write a one sentence summary of the section select key words from the section list main ideas answer questions
2. read one section at a time of a passage with no headings	all of the above write a heading that specifies the content

We began this chapter by describing how readers use comprehension questions to limit their interaction with a text, yet we recommend that they "answer questions" as a comprehension check. What kinds of questions will guide readers into the text and not simply encourage them to search for matching wording? The following example provides an answer to this question.

Let's say that the class has been asked to read a three-page article that describes and explains nine different behaviors characterizing the social organization of a herd of elephants. Traditionally, such a reading would be followed by a set of comprehension questions presented in the same order in which the information appears in the passage. Such a set of traditional comprehension questions for the passage about elephants follows.

Traditional comprehension questions
1. What is the theme of this article?
2. Based on the tone, is the article in favor of or against elephants?
3. Is the fight between males for the leadership of the herd a fight to the death?
4. When do baby elephants learn to use their trunks?
5. What do male elephants use their trunks for? females?
6. What is a matriarchy?
7. To what does the phrase *steps according to age* refer?
8. Are elephants violent or peaceful animals?
9. How is the care of young elephants shared between all members of the herd?
10. Is the organization of the herd democratic?
11. What is a herd of elephants made of?
12. Do the males remain in the herd in which they are born for their entire lives? Do the females?

13. Which of the behaviors described in the article are instinctive and which are learned?
14. What information in the article supports the idea that elephants are intelligent, difficult, active, powerful, and fun-loving?
15. On what is the social organization of a herd of elephants based?

These comprehension questions can easily be transformed into task-based classroom activities, as in Activity H. Specific questions from the list above are indicated in parentheses. As you read Activity H, ask yourself which is better for the language learner, traditional comprehension questions or a task-oriented guided interaction?

Activity H. Guided Interaction

Step 1. Since this is a relatively long reading, it would be best to read it section by section. After reading each section fairly quickly, pause to collect your thoughts by writing a sentence that captures the main idea of the section. Compare your sentences with those of a classmate. Do you agree on the main ideas?

Step 2. Go back and reread each section, paying more attention to the details. Using a highlighter, identify key words or phrases that will help you remember what you have read. At the end of each section, look at what you have highlighted. Does it spark your memory? Compare the words and phrases you have highlighted with those of your classmates. Have you chosen different words?

Step 3. Based on what you have read, check off the statements that are true.

☐ From the tone of the article, it is evident that the author is pro-elephant. (question 2)

☐ Even though elephants are normally quite peaceful, they are capable of tremendous violence. (question 8)

☐ An elephant herd is a democratic unit. (question 10)

☐ Elephants and humans share similar preoccupations with their young. (question 9)

Step 4. Complete the following statements.

1. A herd of elephants is composed of . . . (question 11)
   a. males and females in more or less equal proportions.
   b. more males than females.
   c. one male and various females, like a harem.

2. The care of the young is . . . (question 9)
   a. shared equally among males and females.
   b. the responsibility of the males.
   c. the responsibility of the females.

3. Of the young that are born in a herd. . . (question 12)
   a. the males and females are members of the same herd for all their lives.
   b. the males and females form subgroups, which eventually leave the herd.
   c. the males leave the herd but the females remain.
   d. the females leave the herd but the males remain.

Step 5. Working with two or three classmates, make a list of all the behaviors described in the article. Then share your list with the rest of the class, adding to your list whatever behaviors you might have missed. Finally, as a class, indicate if each behavior is instinctive or learned. (question 13)

Step 6. According to the introductory paragraphs, elephants are intelligent, difficult, active, powerful, and fun-loving animals. As a class, identify the information in the article that supports the idea that elephants really are as they are described. (question 14)

Pause to consider . . .

the pros and cons of having learners read in class. Some instructors believe that reading is an activity learners should do at home, not in class. Is reading instruction so different from other aspects of language instruction? In what way(s) is the Guided Interaction no different from other kinds of in-class activities?

Assimilation

If the Preparation phase was to build a bridge between the readers and the text and the Guided Interaction phase was to lead readers across the bridge, then the Assimilation phase is the building inspection. You want to be sure that all the pieces are in place and that the experience of crossing the bridge will be memorable.

Most lesson frameworks for reading end with the Guided Interaction phase. Once comprehension is checked and verified as accurate, the reading lesson is over. However, we advocate continuing the lesson based on the content of the reading. For, after all, why do we read? The answer to this question is varied. We read to pass the time in the dentist's waiting room and to focus our attention on something other than the sound of a drill. We read to keep abreast of the latest world events. We read to fall asleep at night. But those purposes do not reflect reading in an academic setting. Why do we do that? Reading in an academic setting is equated with reading to learn, which means that the content of what we read is important. We read to get the information and do something with it. At times, all we do with the information is give it back to the professor on a test; at other times we discuss it; and sometimes we write papers about it. The purpose, then, of the Assimilation phase is to encourage second language readers to learn from what they have read. To accomplish this goal, we present tasks and activities that are study-skills oriented: ways to organize information in order to learn that information. Some common techniques that can be considered study-skills oriented are:

- to associate a person's name with places and/or events
- to identify main ideas and the key words associated with those ideas
- to write a test based on content

- to write questions for the passage as a whole or the various subsections of a passage
- to outline a passage
- to classify information as main idea, supporting information, and details
- to identify the themes treated in a passage
- to create a poster of the contents of a passage
- to write a summary
- to establish cause/effect relationships, problem/solutions, advantages/disadvantages
- to draw a semantic map or a Venn diagram of the content
- to fill in a chart or table

The Assimilation phase overtly focuses the language learners' reading experience on information. As the instructor, you must determine what information you want them to learn, which is based on the reason(s) you selected the text in the first place. In the assimilation phase, the readers are given a task or series of tasks in which they organize the information in the text. By carrying out an organizing task, the readers internalize the content of the reading, thereby ensuring that they are reading to learn.

Activity I. Assimilation

Step 1. Review what you did in the Preparation and Guided Interaction activities. Then, complete the semantic map below without rereading the article (if you can).

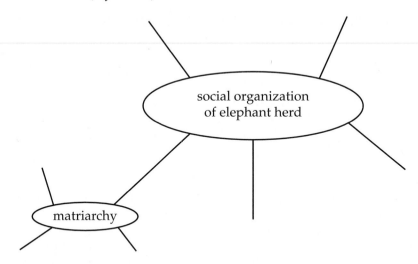

Step 2. You have three options for working with the semantic map.

    Option 1. Using only the semantic map, write a summary of the article you read.

    Option 2. Using only the semantic map, write a short quiz on the content of the article. Try not to be too detail oriented with your questions. After all, you should write a quiz that you think is fair. You should also write a quiz that you would be willing to take!

Option 3. Using only the semantic map to guide you, write three essay questions covering the content of the entire article. As you write the questions, think about keeping the answers to two or three paragraphs. Remember, the questions you write just might be the ones your instructor uses on the exam!

Pause to consider . . .

the thought processes a learner would have to use in order to write test questions. How does writing a test or writing test questions get readers to assimilate the content of what they have read? What would you do with the questions the learners submitted to you? Would you use them on a test? Would you edit them and give them back to the whole class on a handout?

Through task-based activities, students interact with the content of a text a number of times; they read and reread. But each time they do, they are engaged in another activity as they complete another task. They are given something new to think about and do each time they read. Each act of reading has a purpose: the readers' search for meaning.

PERSONALIZING THE CONTENT OF A TEXT

An important aspect of reading, often not taken into account in early-stage second language instruction, is an exploration of what Grellet calls the communicative function of a text. Outside of classroom settings, authors frequently expect readers to respond to the content of the article. As Grellet argues,

> exercises must be meaningful and correspond as often as possible to what one is expected to do with the text. We rarely answer questions after reading a text, but we may have to
>
> - write an answer to a letter
> - use the text to do something (e.g., follow directions, make a choice, solve a problem)
> - compare the information to some previous knowledge
>
> (Grellet 1981, p. 9)

Each of Grellet's examples can be exploited in the language classroom. Exploring the communicative function of a text can also be thought of as *personalizing its content*. Once readers gain information from a text, can they then relate to it personally and, therefore, more meaningfully? Can they apply the content to themselves, to their experiences, to the world as they know it? The following activity exemplifies how the content of an article on animals' sixth sense can be related to the readers' lives. To use Grellet's terms, the readers will compare the content of the article to previous knowledge.

Activity J. Communicative Function of a Text. Apply what you learned about animals' sense of direction to your own experiences by describing the sense of direction of various members of your family. Use the words and phrases below that you think are appropriate. A model is provided.

MODEL: My father has the sense of direction of a turtle because it is a mystery how he always knows how and where to go when we visit a city for the first time. He never needs a map.

Family Member	Animal	Category
mother	bird	always knows where north is
father	reptile	when given directions, memorizes them immediately
sister	locust	always gets lost when visiting a city for the first time
brother	butterfly	needs a detailed map in order to find someone's house for the first time
grandfather	bee	
grandmother	turtle	

The following activity demonstrates how learners can personalize the content of the reading about elephant behavior. In this activity, they relate the reading to the world as they know it.

Activity K. Communicative Function of a Text

Step 1. Working with two or three classmates, put the number that corresponds to your own opinions next to each of the following sentences.
We believe that for the majority of people our age,
  1 = it is important. . .
  2 = it will be important some day. . .
  3 = it is not very important. . .
   a. _____ to have a leadership role in whatever group one is associated with.
   b. _____ to live in a safe and protected area.
   c. _____ to lead an active social life.
   d. _____ to count on child care while at work.
   e. _____ to have various opportunities to find companionship.
   f. _____ to make friends.
   g. _____ to advance professionally.
   h. _____ to have economic security in old age.
   i. _____ to have a place to live in old age.
Step 2. Compare your answers with those of the rest of the class by indicating how many people responded to each item with a "1," a "2," or a "3."

Step 3. Which items were most important to the majority of the class? Which were not important? Does the class agree on what to look for in life?

Step 4. Go back over the sentences, but this time indicate with the letter "E" those statements that can apply to elephants. Then explain what information from the article supports your choices. In what ways are humans and elephants similar?

> *Pause to consider . . .*
>
> the contribution of the content of readings to interactional activities. Activities J and K could also be done without having read an article about anything. In this case, references to the articles would have to be eliminated. Go back through Activities J and K, locating references to the articles. If you were to eliminate those references, would the activities still be worth doing? In other words, are they good activities? What does adding content do for the activities?

SUMMARY

In this chapter we have explored what it means to comprehend written language, focusing in particular on what is involved in comprehending a second language. We first presented an interactive model of reading, one in which a variety of knowledge sources come into play. An important feature of interactive models is that the knowledge sources do not operate sequentially but simultaneously, that each knowledge source can influence the other. Interactive models of reading led to reexamining the role of readers and texts in comprehension. Under the rubric of schema theory, a great deal of research was carried out into the contributions that individual readers make to comprehension. We presented four functions of schema: to disambiguate, elaborate, filter, and compensate. We then examined the effects of text characteristics on comprehension, demonstrating that language does affect comprehension in a variety of ways: lexical choice, the organization of information, and level of language proficiency.

We then proposed and described an instructional approach to reading that comprises a lesson framework to surround the text and activities to go beyond the text. The approach reflects what is known about how the mind processes information. Reading is a mental activity during which textual elements are taken in and acted on by linguistic processes mediated by the individual reader's characteristics. The approach also reflects what we know learners do with texts when left to their own devices. They read word for word, translating on the page and in their heads; such practices should be avoided. Finally, the approach emphasizes the communicative function of texts. In developing this approach, we have shown how research on the interactive nature of reading can be transferred to the second language classroom. In effect, our approach promotes reading instruction as the *interaction* between a reader and a text.

KEY TERMS, CONCEPTS, AND ISSUES

look-back-and-lift-off strategy
translation approach to comprehension
interactive model of reading
schema theory
knowledge sources
interaction of knowledge sources
comprehension
blueprint metaphor for texts
readers' contributions to comprehension
function of schema
   disambiguate
   elaborate
   filter
   compensate
effects of text features on comprehension
   vocabulary
   organization of information
interaction of reader contributions and text characteristics
instructional framework for reading lessons
   preparation (activating appropriate schema)
      brainstorming
      titles, headings, and illustrations
      world knowledge
      pretest/posttest
      scanning
   guided interaction
      management strategies
      comprehension checks
   assimilation
      various techniques
reading to learn
personalizing the content

EXPLORING THE TOPICS FURTHER

1. *Descriptions of what learners do with texts.* An early pioneer in research on what language learners were actually doing with texts was Carol Hosenfeld (1977, 1984). For analyses of what readers do with texts within an interactive framework, see Lee (1990) and Bernhardt (1986).
2. *Readers' contributions to comprehension.* One of the best works on this subject is Bransford's book, *Human Cognition.* While we recommend you read the entire work, you might select the chapters specifically related to Schema Theory (Bransford 1979, Chapters 5 and 6).
3. *Lesson frameworks.* Grellet's (1981) book was extremely influential in American foreign language instruction. Her framework was adapted and popularized by Philips (1984). Other authors with useful suggestions for reading instruction are Bernhardt (1991), Barnett (1989), Dubin, Eskey, and Grabe (1986), and Swaffar, Arens, and Byrnes (1991).

CHAPTER 11

Writing and Composing in a Second Language

> *. . . writing will be used as a generic term to refer to all of the various activities that involve transferring thought to paper. Writing that focuses primarily on the conventions of language form, i.e., grammatical or lexical structure, will be termed* transcription. *The term* composition *will refer to the skills involved in effectively developing and communicating an idea or making a point.*
>
> (Dvorak 1986: 145)

INTRODUCTION

Some have referred to reading as the forgotten skill in language instruction. We suspect, however, that writing is probably the area in which language classes offer the learner the least. Think about your own language learning experiences. How much writing (that is, transcribing and composing) did you do? Answer the following questions about writing in general, and about writing in a second language in particular, based on your own experiences.

1. What do grocery lists, recipes, letters of complaint, poems, and essays have in common?
   a. The same person who writes them is the one who has to read them.
   b. The writer and the reader are presumably different people.
   c. They all have words on a page.
   d. They really don't have much in common.
   e. Other
2. In what ways do the above writing samples differ? Indicate all that apply.
   a. length
   b. the intended audience
   c. purpose
   d. handwritten versus typewritten
   e. other _____
3. How much and what kind of writing did you do in the first two years (or two courses) you studied your second language? Indicate all that apply.

   a. fill in the blank sentences and/or paragraphs
   b. letters
   c. diaries or journals
   d. note taking from lectures or readings
   e. poems, stories, and/or dramas
   f. invitations
   g. essays
   h. compositions
   i. other _____

4. Do you feel the writing you described in (3) above made you a better writer?
   a. Without a doubt, yes!
   b. I think so.
   c. Maybe not.
   d. Definitely not.
   e. not applicable

5. Which of the following describe your writing experiences in your second language? Indicate all that apply.
   a. I was alone at home.
   b. My biggest problem was finding a way to say what I wanted to say.
   c. I was worried about making sure my grammar was correct.
   d. I hardly ever reread what I wrote before handing it in.
   e. Except for correct grammar, it didn't matter to my instructor what I wrote.
   f. I learned more about good writing from my language classes than from my English (i.e., native-language) classes.

As you read this chapter, keep your responses in mind. You will probably discover that your own experiences support the distinction between transcription and composition.

We have defined *communication* as the expression, interpretation, and negotiation of meaning. This definition is applicable not only to oral language but to written language as well. We express ourselves in writing as well as speaking. A grocery list can be considered an act of communication: you can write the list for yourself or for someone else, but its purpose is to have someone do something. Although writing a grocery list might be an act of communication, is it the kind of activity that has a place in the language classroom? Possibly. Does writing a grocery list make you a better writer? Probably not.

In this chapter, we explore second language production in a written mode. With the goal of making language learners better writers, we distinguish between transcription-oriented practices and composing. To begin, we describe a theory of writing that has gained tremendous acceptance in language teaching circles. We then develop an instructional framework that applies the various elements of this theory to the classroom.

A COGNITIVE-PROCESS THEORY OF WRITING

In 1981, Flower and Hayes put forth a cognitive-process theory of writing that is the most frequently cited theory in foreign language instructional circles.

Critics of the theory claim that it is not a model but merely a description. No matter what it is called, the theory emphasizes mental processes, which are the focus of our framework. Flower and Hayes organize their model/description around three components: (a) the task environment, (b) the writer's long-term memory, and (c) writing processes. Various elements make up each of the components of the model. Before describing and explaining them, we must note that the Flower and Hayes model is not a stage model. Whereas stage models sequence activities (one event occurs and then another one follows it), a cognitive-process model describes thought processes. These processes or mental events might or might not occur, and (unlike stage models) the processes influence each other. (In Chapter 10, we saw how the idea of mutual influence among processes characterizes interactive models of reading.)

We now summarize the Flower and Hayes (1981) model of writing.

Task Environment

The Rhetorical Problem. The *rhetorical problem* is a complex notion comprising concepts such as situation, audience, and a writer's own goals in writing. Good writers take all these into consideration, weighing one against the other. Poor writers, on the other hand, often reduce the rhetorical problem to "completing the assignment." Whereas the latter might be straightforward, economical, and very pragmatic, it seriously underestimates the task at hand because writers respond only to the rhetorical problem they set for themselves (not necessarily the one an instructor thinks the materials set). The good writer will see the complexity of the problem; the poor writer will reduce, minimize, or somehow underestimate it. The goals that good writers and poor writers set for their writing depend very much on the way they define the rhetorical problem. Writers attempt to solve a rhetorical problem by writing. What they produce is the *written text,* which is also an element of the task environment.

> ## *Pause to consider . . .*
>
> a particular rhetorical problem. Let's say the following item appears on the final exam for a course on language teaching methodology: *Define and explain "comprehension."* What is the rhetorical problem faced by the writer?

The Text Produced So Far. Once writing has begun, the text enters the task environment (and some would say the text is part of the task environment even before a word is committed to print). The importance of the written text is that it constrains what the writer does next. For example, a title can constrain the content of a paper. A topic sentence can constrain the organization of a paragraph. And so, the *text produced so far* constrains, to one degree or another, what comes next. The word *constrain,* in this context, means to provide direction. If the text does not sufficiently constrain the writer, the result is often incoherence. On the other hand, the text can constrain too much, to the extent that the writer tries to move only forward with the prose rather than backward to reexamine what has been written.

As stated earlier, the components and elements of the model work with each other. Flower and Hayes point out that the written text competes with other elements in the model that also direct the composing process, namely, the writer's plan for addressing the rhetorical problem and knowledge stored in long-term memory.

The Writer's Long-Term Memory

A writer's *long-term memory* refers to the storehouse of knowledge the writer possesses or has access to in sources such as books and data banks. Long-term memory can also include the writer's schema for writing, so that a cue in the assignment can trigger a whole network of stored information. If told to "contrast the two approaches. . .", the cue "contrast" might trigger many rhetorical devices and plans for approaching the task. In addition to triggering long-term memory, an issue of equal or greater importance is reorganizing or adapting that which is in memory to fit the demands of the task at hand. Flower and Hayes mention other types of knowledge the writer possesses such as knowledge of the audience. Do you know the instructor or professor for whom you are writing? Do you have experience writing for him or her? Those experiences form part of the network of information the writer potentially uses.

Writing Processes

Planning. *Planning* in the Flower and Hayes model does not refer to an external (physical, concrete) outline but rather to an internal, mental representation of the knowledge to be used in writing. A number of subprocesses are entailed in planning, among them generating ideas, organizing ideas, and goal setting. *Generating ideas* includes retrieving information from long-term memory; the ideas might be well developed and organized or fragmentary and unconnected. When unconnected, the process of idea generation helps writers make meaning or sense out of the information. Ideas are grouped, categories identified, ideas hierarchized; the text is ordered, and perhaps new concepts are formed. *Organizing ideas* and *goal setting* are related subprocesses because the latter often guide the former. There are many types of goals writers set for themselves: procedural ("I'll start with a definition of the term *meaningful*") and content related ("I have to relate written input to oral input"). Flower and Hayes emphasize that the most important aspect of goal setting is that writers themselves set their own goals (which accounts for some differences from writer to writer). Obviously, if a writer does not set a goal, it will not be met. Furthermore, the nature of the goal itself is important. If a writer's goal is merely to write one hundred words rather than to convince the reader of another point of view, the quality of the product will be different. Goal setting accounts for some of the individual differences between good and poor writers.

Translating. The process by which writers render thought into visible language is referred to as *translating*, which involves the physical act of writing. The process of translating requires writers to decide what they attend to consciously. If spelling and grammar (formal demands) take up too much conscious attention, then the task of translating can interfere with the process and subprocesses of planning. Writers, after all, can juggle only so many processes at once; they are what might be called "limited-capacity" processors.

Reviewing. *Reviewing* consists of two subprocesses, *revising* and *evaluating*. Writers may review the text produced so far in order to change it or use it as a springboard forward. Reviewing can be either a planned periodic activity ("stop after each paragraph and assess") or an unplanned response (the feeling that something "isn't quite right"). The subprocesses of evaluating and revising, along with generating as a planning subprocess, are distinguished by the fact that they can interrupt any other process at any time during the act of writing. This might be beneficial to some writers but might paralyze others. Reviewing, evaluating, and revising are writing processes and subprocesses that seem particularly difficult to develop in both first and second language writing.

The Monitor. The *Monitor* is an internal writing "strategist" that informs the writer when to move from one process or subprocess to another; when to continue generating ideas; when to stop and move to or engage another process or subprocess; and when to stop reviewing and continue translating. In native-language writing, the Monitor develops over time with cognitive maturity. That is, children seem to have an underdeveloped Monitor: they might easily generate ideas but lack the kind of Monitor that tells them they need to generate a few more or review what they have written.

Summary

The Flower and Hayes model does not describe the inner workings of a neurophysiological network. Rather, it attempts to account for and explain the diverse set of thoughts and thought processes writers engage while writing. Writing is, in this model, a "thoughtful process." In the remainder of this

---

*P*ause to consider . . .

whether or not the Flower and Hayes model applies to all types of writing. The epigraph at the start of this chapter defines *writing* as a generic term to refer to all activities involved in transferring thought to paper. Grocery lists and essays involve the transfer of thought to paper. Does the model apply to grocery lists just as well as it does to essays?

chapter, we examine the thought processes writers engage under two sets of stimuli: transcription-oriented writing practices and composing-oriented activities.

TRANSCRIPTION-ORIENTED WRITING PRACTICES

In regarding writing as a thoughtful process, we must consider writing activities as multidimensional tasks. Whether or not the task specifies them, all writing tasks involve the writer's long-term memory, task environment (as the writer conceptualizes it), and writing processes. Let's examine some typical writing activities for language learners, keeping in mind the multidimensionality of the task. Transcription-oriented practices, as Dvorak (1986) notes, involve writing that focuses primarily on the conventions of language form, namely, grammatical or lexical structure. These activities focus learners' attention on the subcomponents of writing, emphasizing the processes of putting ideas into visible language (what Flower and Hayes term *translating*, a word that has additional connotations in language instruction).

In Activity A, which is typical of the writing practices included in textbooks, students are provided a list of words they must use to write a paragraph. As you read the activity, consider the act of writing according to the Flower and Hayes model. What long-term memory is involved? How will the writer define the task environment? What are the relative contributions of the writing processes of planning, translating, reviewing, and monitoring?

Activity A. Families. Use at least ten of the following words to write a short composition about families. Underline each word used from the list in your composition.

parents	education	neighborhood
grandparents	goals	house
siblings	vacations	friends
occupations	weekends	dinner
chores	weekdays	mornings

The rhetorical problem defined for the writers is to produce a text with ten targeted lexical items. The text-produced-so-far will probably constrain their writing in a purely quantitative way. That is, their concern will not be so much what they write but whether or not they have used particular lexical items. This is the case because their knowledge of the topic and audience (their long-term memory) includes not only what they know about families but what they know about *this type of assignment*. Specifically, the grade will most likely reflect whether or not they include ten targeted words and not what they say about families. The writing processes of monitoring and reviewing will most likely focus on counting to ten. Planning can be minimal since content is not as important as form. Whereas instructors might think the word list will stimulate the learners to think about content, the list functions to guide them, but *guide* in this context is synonymous with *restrict*.

Whereas Activity A focuses the writers on lexical items, Activity B focuses them on sentence structure, namely, word order. Each column contains a different part of speech (adverbs, nouns and pronouns, verbs) that the writers must use to build sentences. How will second language writers approach the task? What is the rhetorical problem? What writing processes will predominate?

Activity B. Your Family. Write a composition about your family, using the elements in the three columns as a guide.

A	B	C
frequently	I	visit
from time to time	father	call
hardly ever	mother	talk
whenever	siblings	see
always	we	listen
never	they	value

Our analysis of Activity B is similar to that of Activity A. The rhetorical problem the writers will establish for themselves will be to use the elements of the three columns, thereby focusing on form over content. Planning processes will involve constructing and ordering individual sentences. Reviewing will most likely focus not on what was written or how it was phrased but on which items in the lists were used.

The list to which writers respond can also be a list of questions, not just words and phrases. In Activity C, writers are to build a short composition prompted by a series of questions. Some might wonder why Activity C is included under the heading of transcription-oriented practices when it seems the most "composition-like" of the activities presented thus far. As you read it over, consider the task environment writers create for themselves, what they access from long-term memory, and what writing processes will be engaged. Consider also the Kinginger (1990) and Brooks (1990) research we presented in Chapter 5 to demonstrate how learners take seemingly communicative activities and turn them into drill-like practices.

Activity C. Compare and Contrast. Write a short composition contrasting today's family with the family of three generations ago. Use your answers to the following questions as a guide to writing.

1. How big are families now? How big were they then?
2. How long do people expect to live now compared to then?
3. Is the woman's place still in the home?
4. Do people have more economic opportunities now?
5. Do people have more educational opportunities now?

What is the rhetorical problem for the language learner: to write a composition or to answer the questions? Learners will most likely underestimate and underspecify the rhetorical problem in order to answer the questions. What knowledge of the audience will learners access from long-term memory? In other words, what will they think the instructor wants? Learners will most likely see that this composition requires the use of imperfect aspect to describe the past and thereby focus on form. What planning will take place? The writers' plan will probably be no more elaborate than to answer the questions. What will they review? They might review the verb forms; they might not.

Pause to consider . . .

possible variations on Activity C. Some instructors find that when prompt questions are written in the target language, learners simply answer using the words and wording of the questions. (This technique parallels the reader's technique of "looking back and lifting off.") When the prompt questions are in the native language, learners still answer them but have to come up with the target language themselves. Are prompt questions an effective device for eliciting a thoughtful composition? Do they contribute to the tendency among learners to underspecify the rhetorical problem? Would writers reconceptualize the rhetorical problem if an instructor said no more than: Write a composition comparing and contrasting today's family with that of three generations past?

In this section, we used the three components of the Flower and Hayes model (task environment, long-term memory, and writing processes) to assess common writing practices in second language classrooms. What we found was that writers underestimated and underspecified the rhetorical problem, reducing it to merely "complete the assignment." Such reductionism has ramifications for both long-term memory and writing processes. Once writers underspecify the rhetorical problem, they tend to access from long-term memory only that knowledge of the audience satisfying "what the instructor wants." Their writing goal simply becomes meeting what they perceive to be the instructor's desires. With transcription-oriented practices, planning and reviewing processes are minimized, defined only in terms of the rhetorical problem.

COMPOSING-ORIENTED ACTIVITIES

We propose quite a different approach to second language writing, one that exploits the components of the Flower and Hayes model, especially what we've termed "thoughtful processes." In such an approach, writing activities must help determine writers' conceptualization of the rhetorical problem and engage higher-level planning and reviewing processes. Let's examine a series of activities that engage second language writers in a variety of cognitive processes all leading toward writing a composition. Even though transcription-oriented activities are more common than compositions in beginning language instruction, the following composition activities were designed with first-year language learners in mind. Activities D through F can be considered prewriting exercises and Activity G the writing phase. In each of the prewriting exercises, the learners are given options to consider. These options require them to make choices, to consciously decide on the direction their composition will take. As you read these activities, note beside each step what elements of the Flower and Hayes model are being applied.

Activity D. Generating Content

Step 1. To each group of three or four students, the instructor will assign one of the following topics.
    a. family life at the turn of the century
    b. family life today

    Each group will have ten minutes to make a list of as many ideas as possible relating its topic to each of the following.
    1. family size
    2. economic opportunities
    3. educational opportunities
    4. male and female roles
    5. society

Step 2. Report to the rest of the class the ideas your group has generated. Create a master list on the board of the ideas generated on each topic. Are there any other ideas you can think of to add to the lists?

Step 3. Each member of the class should copy the lists from the board to use later in writing.

Activity E. Selecting an Audience and Purpose

Step 1. Keeping in mind the ideas the class generated in Activity D, think about an audience for your writing. Select an audience from the following list or propose one yourself.

     a. high school students you are addressing as part of a college
recruitment program

     b. the readers of the school newspaper

     c. the members of a businesswomen's organization

     d. the members of a church council

     e. the Panhellenic council that governs fraternities and sororities on
campus

     f. other suggestions _____

Step 2. Select one of the two topics. Then form groups of three with others
working with the same topic and list your audience's characteristics.
Report your list to the rest of the class. Try to help other groups by
proposing characteristics they may not have considered. Take down
any suggestions your classmates offer you.

Activity F. Planning and Organizing

Step 1. Now that you have an audience, what will you say to them? Working
in the same groups as in Activity E, examine the lists of ideas you
prepared for Activity D and indicate what information you might
include in your composition.

Step 2. Working individually, prepare an outline of the composition. Once
each of you has an outline, present them to each other. Have your
partners thought of some things you didn't?

Step 3. (Option) Present your outline to someone who selected a different
audience and listen to them present theirs. Can you offer any ideas or
suggestions?

Activities D, E, and F engage learners in thoughtful considerations of the task
environment, the writer's long-term memory, and some writing processes.
These activities serve to specify the rhetorical problem (which learners might
underestimate) and lead them to a preliminary plan for writing the composition.

Pause to consider . . .
_____

the nature of the interaction encouraged in Activities D through F. In
Chapter 8, we advocated the use of oral activities that allow for the
expression, interpretation, and negotiation of meaning. Although Activities
D through F are writing oriented, will they also promote language
development in the learners? Why or why not?

     Once a certain amount of preparatory work has been undertaken, writing
the composition should begin. Whereas Activities D through F set the stage,
Activity G is about writing. At some point writers must write, but they must
also be encouraged to engage the processes Flower and Hayes describe. Note
the function of the questions in Activity G.

Activity G. Composing

Step 1. Take your outline and list of ideas and keep them handy as you write a composition directed at the audience you selected. Suggestion: Write a draft of the work and let it sit for two days. Do not think about it or read it. At the end of two days, pick it up and read it. As you do, answer the following questions.

    a. content: Are these still the ideas you want to include?

    b. organization: Does the order in which the ideas are presented help you get your message across to the audience?

If you answer "no" to either question, rewrite some of your composition.

Step 2. Once you think your composition is good enough to hand in, review the language you used.

    a. verbs: Are the forms, spelling, and accents correct?

    b. adjectives: What noun do they go with? Do the adjectives agree?

    c. [*other elements of the language on which you wish learners to focus*]

Activities D through G help writers become conscious of the elements of good writing. Not only will the composition—the product of writing—in Activity G be better than the one generated in Activity C, but the way the writers write (the process through which they generate the product) will be qualitatively different.

***P**ause to consider . . .*

writing as a social, rather than private, act. In Chapter 10, we asked you to consider reading as a social act. In what ways have we construed writing, too, as a social act?

SUMMARY

Written language is not merely the printed counterpart of oral language. In other words, written discourse is not the same as oral discourse. A principled examination of writing led to Flower and Hayes' cognitive-process theory of writing. Their model describes and details what happens in the minds of writers as they go about developing and communicating an idea. The three major components of their model are the task environment, a writer's long-term memory, and writing processes. An important feature of their model is that these components (and the subprocesses they entail) can and do interact with each other. Many events take place in the mind of the writer before, during, and after pen is put to paper (or fingers put to the keyboard). Using their model as a basis, we presented and analyzed some transcription-oriented practices common in beginning language instruction. While there is arguably some value in engaging language learners in these activities, the activities were found deficient in terms of promoting the learners' development as writers. To promote the development of writing skills, we proposed a series of classroom activities that reflect the mental processes that comprise the act of writing. These activities encouraged learners to work together to generate content, select an audience and purpose, and plan and organize the composition. Each activity was structured with options from among which the learners must choose. In other words, the learners were directed to make decisions. In the final activity, they were directed not only to compose, but also to review and evaluate the content and form. Although composition instruction is traditionally delayed until more advanced language courses, a thoughtful approach to writing can be incorporated into beginning language classes.

KEY TERMS, CONCEPTS, AND ISSUES

writing
  transcription
  composition
cognitive-process theory of writing
stage models versus interactive models
task environment
  rhetorical problem
  the text produced so far
writer's long-term memory
writing processes
  planning
    generating
    organizing
    goal setting
  translating
  reviewing
    evaluating
    revising
  monitoring
transcription-oriented practices
  application of cognitive-process theory
underspecification and underestimation of rhetorical problem
composition-oriented practices
  thoughtful approach to L2 writing

EXPLORING THE TOPICS FURTHER

1. *Writing activities.* Idea books include Raimes (1983), Hedge (1988), and Prince (1990).
2. *Research on Second Language Writing.* Kroll (1990) collected a series of essays on second language writing research that provide insights for classroom practice. See also Omaggio Hadley (1993, Chapter 7), Dvorak's essay (1986), and Krashen's monograph (1984).
3. *Task formulation and problem solving.* Paulson's dissertation (1993) on second language writing clearly demonstrates that how the writing task is posed affects the quality of the outcome. He also discusses the idea that engaging language learners in problem solving is perhaps the key to better writing.

CHAPTER 12

Issues in Testing Reading and Evaluating Writing

*issue (ish'-oo) n. 1. a point of discussion,
debate, or dispute. 2. a matter of wide public
concern. 3. in question, in dispute.*
American Heritage Dictionary

INTRODUCTION

We have already presented a variety of considerations and concerns regarding testing. In Chapter 7, we reviewed Carroll's four considerations in testing: economy, relevance, acceptability, and comparability. We also presented two other concepts in that chapter, washback effects and the principle of testing what and how you teach. In Chapter 9, we summarized the debate on unitary versus componential abilities and the need for uniform administration and interrater reliability. While these considerations were discussed in the context of testing specific language features, they are applicable to all testing situations. We now build on these concepts by addressing issues concerning testing reading comprehension and evaluating writing. We begin with reading.

SOME ISSUES IN TESTING READING

The Purpose of the Test

Bachman (1990) reminds us that not all tests are created for the same purpose. Within an educational setting, tests serve a variety of purposes. For example, a classroom test can indicate progress and achievement. Tests can also be diagnostic, indicating strengths and weaknesses. Entrance tests discriminate among applicants; placement tests direct learners to particular courses. Each of these tests might include an examination of reading comprehension but approach it in different ways. For example, whereas a placement test might have all the items written in the test taker's native language, a classroom test might have them in the target language, particularly if all classroom instruction is carried out in the target language. Placement tests and entrance tests might favor the use of a single task type (such as multiple choice) due to its ease of scoring, whereas a classroom test or diagnostic test might use a combination of task types (multiple choice, open ended, cloze procedures).

Task Type and Language of Assessment

Wolf (1993a) reviews and interprets selected literature on testing second language reading comprehension. The result is a series of recommendations concerning test-item construction. Wolf's discussion focuses on the effects on learners' responses of task type and the language of assessment. Research directly comparing task types clearly demonstrates that the task influences the outcome (Shohamy 1984; Lee 1987b; Wolf 1993b): some tasks allow learners to demonstrate their comprehension better than other tasks do. Some might reduce these findings to saying that multiple-choice questions are easier than open-ended questions because the test taker simply selects among options in one but actually has to produce something in the other. Nevertheless, we cannot dismiss the fact that the format of a test might determine the decisions we make about the test taker.

Research on the language of assessment examines the use of reading test items written in the test takers' native or target language. The results consistently show that language learners perform better on items/tasks written in their native language (Hock and Poh 1979; Shohamy 1984; Lee 1986a, 1987b; Wolf 1993b). These results hold for beginning as well as advanced foreign language learners; surprisingly, they also hold for language learners who are completing high school in which the medium of instruction is the target language. The application of these results to classroom testing can be summarized as "biasing for the best." In other words, what does the test giver want to test: what the readers know/understand or what they do *not* know/understand?

---

*P*ause to consider . . .

the relevance of the curriculum to testing. The research mentioned above was carried out without consideration given to the curricula in which the learners were enrolled. If all instruction is carried out in the target language, should the test then be given in the learners' native language just because research has shown that their scores will probably be higher?

Item Construction

Whereas in the foregoing discussion we examined general issues about testing, we now explore individual item construction. A test is only as good as the questions asked. If a test item can be answered correctly without the test taker reading the passage, then the item is not passage dependent and, thus, not a good test item (Johns 1978; Perkins and Jones 1985). If test items encourage test takers to read only sections of a passage or to do only a surface reading of the passage, then the items are not good ones (Cohen 1984). If items test only isolated facts or details, they can be answered based on understanding only words and phrases and not the entire passage; such items are not good ones

(Swaffar and Wälterman 1988). Based on her review of the research, Wolf recommends the following guidelines for constructing individual test items:

> 1) that all items be passage dependent; 2) that items test information from different levels of the passage, that is, main ideas as well as details; 3) that all distractors be plausible; 4) that items paraphrase information in the passage so that learners cannot match words and phrases from the item to the passage; and 5) that test takers not be allowed to refer to the passage while performing the comprehension tasks, thereby discouraging surface reading of the passage. (1993a:327)

***P**ause to consider . . .*

withholding the passage during testing. How does the idea strike you? How will the idea strike the test takers? Can you suggest other ways to achieve the goal of avoiding surface readings?

FROM CLASSROOM ACTIVITIES TO READING TESTS

Processes and Products

Recall that *comprehension* was defined in Chapter 10 as the process of relating new or incoming information to information already stored in memory. All attempts to test and evaluate comprehension are problematic because the process is internal to the reader (it happens in the mind) but tests require external manifestation of mental processes. Some argue that "testing comprehension" is an oxymoron: eliciting external manifestations of mental processes in a classroom testing situation is simply not possible. Others argue that testing reading comprehension is a matter of testing what a reader learned from the text. In other words, testing assesses the accuracy of the *result* of relating incoming information to information already stored in memory. Thus, although comprehension is a process, the process yields a product. This view holds that what is important in testing is not *how* a reader comprehends but *what* is comprehended. This debate will not be easily resolved.

Throughout this book, we have advocated that tests reflect classroom activities. We will examine testing reading comprehension from two perspectives, both consistent with this position. The first focuses on content—a product-oriented approach. The second focuses on applying skills learned to a new reading situation—a process-oriented approach. There are advantages to both approaches.

Focus on Content

Krashen and Terrell (1983) recommend constructing tests that encourage learners to engage in acquisition activities, either during class activities or while studying. Their recommendation lies at the heart of the *washback effect* from testing to instruction; it can be applied to reading tests as well as to other kinds of testing. Our position is that reading tests should be constructed to encourage learners to read more. The more language learners read, the better readers they become and the more language they acquire. Krashen refers to this phenomenon as "the power of reading" (Krashen 1993). The test sections below are derived from classroom activities, thereby demonstrating to learners that they are responsible for the class assignments and that they must read and reread the assigned texts in order to prepare for the test.

When writing a test that focuses on content, you will want to focus on the Guided Interaction phase, the Assimilation phase, and the communicative functions of texts; Activities H, I, and K, respectively, illustrated these three aspects of reading in Chapter 10. We display each Activity again for your convenience, followed by a test version of the same activity.

Activity H. Guided Interaction

Step 1. Since this is a relatively long reading, it would be best to read it section by section. After reading each section fairly quickly, pause to collect your thoughts by writing a sentence that captures the main idea of the section. Compare your sentences with those of a classmate. Do you agree on the main ideas?

Step 2. Go back and reread each section, paying more attention to the details. Using a highlighter, identify key words or phrases that will help you remember what you have read. At the end of each section, look at what you have highlighted. Does it spark your memory? Compare the words and phrases you have highlighted with those of your classmates. Have you chosen different words?

Step 3. Based on what you have read, check off the statements that are true.

☐ From the tone of the article, it is evident that the author is pro-elephant.

☐ Even though elephants are normally quite peaceful, they are capable of tremendous violence.

☐ An elephant herd is a democratic unit.

☐ Elephants and humans share similar preoccupations with their young.

Step 4. Complete the following statements.

1. A herd of elephants is composed of . . .

a. males and females in more or less equal proportions.

b. more males than females.

c. one male and various females, like a harem.

2. The care of the young is . . .

a. shared equally among males and females.

b. the responsibility of the males.

c. the responsibility of the females.

3. Of the young that are born in a herd . . .

a. the males and females are members of the same herd for all their lives.

b. the males and females form subgroups, which eventually leave the herd.

c. the males leave the herd but the females remain.
d. the females leave the herd but the males remain.

Step 5. Working with two or three classmates, make a list of all the behaviors described in the article. Then share your list with the rest of the class, adding to your list whatever behaviors you might have missed. Finally, as a class, indicate if each behavior is instinctive or learned.

Step 6. According to the introductory paragraphs, elephants are intelligent, difficult, active, powerful, and fun-loving animals. As a class, identify the information in the article that supports the idea that elephants really are as they are described.

Section A. (Based on Activity H, Steps 3 and 4)

Based on your reading of "The Secret Code of Elephants," comment on three of the following ideas. Be sure to cite specific information from the passage that supports your statements.

a. tone of the article
b. organization of the herd (leadership and makeup)
c. care of the young
d. violence among elephants
e. allegiance to the herd as the young grow older

Section B. (Based on Activity H, Steps 5 and 6)

1. We often hear that animal behavior is instinctive, that animals survive in the wild because they have the instincts to survive. How true is this statement for elephants? Refer to specific information from the article when answering.

2. According to the authors, elephants are intelligent, difficult, active, powerful, and fun-loving animals. Do you agree or disagree with the authors? Be sure to cite specific information from the article to support your opinion.

Test Sections A and B parallel the in-class Guided Interaction activities. The test requires learners to produce evidence of their comprehension of the passage; in each case, learners must cite specifics from the passage to support their views. Another option for testing the content of the passages is to use an Assimilation activity. Activity I from Chapter 10 is reproduced below, followed by Sections C and D incorporating its content.

Activity I. Assimilation

Step 1. Review what you did in the Preparation and Guided Interaction activities. Then, complete the semantic map on page 232 without rereading the article (if you can).

Step 2. You have three options for working with the semantic map.
    Option 1. Using only the semantic map, write a summary of the article you read.
    Option 2. Using only the semantic map, write a short quiz on the content of the article. Try not to be too detail oriented with your questions. After all, you should write a quiz that you

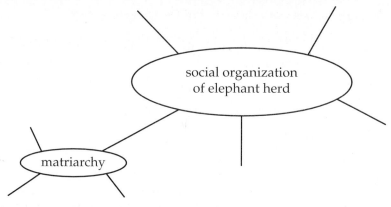

think is fair. You should also write a quiz that you would be willing to take!

Option 3. Using only the semantic map to guide you, write three essay questions covering the content of the entire article. As you write the questions, think about keeping the answers to two or three paragraphs. Remember, the questions you write just might be the ones your instructor uses on the exam!

Section C. (Based on Activity I, Steps 1 and 2)

1. Draw a semantic map of the article using the social organization of the herd as the central organizing concept.
2. Use the map to summarize the article.

Section D. (Based on Activity I, Step 2 options)

1. Take the quiz you wrote in class.
2. Answer the essay questions you wrote in class.

Recall that in Activity K, learners are asked to personalize the content of the reading about the secret code of elephants, relating it to the world as they know it. Test Section E builds from this activity and demonstrates that both comprehension of the passage and class participation are important.

Activity K. Communicative Function of a Text

Step 1. Working with two or three classmates, put the number that corresponds to your own opinions next to each of the following sentences.

We believe that for the majority of people our age,

> 1 = it is important . . .
> 2 = it will be important some day . . .
> 3 = it is not very important . . .

a. _____ to have a leadership role in whatever group one is associated with.

b. _____ to live in a safe and protected area.

c. _____ to lead an active social life.

    d. _____ to count on child care while at work.

    e. _____ to have various opportunities to find companionship.

    f. _____ to make friends.

    g. _____ to advance professionally.

    h. _____ to have economic security in old age.

    i. _____ to have a place to live in old age.

Step 2. Compare your answers with those of the rest of the class by indicating how many people responded to each item with a "1," a "2," or a "3."

Step 3. Which items were most important to the majority of the class? Which were not important? Does the class agree on what to look for in life?

Step 4. Go back over the sentences, but this time indicate with the letter "E" those statements that can apply to elephants. Then explain what information from the article supports your choices. In what ways are humans and elephants similar?

Section E. (Based on Activity K)

1. Indicate which of the following items were important to the class.

    a. _____ to have a leadership role in whatever group one is associated with.

    b. _____ to live in a safe and protected area.

    c. _____ to lead an active social life.

    d. _____ to count on child care while at work.

    e. _____ to have various opportunities to find companionship.

    f. _____ to make friends.

    g. _____ to advance professionally.

    h. _____ to have economic security in old age.

    i. _____ to have a place to live in old age.

2. The class discussed ways in which elephant and human behaviors are similar. First, summarize both sides of the discussion. Then, state which side you agree with using specific passage information to support your point of view.

Pause to consider . . .

how many test sections are needed to evaluate reading. On a midterm or final exam, what percentage of the test should be dedicated to reading? How many reading test sections should there be?

Focus on Skills Application

The alternative to testing content is to test the application of reading skills to a new reading. The teaching-testing philosophy behind this practice is that the assigned class readings are themselves not important. The act of reading and the accumulation of reading skills should instead be the focus.

   To focus on the application of reading skills, you would construct a series of test sections whose structure mirrors that of class activities: Preparation, Guided Interaction, Assimilation, and the communicative functions of texts. Section F is an example of how to adapt the Preparation-oriented in-class formats from Chapter 10, Activities A and G, for a test. (The adaptation of guided interaction, assimilation and communicative function activities to testing formats was demonstrated in the previous section.)

Activity A. Brainstorming with the Whole Class

Step 1. As a class, generate a list of all the ideas you associate with weddings. Come up with as many different ideas as possible in five minutes.

Step 2. As rapidly as possible, skim the text to determine whether or not the ideas on the board *(or overhead)* are actually in the reading. All you have to do is say whether or not the information is there; you do not have to know (not yet anyway) what the author says about that information. You have five minutes.

Step 3. Share what you found with the rest of the class. As you do, erase from the board all those ideas that are *not* in the text. Do you all agree?

Activity G. Scanning

Step 1. Find the following three words in the text and underline the sentences in which you find them.
   a. *feudalism*   **b.** *stewardship*   **c.** *tithes*

Step 2. Working with two or three classmates, either write a definition of each of the words or list as many things as you can think of that you associate with each.

Step 3. Share your work with the rest of the class. Are you all sure what these words mean?

Section F. (Based on Activities A and G)

1. Find the following three words in the text and underline the sentences in which you find them.
   a. *feudalism*   **b.** *stewardship*   **c.** *tithes*
Then write a definition of each of the words.

2. Now, skim the passage to determine whether or not the following topics are covered in the reading.

YES	NO	
☐	☐	**1.** inheritance laws for titles and property

☐   ☐   **2.** women's rights

☐   ☐   **3.** the effects of war on the economy

> ***P****ause to consider . . .*
>
> the appropriate text for a testing situation. Review page 198 contains the guidelines suggested by Swaffar and her colleagues for selecting texts to teach.
> Which of these apply to testing as well?

SOME ISSUES IN EVALUATING WRITING

In Chapter 11, we distinguished between transcription-oriented practices and composition activities. The evaluation of transcription-oriented practices is a fairly simple, straightforward issue: you would grade according to the intent of the practice. If the writers were directed, as in Chapter 11's Activity A (on page 219), to include ten targeted words, the grade should reflect the presence or absence of these words. If, as in Activity B (on page 220), the focus of the activity is sentence structure and word order, then the grading should reflect only those elements. Composition activities, however, engage qualitatively different thinking processes and yield a qualitatively different product than do the transcription-oriented Activities A and B. We focus our discussion on issues concerning the evaluation of compositions.

Responding to Form

Responding to form, otherwise known as "error correction" or "corrective feedback," is perhaps the most debated issue in language instruction. It goes far beyond composition. The underlying question is whether corrective feedback is effective: in the case of composition, does corrective feedback improve learners' writing? The answer is yes and no. Some research supports the idea that responding to form brings about changes in learners' writing (see, for example, Lalande 1982), whereas other research does not (see Semke 1984). Still other research (Robb, Ross, and Shortreed 1986) suggests a middle ground. Let's review these studies.

Lalande compared two methods of treating errors in the writing of second-year university learners of German. In the first method, instructors corrected errors and learners rewrote their compositions incorporating the corrections. In the second method, instructors coded the errors (for example, using *Nag* to indicate noun-adjective-agreement errors and *T* to indicate an error in tense selection). Learners then had to rewrite their compositions addressing these errors. Additionally, learners in the second method had to track the number and types of errors they made on each composition. Lalande found that learners in the second method improved their linguistic accuracy in writing more than did learners in the first method, although only to a small extent.

Semke (1984) compared several methods of providing feedback to first-year university learners of German. Instructors used one of the following methods:

- commenting on the content
- correcting errors
- commenting on the content and correct errors
- coding errors for learners to then self-correct

At the end of the quarter, learners who received comments only were superior to all other groups. Not only did they write more (they produced longer works), they also wrote more accurately (with fewer grammatical errors) than did the other groups.

Robb, Ross, and Shortreed (1986) expanded considerably on the designs of Lalande and Semke. They tracked learners over a year-long period, used multiple methods of feedback, and scored the compositions along a variety of lines. The methods used were:

- correcting errors
- coding errors
- highlighting errors but not correct or code them
- indicating in the margin the number of errors made

They found that writing improved less as a result of feedback on errors than by having additional opportunities to write. Labor-intensive methods of providing feedback, such as correcting and coding errors, did not produce results commensurate with the instructor's investment of time. Moreover, when instructors respond to form, so do learners. That is, since instructors were indicating surface errors, rather than errors in meaning, learners responded by focusing their attention on changing the surface features, not their meanings.

Pause to consider . . .

the parallel between this line of research on writing and the research insights presented in Chapter 2. Can you draw a parallel between stages of language development and the improvement in linguistic accuracy that results from having more opportunities to write?

Responding to Content

Writing involves not only form but content. The cognitive-process approach to composition described in Chapter 11 focuses learners on the expression of meaning. Feedback on such compositions should include responding to the content (the intended meanings) whether or not one responds to form. The type of instructor response should encourage writers to express themselves better. The instructor, acting on behalf of the intended audience, will in effect negotiate written meaning with the writer. This concept is essential for formulating a coherent approach to teaching and evaluating writing. Yet, as research shows, we must carefully construct our responses to content.

Zamel (1985) examined the comments, reactions, and markings that appeared on compositions assigned and evaluated by fifteen instructors teaching their own university-level ESL classes. She found that, by and large, instructors:

- make vague comments about abstract rules and principles that learners are unable to interpret
- correct on a clause-by-clause basis without considering the text as a whole
- respond to some problems but not others so that their reactions appear arbitrary and idiosyncratic
- tend to give conflicting signals about what to improve when providing overall comments and suggestions
- tend not to review their feedback when reviewing a revised composition and so accept revisions that address surface-level language errors

Overall, Zamel found that the instructors were poor communicators who faulted their students for being imprecise and vague but were themselves no better at communicating their responses.

Pause to consider . . .

your own writing experiences. Which of your instructors provided you the type of feedback that made you a better writer? Which provided feedback that was confusing or even contradictory? What type of feedback would/do you give learners?

Responding to Drafts

As Zamel found, even instructors who responded to content accepted revisions of the work with only changes in surface errors. This practice is questionable on two levels. First, we have seen repeatedly that learners "read" their instructors. If the instructor accepts rewrites that only address grammatical errors, then learners will most likely interpret the intent of the writing to be correct form production. On the other hand, learners may not know how to address content-related issues in their rewrites. Their practice of correcting only the grammatical errors is a call to the instructor to teach them how to address other issues. Colomb and colleagues (1991) recommend that instructors respond only to the content of a draft and not to formal errors, even though learners find it easier to focus on their formal errors than they find it to work on their expression of meaning. But the issue is also one of instructor effort. Why respond to formal errors before the writer has produced the "final" version that includes all the content? Here is an example. The following two samples of writing are a second language learner's draft and a rewrite of a definition of the term *meaningful*. As you read them, consider the ways in which an instructor would waste time responding to the formal errors in the draft.

> *Draft*
> If activity "meaningful" then learner required to interpret/compre-hend the language so to complete the activity. If activity "meaning bearing," not only meaningful, but it must require a personal/affec-tive response by learner.

> *Rewrite*
> Both *meaningful* and *meaning bearing* are terms to categorize activities. Meaningful activity require learner comprehend/interpret item lan-guage in order to carry out the activity. Meaning-bearing activity meet criteria for meaningful but also require learner provide some type of evaluative response to item. Examples of evaluative responses are per-sonal and affective responses, assessments of the information, etc.

P*ause to consider . . .*

the kind of response to the content of the draft that would focus the writer on addressing the meaning. What would you say to a second language learner who wrote the draft of the definition in order to focus the writer on content and meaning?

Holistic versus Analytical Scoring

We first introduced holistic and analytical scoring with reference to oval test-ing. A discussion of these two types of scoring criteria is relevant to evaluating writing. Whether you use holistic or analytical scoring procedures, you are ap-plying criteria in order to evaluate a composition. Holistic scoring results in an overall assessment of the work, reflected in a single score, rating, or grade based on descriptions of performance at a variety of levels. The rater evaluates the "fit" between the composition and the description. Examples of holistic descriptions are the ACTFL Proficiency Guidelines and the TOEFL Test of Written English. The TOEFL Test of Written English has six levels. The follow-ing description corresponds to Level 4; writing samples that "fit" this descrip-tion would be rated a "4."

- is adequately organized and developed
- uses some details to support thesis or illustrate an idea
- demonstrates adequate, but possibly inconsistent, facility with syntax and usage
- may contain some errors that occasionally obscure meaning

Analytical scoring is analogous to componential scoring, which was discussed in Chapter 9. Each component of the composition is evaluated (scored, rated, or graded); the component scores are typically added together to yield a final evaluation. Whereas holistic level descriptions collapse a number of categories into one level, the analytical criteria expand the descriptions of each category. Lee and Paulson (1992) developed the analytical scoring criteria listed in Figure 12.1. As you read them, note that the categories are not weighted equally. The weightings should reflect the importance of the category. One way to determine importance is to consider how it was treated during instruction.

Whether you select holistic or analytical scoring criteria, you must ensure that (1) writers are both aware and knowledgeable of the criteria, and (2) the criteria are applied consistently to all writers. When learners know how they will be evaluated, they can write with the criteria in mind. For example, if writers do not know that vocabulary use will be assessed, they may not review their use of vocabulary. Some educators recommend teaching learners how to apply the evaluation criteria to their own and to their peers' compositions as a means of familiarizing them with the criteria. Consistent application of criteria is a fundamental consideration in all testing situations. You are already familiar with the term *interrater reliability* (from Chapter 9) to describe a situation in which two different raters agree on an evaluation. An issue that arises in composition grading is that of *intrarater reliability,* in which the same rater applies the criteria consistently across all the compositions he or she evaluates. When raters are tired, they might not make the same judgments that they do when they are alert. After evaluating fifteen compositions without resting, level distinctions can become blurred.

Pause to consider . . .

other categories for analytical criteria. Among them are:

> thought organization
>
> quality of arguments/explanations
>
> surface features/mechanics (handwriting and spelling)
>
> communicative quality (ease of reading)
>
> expression
>
> cohesiveness
>
> comprehensibility
>
> stylistic techniques

On what basis do you choose one category over another? What weighting would you give to the category?

Evaluation Criteria for Compositions

Content (Information Conveyed)   **Points**

- minimal information; information lacks substance (is superficial); inappropriate or irrelevant information; or not enough information to evaluate   19
- limited information; ideas present but not developed; lack of supporting detail or evidence   22
- adequate information; some development of ideas; some ideas lack supporting detail or evidence   25
- very complete information; no more can be said; thorough; relevant; on target   30

Organization

- series of separate sentences with no transitions; disconnected ideas; no apparent order to the content; or not enough to evaluate   16
- limited order to the content; lacks logical sequencing of ideas; ineffective ordering; very choppy; disjointed   18
- an apparent order to the content is intended; somewhat choppy; loosely organized but main points do stand out although sequencing of ideas is not complete   22
- logically and effectively ordered; main points and details are connected; fluent; not choppy whatsoever   25

Vocabulary

- inadequate; repetitive; incorrect use or non-use of words studied; literal translations; abundance of invented words; or not enough to evaluate   16
- erroneous word use or choice leads to confused or obscured meaning; some literal translations and invented words; limited use of words studied   18
- adequate but not impressive; some erroneous word usage or choice, but meaning is not confused or obscured; some use of words studied   22
- broad; impressive; precise and effective word use and choice; extensive use of words studied   25

Language

- one or more errors in use and form of the grammar presented in lesson; frequent errors in subject/verb agreement; non-Spanish sentence structure; erroneous use of language makes the work mostly incomprehensible; no evidence of having edited the work for language; or not enough to evaluate   13
- no errors in the grammar presented in lesson; some errors in subject/verb agreement; some errors in adjective/noun agreement; erroneous use of language often impedes comprehensibility; work was poorly edited for language   15
- no errors in the grammar presented in lesson; occasional errors in subject/verb or adjective/noun agreement; erroneous use of language does not impede comprehensibility; some editing for language evident but not complete   17
- no errors in the grammar presented in lesson; very few errors in subject/verb or adjective/noun agreement; work was well edited for language   20

Total points _____ /100

FIGURE 12.1. *Source:* Lee and Paulson (1992) (p. 33)

SUMMARY

In this chapter, we discussed a number of issues surrounding the testing of reading and the evaluation of writing. These issues can be added to the list of considerations we presented in Chapters 7 and 9. We began by considering that different tests have different purposes. Thus, any decision about the test (from task types to evaluation criteria) must be made in the appropriate context. As we have done in previous chapters on testing, we adapted classroom activities as test sections, underscoring our position to test what and how you teach. We presented two approaches to testing reading: one that focused on content and another that focused on the application of skills. Focusing testing on content would lead the learners to read and reread, to go beyond a surface reading of the assigned passages. Focusing testing on applying skills would lead the learners to appreciate the instructional framework (the *how* of reading) rather than the content (the *what* of reading). Either approach to testing is consistent with the type of instruction advocated in Chapter 10. We then presented several issues in evaluating writing, including research on the effects of feedback provided to learners, whether and when to respond to form and/or content, and the use of holistic versus analytical criteria. Like teaching, testing involves making decisions. Decisions about tests, however, seem to have greater emotional consequences for learners. Although you might be able to motivate learners with tests and thus reinforce your classroom practices, you could also unmotivate them and undermine your classroom practices. Whatever decisions you make about testing, you must be able to justify them not only to yourself but to the learners.

KEY TERMS, CONCEPTS, AND ISSUES

demonstration of comprehension
purpose of tests
knowledge
task type
language of assessment
   bias for the best
   curricular considerations
item construction (guidelines)
   passage dependency
   levels of information
      main idea versus detail
   paraphrasing
   surface readings
process versus product
   mental processes
   external manifestations
focus on content
   washback effects
focus on skills application

evaluating writing
  responding to form
    various treatment methods
    effectiveness
    labor-intensive feedback
  responding to content
    negotiation of meaning
  responding to drafts
    form versus meaning
  holistic scoring
    level descriptions
  analytical scoring
    categories
    weights
intrarater reliability versus interrater reliability
writer's knowledge of criteria

EXPLORING THE TOPICS FURTHER

1. *Testing reading.* Lee (1989) takes an expository passage and develops an instructional framework to support it; he then adapts the framework for testing purposes. See also Swaffar, Kern, and Young (1989) for a similar treatment.
2. *Issues in test construction.* Wolf's review (1993a) is quite comprehensible and makes several practical recommendations. See also Bachman (1990) and Omaggio Hadley (1993) (Chapter 9).
3. *Evaluating writing.* Semke's (1984) article is quite readable. See also selected chapters in Kroll (1992).
4. *Evaluation instruments.* One of the most widely used analytical scoring instruments is the ESL Composition Profile developed by Jacobs and colleagues (1981). See Omaggio Hadley (1993) (Chapter 7) for a discussion that advocates holistic over analytical scoring.

PART V

A Look Forward

Most if not all textbooks include statements at the beginning of a chapter about the communicative or proficiency objectives for the upcoming material, as in "After studying this chapter you will know how to discuss daily routines." In most cases, the only connection between activities in that chapter is that they all have something to do with daily routines, not that these routines build on each other and work toward a goal. In this chapter we present the idea that activities in a chapter should lead to a concrete end. The end (or goal) we advocate is an information exchange task that is constructed in such a way as to encompass all the vocabulary, grammar, and language functions presented in the chapter. To arrive at such a goal, subgoals, represented by smaller information exchange tasks, should cap off strings of activities. As an instructor and learners move forward through a chapter, they will see that the parts of the lesson allow them to do something later in the lesson.

CHAPTER 13

Building Toward a Proficiency Goal

goal (gōl) n. *the purpose toward which an endeavor is directed; an end; objective.*
American Heritage Dictionary

INTRODUCTION

If you were to state an objective for a first-semester language class, what would it be? Would you phrase it in terms of material to be covered, say, certain chapters in a textbook or certain grammatical structures and vocabulary groups? If you were to state an objective for a lesson, what would it be? Have you ever heard an instructor say, "This week we will cover pages 250–271"? Which of the following sound familiar, if any?

- *This week we will complete Chapter 4.*
- *This week we're studying the past tense.*
- *This week we're on food.*
- *This week we will learn how to describe people's physical appearances.*

Of concern to many language teaching professionals is the nature of communicative objectives or proficiency goals. Many states have guidelines for language instruction at the secondary level that include proficiency goals: "The goals of language instruction are to . . ." or "Learners should be able to . . ." The Proficiency Guidelines developed by the American Council on the Teaching of Foreign Languages have been adopted in various ways by some educators in order to establish teaching objectives. But these are long-term goals, goals that suggest what a learner should be able to do *after* some extended period of time, such as two years of classroom language learning or upon completion of a major in the language. Practicing instructors, however, are generally concerned with the more immediate context in which they work and thus are particularly concerned with day-to-day and week-to-week objectives. In particular, they are concerned with class-hour and lesson objectives.

In this chapter, we explore the nature of lesson goals and examine how the various pieces of a lesson fit together. We are especially interested in the idea of reaching a lesson-final communicative objective. The question that underlies our discussion is, What do we want our learners to be able to do after a week or two of instruction *following* completion of a lesson? We first review the concept of a lesson goal.

245

Imagine that you have decided to build a gazebo in your backyard. You have lumber, screws, braces, tools, and some kind of plan for constructing the gazebo. You may work very hard and, depending on your skill and knowledge of building, spend one week, two weeks, various weekends, or some other amount of time on the construction of your gazebo. How do you know when you have finished? The answer is simple. You know you have finished when you have completed the gazebo. You can look at it, touch it, point to it, and say, "I'm done." In essence, the gazebo itself was your goal, and when the gazebo is up and standing you know you have reached your goal.

Now let's compare the building of a gazebo with a typical lesson in communicative or proficiency-oriented textbooks. Following are goal statements from various textbooks currently in use.

- *In this lesson you will learn to talk about daily routines.*
- *Language function: describing one's daily routine.*
- *In this chapter you will learn to make plans with someone, talk about your daily schedule, and tell time.*
- *After studying this chapter, you will know how to discuss daily routines.*

As an instructor or as a student, how do you know when you have reached the chapter objective? What can you point to and say, "This is it. Now I know I'm finished"? In short, what is your "gazebo" for the lesson? With most existing materials, communicative goals or proficiency objectives are often stated, but the statements tend to be vague. There is little in the materials that tells the learner or the instructor when a goal has been reached. In most cases, a lesson is completed when learners and instructors get to the last page of the chapter in the textbook.

Perhaps the reason for the vagueness of these stated proficiency goals becomes evident if we ponder for a moment the tools provided in lessons on "daily routines." What vocabulary, grammar, and interactional patterns are part of the lesson on daily routines? Before looking at what textbooks have to offer, consider the typical daily routine of a university student. We requested that a group of students describe their daily routines, asking them to mention at least three things about their mornings, three things about their afternoons, and three things about their evenings. Following is a composite of what a typical student's day might look like based on this particular group of students.

> I get up in the morning around 9:00. I sometimes eat breakfast but usually I just go to my first class. In the afternoon, I have classes and often go to the library to study. I eat a quick snack when I can. In the evening I work until 11:00 at night. I study a little when I get home, but sometimes I just watch "Nick at Night" then go to bed.

Compare this real-life typical routine with what is found in several textbooks published in the past ten years. Textbook X includes the following on the first page of Chapter 12: "Communication goals: talking about everyday events and actions . . ." In the vocabulary section under *Everyday Life,* learners are presented with the following sentences accompanied by drawings depicting a man and woman.

They wake up and they get up.

They brush their teeth.

She puts on her makeup.

They get dressed.

They take off (i.e., *they leave for the day*).

They go to bed.

They fall asleep.

After this presentation is a grammar section titled "Reporting everyday events: pronominal verbs." In this section, learners study the form and use of reflexive pronominal verbs. This is followed by four practices, each of which asks learners to use a reflexive verb in every sentence that they produce.

Textbook Y includes the following goal in Chapter 3: "In this chapter you will learn some ways to . . . talk about daily routines." The first thing one encounters is a description of Alice's routine:

She wakes up.

She gets up.

She takes a shower.

She gets dressed.

She gets undressed.

She brushes her teeth.

She goes to bed.

She falls asleep.

All of the above would require reflexive verbs in the target language. There are various activities that follow:

a. Say what time you do the following.

EXAMPLE: Wake up
(reflexive verbs are used here)

b. Match the phrase to the word in the vocabulary list that it defines.
(reflexive verbs matched with items like soap, toothpaste, and so on)

c. Put the following activities in the order you do them.
(most are actions that require reflexive verbs, as in Alice's routine above)

d. Personal questions

EXAMPLE: What time do you normally get up?

e. You and your partner have been invited to audition for a soap opera about student life. Unfortunately, the script is incomplete. Complete the minidialogue below and practice for your audition. (The missing parts require reflexive verbs.)

After these activities, which seem to teach new vocabulary, is the following:

Presentation of reflexive verbs. Form and position of pronoun.

a. Complete the slash (dehydrated) sentences using reflexive verbs.

b. Combine elements from each column to make real statements. (reflexive verbs)

c. You are doing a survey on personal hygiene for a company that manufactures such items as soap, perfume, and deodorant. Luckily you do the survey by phone and it is completely anonymous, since some of the questions are somewhat personal. Your friend has agreed to allow you to practice on him/her. Use the formal form in the questions . . .

	EVERYDAY	OFTEN	SOMETIMES	NEVER
take a bath with cold water	☐	☐	☐	☐
brush your teeth	☐	☐	☐	☐
shave	☐	☐	☐	☐
comb your hair	☐	☐	☐	☐

d. Answer the following questions about your family.

EXAMPLE: Who gets up early in the morning?

If we step back and look at these samples from various textbooks, we see that the focus of so-called daily routines is the use of reflexive verbs. While reflexive verbs are an important grammatical concept, how important are they for talking about daily routines? Recall the typical student routine described at the outset of this section, and note that students did not mention such actions as combing their hair, brushing their teeth, taking a shower, shaving, putting on clothes, taking off their clothes, falling asleep, or the kind of water they shower with. Undoubtedly there is some variation here; some people might say, "I got up and took a shower, then I ate breakfast." However, most people spare us the details of their personal hygiene and the minute-by-minute account of their morning preparatory habits. In other words, in normal conversational situations only a few reflexive verbs seem necessary to talk about daily routines *from the learner's point of view.*

The point, then, is that topicalized or contextualized grammar is not equivalent to a communicative or proficiency orientation. True communicative- and proficiency-oriented instruction cannot be grammar driven. Moreover, in many cases a communicative goal cannot be equated with (or reduced to) a particular grammatical item. In those textbooks in which communicative goals are apparently equated with grammar, then the linguistic tools provided might not be what is needed to realize the stated communicative goals. What is evident from the preceding examples on daily routines is that the stated communicative goal is actually window dressing for a predetermined grammatical point; grammar is not at the service of communication.

*P*ause *to consider . . .*

why daily routines look the way they do in many current textbooks. Why do you think textbook authors and their publishers have equated "daily routines" with so-called reflexive verbs? As you think about this, you may wish to review some of the ideas and observations from Chapter 1.

RETHINKING LESSON GOALS

The problem with many proficiency goals in commercial materials is not so much the goal statement but what happens in the lesson itself. As we saw in the previous section, a good communicative goal such as describing one's daily routine turns out not really to be the goal at all. What is needed in language lessons is a "gazebo," something that signals to learners and instructors that a goal has been reached.

Information-Exchange Tasks

We start by exploring the idea of a proficiency goal as some kind of information-exchange task, a task requiring students to exchange information and use it in some way. We introduced these types of tasks in Chapter 8, and we are now ready to situate them in a more focused context: achieving a lesson-wide proficiency goal. For example, to teach toward a goal such as "talking about everyday events and actions," we suggest that *instructors could adopt an information-exchange task as a lesson objective.* The stated proficiency goal of a lesson would then correspond to a particular task. Having a particular task that represents the lesson's communicative objective, instructors and learners can point to it and say, "When we can do this task, we have reached the goal for this lesson."

In addition, instructors and learners can more easily see how the vocabulary, grammar, and other language features of a lesson fit together to realize a concrete objective. How is this so? An interactive information-exchange task implies a lesson blueprint that suggests what learners need to know and what they need to be able to do in order to complete the task. More specifically, once a task is identified we can ask questions such as the following:

- What vocabulary do learners need to have under control to complete this task?
- What grammar or pieces of grammar do the learners need to be able to comprehend or produce to complete this task?
- What functions of language will they need to perform (e.g., asking questions, making declarative statements, listing items, narrating with connective devices)?
- What content (information on a given topic) needs to be included?

These questions suggest that lessons have divisible parts or sections that can be thought of as smaller goals—lesson subgoals—along the way. In short,

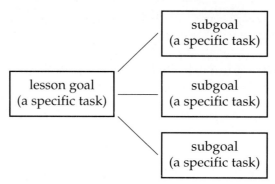

FIGURE 13.1. Lesson Goals Imply Lesson Subgoals

a lesson goal that is represented by an interactive information-exchange task allows an instructor to map out the lesson, specifying subgoals along the way. This is illustrated in Figure 13.1.

We can illustrate this concept with a concrete idea. Returning to our proficiency goal of talking about daily routines or everyday events, let's imagine an interactive information-exchange task such as the following. It can be used in just about any language.

Activity Z. In this lesson-final activity, you will prepare a series of quiz items for your instructor to use. In order to do so, you will need to interview someone about his or her daily routines as well as offer examples about your own daily routine in order to make contrastive and comparative statements.

Step 1. Using the chart below, fill in at least three things that you tend to do each morning, three things that you tend to do every afternoon, and three things that you tend to do every night. Include when you get up and when you go to bed. Be sure to use proper verb forms to talk about yourself.

	I . . .	My classmate . . .
morning		
afternoon		
evening		

Step 2. Now interview someone in the class with whom you have not worked much during this lesson. Ask your partner specific questions to find out if he/she does the same things. For example, if you wrote for yourself *I study for 2 hours* in the afternoon box, ask your partner,

"When do you study?" and "How long do you tend to study?" The idea here is to get information so that you can write a series of contrastive and comparative statements. (Be sure to frame your questions correctly and jot your partner's information down.)

Step 3. Using the information that you have obtained in Steps 1 and 2, write three true-false questions and three multiple-choice questions comparing and contrasting you and your partner. Here are some samples:

> Ex: True   False   1. I get up early, but David gets up late.

> Ex: David works in the evening. In the evening I . . .
> **a.** work too.   **b.** watch TV.   **c.** study.

Step 4. Turn in to your instructor a neat copy of your chart and your list of true-false and multiple-choice questions.

Vocabulary

As we examine this task we can ask ourselves, What vocabulary does the learner need to know in order to complete this task? Although we can't foresee every single lexical item a particular learner might need, common sense and experience in actual communication suggests to us that learners need vocabulary such as *get up, go to bed, eat, take a nap, watch TV, go to class, study, work, go the gym, exercise,* and so on. In addition, they need time expressions such as *in the morning, in the afternoon, in the evening, for _____ hours.* They may also need to know how to express a particular time *(at 10:00, at 12:30).* They will probably need to express days of the week *(Monday, Tuesday),* since schedules and routines may vary depending on the day. They also need connectors such as *but, and,* and *however* in order to make the comparative and contrastive statements in Step 3 of the task.

Thus, we see that several lesson subgoals might include work with these lexical items. One subgoal could be a short task that works with just the actions and events (introduced and practiced first using third-person verb forms).

Activity A. Make a list of eight statements about a typical student's day. Scramble the list and read it to your classmates. They should write down your statements and see if they can put the daily actions in the order in which the typical student would most likely do them. Did everyone match your order?

An alternative might be something like the following.

Activity A (alternative).

Step 1. Make a list of three daily activities a student does that you don't think your instructor does. Also make a list of three daily activities a student does that you think your instructor does as well.

Step 2. A volunteer should read his or her statements to the class, and someone should write them on the board in two columns. After the volunteer finishes, classmates should continue reading *new* statements aloud in order to make the two lists on the board as complete as possible. In the end, your instructor will tell you if you are correct about your statements.

Either of the two activities could serve as a lesson subgoal task. Thus, as learners and instructor work through vocabulary activities with daily actions, they are actually working toward one of the two tasks above. When they get to the task and complete it, they have completed a lesson subgoal for talking about daily routines. That is, *they can make statements about another person's daily routine, an ability necessary to perform Step 3 of the lesson-final task, Activity Z.*

Pause to consider . . .

why actions and events for daily routines might be introduced and practiced via third-person verb forms. There are two advantages in doing this. The first is that the vocabulary practice also serves as a grammar practice. Although learners are learning vocabulary related to daily routines, they are getting exposure to and practice with third-person singular verb forms at the same time. In this way, the subgoal task, Activity A, serves double duty; it represents both a vocabulary subgoal and a grammar subgoal. (We will examine grammar in the next section.) The second advantage to introducing verb-related vocabulary via third-person forms is a practical one. Recall from Chapter 3 that we advocate the use of visuals to help make input comprehensible. When using such visuals with people in them we are naturally speaking in the third person. For example, "See this lady? She is a doctor. We are going to talk about her daily routine. She gets up early. She drinks coffee and reads the newspaper, etc." What would happen if you didn't start with the third person? In what way(s) would introducing the vocabulary be more difficult?

Subgoal tasks for days of the week, time expressions, and specific times of the day could be developed as well, as in the following examples.

Activity B

Step 1. Write a series of statements about how many classes you have on each day of the week. Leave a blank after each one.

EXAMPLE: I have three classes on Monday. _____

Step 2. Now go about the room telling different people about your classes and asking them if their day is the same. If it is, get that person's signature in the blank. If not, move on to someone else. You must try to obtain five different signatures for the five different days of the week. Be prepared to answer questions that your instructor will ask when you are finished obtaining signatures.

EXAMPLE: *You say:* I have three classes on Monday. Do you?
Other person: Uh-huh. *(or)* Nope, I don't.
You: Sign here, please! *(or)* Oh, well. Thanks.

Activity C

Step 1. Using the time expressions you have been learning in this lesson, indicate when you do the following activities on a particular day of the week. The last items indicate that you should come up with two activities not on the list.

EXAMPLE: On Saturday, I watch TV in the afternoon.

watch TV
study
have your first class
get up
go to bed
work (if you have a job)
_____?_____
_____?_____

Step 2. Break into groups of three and present your statements to the two other people. They should indicate whether they do the same or not. When you have finished, they should add any activities that they do that you did not mention. Are your schedules fairly similar?

EXAMPLE: *You say:* I watch TV on Saturday, but usually in the morning.
             Other person: Me, too.
                   (or)
             Other person: Not me. I only watch TV at night.

Activity D

Step 1. Select the day of the week that is your busiest and make a schedule of that day below. Write in things such as "Chemistry class," "exercise," "I get up," and so forth.

Day of the week: _____

6:00 _____

7:00 _____

8:00 _____

9:00 _____

10:00 _____

11:00 _____

12:00 (noon) _____

1:00 _____

2:00 _____

3:00 _____

4:00 _____

5:00 _____
etc.

Step 2. Now interview a partner, asking questions to find out what his or her day is like. Jot down the information next to your schedule so that you can compare later.

EXAMPLE: What time do you get up?
When is your first class? What is it?
Do you eat breakfast or lunch? When?

Step 3. Comparing the two schedules, decide which of the following statements are true for you and your partner.

1. We are both equally busy on that day.

2. I have more classes than _____.

3. _____ gets up later than I do.

4. I study at night and so does _____.

5. I have more free time than _____ does.

6. _____ does not have any back-to-back classes.

In each of the activities above, we see that the tasks require learners to use language in ways similar to those they will need for the lesson-final task. In Activity B, they are using days of the week to make statements about themselves and to get information from someone else. In Activity C, they must choose time expressions to make statements about themselves. In Activity D, they must use specific times of day to obtain information. These tasks, then, suggest that learners have completed a particular subgoal of the lesson: the ability to use certain vocabulary items to exchange information related to daily routines.

Grammar

We turn now to grammar. What grammatical structures and forms do learners need in order to complete the lesson-final information-exchange task in Activity Z? Here we must be careful, for if we say "present-tense verb forms," this is only partly true. A close examination of the lesson-final task reveals that learners actually *need* only first-person singular forms *(I get up),* second-person singular forms *(You get up),* and third-person singular forms *(He/She gets up).* They need only these three forms of the verb for the task since the task requires only that they make statements about themselves (first-person singular), ask someone else about his/her schedule (second-person singular), and make contrastive statements about themselves and their partners (first-person singular and third-person singular). You might think that learners need first-person plural as well to make statements in Step 3 of Activity Z ("David and I both get up late"). But note that the task doesn't really require this. If you examine the examples in Activity Z again, you will note that in Step 3 learners need to be able to say only the equivalents of "and so do I," "but not me," "and David does, too," and so forth. In short, learners do not need the full paradigm of verb forms in a language to complete this task.

Do learners need reflexive verbs, as in the textbook examples we saw earlier? Again, the answer is incorrect if we say yes. In actuality, learners *need* to use only several common reflexive verbs; full explanation of, and work with, reflexive verbs is not required. Learners can learn the two or three verbs as "special lexical items" that need special pronouns to accompany them. In other words, learners can learn these verbs as lexical items, and as they learn the different forms for first-person singular, second-person singular, and third-person singular, they can simply learn the corresponding pronoun for each form. Following are four activities, the two versions of Activity A that we saw earlier, and two new activities, E and F. (Remember that Activity A does double duty as a vocabulary and a grammar subtask, so we are merely recalling here that learners have already worked with third-person singular verb forms.) Activities E and F represent work with first-person and second-person, respectively.

Activity A (original version). Make a list of eight statements about a typical student's day. Scramble the list and read it to your classmates. They should write down your statements and see if they can put the daily actions in the order in which the typical student would most likely do them. Did everyone match your order?

Activity A (alternative).

Step 1. Make a list of three daily activities a student does that you don't think your instructor does. Also make a list of three daily activities a student does that you think your instructor does as well.

Step 2. A volunteer should read his or her statements to the class, and someone should write them on the board in two columns. After the volunteer finishes, classmates should continue reading *new* statements aloud in order to make the two lists on the board as complete as possible. In the end, your instructor will tell you if you are correct about your statements.

Activity E. Here are three words to describe how regularly you might do something:

> always
> sometimes
> never

Tell the class how regularly you do the following, and see if others say the same about themselves. Is there a pattern in the class?

get up *very* early	study at a friend's house
study all night long	study and watch TV at the
sleep during a class	same time
skip a class	read a novel for fun
take a nap	eat dinner out
walk to campus	watch soap operas
read the newspaper	

Activity F.

Step 1. Read the following paragraph. *[Note: Instructor would have only half the class read the paragraph. The other half would be given a comparable but different paragraph to work with.]*

Mary is a typical student at the University of _____ She gets up early and takes the bus to campus. She has three classes in the morning: Chemistry I, English Literature II, and Japanese I. She eats lunch with a friend and then goes to the library, where she studies for three hours. Then she goes to work at a photocopy shop. She normally works only four hours each day. When she gets home, she eats a light meal and reads a little. She goes to bed early so that she can sleep at least eight hours.

If you were to interview someone in class, what kinds of questions would you ask to find out if that person does the same things as Mary does in a typical day? Remember that another person will not have the paragraph to refer to, so you will have to ask some very specific questions to get all the information you need.

Step 2. Now interview one of your classmates to find out if that person's day is like Mary's. Jot down all information since you may need it later if your instructor asks you to report to the class what you found out. *[Note: Here the instructor pairs learners based on who prepared one paragraph in Step 1 and who prepared the other. Partners take turns interviewing each other in Step 2.]*

The above grammar tasks, like their vocabulary counterparts that we saw earlier, represent subgoals within the lesson. These tasks are like way stations; completion of each signals that a particular objective has been fulfilled as learners work their way toward the lesson-final goal (which is represented by an information-exchange task). Thus, in Activity A, learners demonstrate that they can make simple statements using third-person singular verb forms, an ability necessary for Step 3 of the final task. In Activity E, they show that they can make simple statements to talk about what their daily routines are like, which they will need to do in Steps 1 and 3 of the lesson-final task. In Activity F, learners ask questions using second-person singular verb forms, which are required in Step 2 of the lesson-final task.

---

*P*ause to consider . . .

the ordering of the subgoals and tasks presented so far. The lettering A–F suggests that the subgoals fall into this order, but in reality they might not. One subgoal task can incorporate vocabulary or grammar from a previous subgoal, thus requiring a particular sequencing. Study Activities A–F again carefully and see what sequence they actually represent as currently formulated.

We emphasize here that these tasks are to be preceded by vocabulary presentations and practice (see Chapter 3) and/or structured-input and output activities for grammar (see Chapters 5 and 6). These tasks do not appear out of thin air; like lesson-final information-exchange tasks, these subgoal tasks represent something toward which learners have been working. We explore this in greater detail a bit later.

Functions

In terms of functions, it is clear from the lesson-final task that learners need to be able to make simple statements and ask each other questions. They do not need to string together sentences to create a narrative or produce an elaborate description. The question that arises here is, What do learners need to know—or know how to do—to ask the questions that they need to ask? Do they need all the question words of the target language? It seems that for the lesson-final task of Activity Z, learners actually need only *when, for how long, at what time,* and possibly one or two other time-related question phrases. In addition, they need to know the structure of questions (subject-verb inversion if the second language requires this in question formation, do-support in English, interrogative particle attachment in languages such as Japanese) Although these are typically learned early in language courses, the subgoal tasks frequently require question formation by having learners interview each other and ask questions. In this way, a particular language function that requires certain vocabulary and syntax is systematically recycled before learners arrive at the final task.

We can now develop Figure 13.1 to make it more concrete. In Figure 13.2, we show how a lesson-final information-based task suggests certain subgoals, and we map this out using the activities in this chapter. For the sake of the present discussion, we assume that the numbers 1–30, question words and question formation, and such words as *but, and,* and *too (also)* were learned in a previous lesson. (Note: As was suggested in the "Pause to consider" box on page 256, the ordering of Subgoals 1–6 and Activities A–F is not necessarily the order in which you would actually map-out the lesson.)

ACTIVITIES AND CLASSHOUR GOALS

The discussion of lesson-final goals and lesson subgoals leads us to the question of mapping out both lessons and classhours. It should now be evident that the lesson goal is something to be attained over some period of time (a week, two weeks, ten days). It implies an accumulated set of abilities with grammar, vocabulary, language functions, interactional patterns, and so forth. It is also clear that a lesson subgoal is a stepping stone on the way to the lesson goal. Upon completion of a subgoal task, instructors and learners know that they have completed an important part of a set of materials that is moving toward a concrete end. But how, exactly, does this happen? What is the relationship between subgoals and classhours? What is the relationship between the entire lesson and actual days devoted to the lesson?

In our lesson on daily routines, we have established Activity Z as the information-exchange task representing our lesson-final objective. In turn, we specified six subgoals realized as Activities A through F. It might seem straightforward to suggest that each of these subgoal tasks could be a classhour goal. We could then map out the lesson in the following manner.

Subgoal 1: being able to use vocabulary related to daily routines to talk about someone else (Activity A)

Subgoal 2: being able to use days of the week to talk about schedules and routines (Activity B)

Subgoal 3: being able to use time expressions to talk about daily routines (Activity C)

Lesson-Final Task (Activity Z)

Subgoal 4: being able to use specific time to talk about schedules and daily routines (Activity D)

Subgoal 5: being able to make statements about yourself using first-person singular verb forms (Activity E)

Subgoal 6: being able to ask someone else questions about her/his daily routine using second-person singular verb forms (Activity F)

FIGURE 13.2. Suggested Subgoals Represented by Particular Tasks for the Lesson-Final Task, Activity Z

Day 1: end with Activity A

Day 2: end with Activity B

Day 3: end with Activity C

Day 4: end with Activity D

Day 5: end with Activity E

Day 6: end with Activity F

Day 7: learners do lesson-final task, Activity Z

While in principle subgoals might be good classhour goals, in practice some subgoals encompass material that cannot be learned in just one classhour. In Activity A, for example, learners work with isolated statements in the third-person singular forms in order to use the new vocabulary to talk about classmates and/or their instructor. Considering the basic vocabulary we need to talk about everyday events and activities, the amount of new vocabulary can seem daunting. Here is a list of vocabulary that might need to be introduced *just to get started:*

get up

exercise/run/go to the gym/do aerobics

eat breakfast/lunch/dinner

cook/prepare (a meal)

drink coffee

go to class

skip class

take the bus/walk/drive

read

work

return home

write

watch TV

listen to music

call on the phone/talk on the phone

go out

play (e.g., softball, frisbee)

go to bed

sleep/fall asleep

In addition to this necessarily abbreviated list are: adverbs such as *early, late, for _____ hours, for a while;* places such as *library, laboratory, restaurant, home, dormitory room, cafeteria, bar* (and the prepositions, or case markings, they take); objects and things such as *newspaper, novel, magazine, CD;* and other words associated with the activities in the list. You may recall from Chapter 3 that vocabulary is best introduced via comprehensible input so that learners can make form-word-meaning connections in the second language. Learners will obviously need to hear novel words and expressions dozens of times in the input before being asked to produce it themselves with any degree of confidence. Thus, one suggestion would be to spend two days on the initial vocabulary for talking about daily routines, *making the goal of the first day the ability to comprehend the vocabulary in context and the goal of the second day to produce it as in Activity A.* What an instructor will need, then, is a comprehension- or input-based activity with which to conclude the first day. The following activity is one possibility.

Activity A1. Listen as your instructor describes a typical day for a German university student. Then, decide what inferences you can make and mark each sentence as P (Possible) or I (Impossible).

_____ **1.** He likes to get up early.

_____ **2.** He doesn't have a car.

_____ **3.** He lives alone.

_____ **4.** He's a science student.

_____ **5.** He's not very social.

[*Instructor's script:* Uwe gets up early and eats breakfast. He has a history class in the morning, and then he goes to the library where he works for an hour and a half. Afterwards, he eats lunch in the cafeteria with his friend Anja. After lunch, Uwe returns to the cooperative (the place where he lives) and attends a meeting. After the meeting, he goes back to campus and attends a literature class. After this class, Uwe meets his friends Jörg and Andrea and has an espresso with them at the Cafe Eulenspiegel. When he returns home, he helps prepare dinner. After dinner, he goes out with several friends for a beer. He returns rather late and reads a little before falling asleep.]

We see, then, that our lesson mapping will require two days for the first subgoal, and our new schedule looks something like the following:

Day 1: end with Activity A1

Day 2: end with Activity A

Day 3: end with Activity B

Day 4: end with Activity C

Day 5: end with Activity D

Day 6: end with Activity E

Day 7: end with Activity F

Day 8: learners do lesson-final task, Activity Z

Only experience will help instructors determine what is a lot of material for one day and what is not. Novice instructors and instructors-in-training will want to consult with other instructors on such matters.

---

*P*ause to consider . . .

the role of homework in reaching a subgoal. A possible alternative to splitting up a subgoal (comprehension one day and production another) is to give certain kinds of homework so that learners come to class more prepared than if the instructor started from scratch. Although this seems a good idea, it has some drawbacks. Can you think of some?

We have just seen that, with the basic vocabulary, we might need to spend two days to get students to the point where they can successfully complete Activity A. On the other hand, there may be cases in which two subgoals could be accomplished during the same classhour. Take, for instance, the subgoals represented by Activities C and D: being able to use time expressions (e.g., *in the morning, in the afternoon*) and specific time (e.g., *at 1:00, at 2:30*). Neither of these subgoals is nearly as demanding as that of Activity A. The amount of new vocabulary is minimal, and it might be possible to get to both Activities C and D in one classhour. Likewise, the amount of material to cover in teaching first- and second-person singular might be achievable in one classhour. Our schedule, then, would be altered to look like the following:

Day 1: end with Activity A1

Day 2: end with Activity A

Day 3: end with Activity B

Day 4: Activity C mid-way, end with Activity D

Day 5: Activity E mid-way, end with Activity F

Day 6: learners do lesson-final task, Activity Z

Attaining a Subgoal

How do we reach a subgoal? Another way to phrase this question is, What do classhours look like? While not all classhours would be the same, we can use Day 1 and Day 2 of our hypothetical schedule to suggest what a classhour might look like. Remember that language acquisition always begins with input. So, regardless of whether vocabulary, grammar, or some other aspect of language is the focus, we will want to start with input. Following, then, is a suggested classhour plan for Day 1, the object of which is completing Activity A1 as a subgoal.

Day 1

Instructor introduces the new vocabulary via visuals and comprehensible input (see Chapter 3). This will probably last about 15–20 minutes.

Activity 1. Instructor makes statements and students tell where the activity might take place.

> EXAMPLE: [*instructor*] A student eats lunch.
> [*learner, looking at a list on the overhead*] Cafeteria.
> [*instructor*] Right. A student eats lunch in the cafeteria. But is that the only place?
> [*another learner*] Home.
> [*instructor*] Right. A student eats lunch in the cafeteria or at home. Anywhere else?
> *and so on*

Activity 2. Instructor makes statements about a fictitious student, and learners give their opinion as to whether the statement is typical or not for students at their school.

EXAMPLE: [*instructor*] Robert gets up very early.
[*learners*] Not typical!!!
[*instructor*] He studies at least five hours a day.
and so on

Activity A1. (see above)

The next day, the instructor will probably want to review vocabulary in a comprehension- or input-based manner before leading students into structured output activities. The following, then, is one possible classhour plan.

Day 2

Instructor reviews vocabulary with visuals by holding up two visuals and making a statement. Learners indicate whether the statement goes with visual A or visual B.

EXAMPLE: [*instructor*] This person takes a nap every day.
[*learners*] Picture A.

Activity 1. Using the same visuals as in the review, the instructor holds up a visual and asks learners to name the activity by saying that the person in the picture does the activity regularly.

EXAMPLE: [*instructor holds up a picture of someone reading a newspaper*]
[*learner*] That man reads the newspaper every day.

Activity 2. Instructor provides learners with two columns on the overhead. Column A contains activities listed in infinitive form. Column B contains adverbs, places, objects, and so forth. Using items from both columns, learners must make as many sentences about the typical student at their school as they can in five minutes. Instructor encourages them to agree or disagree.

Activity 3. Instructor gives learners a short text to read, similar to (but not the same as) the one they *heard* in Activity A1. Instructor puts learners into groups of three. Learners have two minutes to read the text. They then turn it over and, without looking, make as many statements about the person's daily routine as they can remember. After four minutes, the instructor calls time and sees which group recalled the most. That group then presents its recalls aloud for the class to judge their truth-value.

Activity A. (see above)

---

*P*ause to consider . . .

the homework assignment that learners might have received before coming to class on Day 2. Which do you think would be a better assignment: one that reviewed the vocabulary via comprehension or one that required the learners to produce the vocabulary? What is your rationale?

As you reflect on the sample classhour plans for Day 1 and Day 2, note that activities are not merely designed to practice the vocabulary and the grammar of a given lesson. Nor are they a simple collection of tasks designed to help fill a classhour. What we see is that *activities are a purposeful endeavor.* They *build toward something.* Activities are completed because the learner needs to know something and be able to do something later in the lesson or later in the class. Activities act as the lumber, screws, sawing, and piecing together that eventually lead to our gazebo, the lesson-final task.

WORK OUTSIDE OF CLASS

Language learning and learning to use language are not confined to the activities completed during class time. An important question to ask is what the learners are doing outside of class as part of their language-learning endeavors. What kind of homework do they have? What kind of laboratory and computer software materials are available to them? It would seem obvious that work done outside of class should somehow be tied to the proficiency objectives of a lesson. Nevertheless, much of what is found in workbook and laboratory assignments reflects the preoccupation with mastery of grammar characteristic of ALM. These materials contain drills, fill-in-the-blank exercises, sentence dictations, and other activities often viewed by learners as busywork. What should learners be doing outside of class?

Continuing our work with the lesson on daily routines, we can ask ourselves a series of questions about outside work that can contribute to a lesson-final goal.

1. Are there opportunities for learners to hear daily routines described? Are there laboratory activities that require learners to focus on comprehending someone else's description of everyday activities? Do these listening activities work at a variety of levels: word, utterance, "extended" narrative, conversational discourse? Do the activities ask learners to compare their own routines with those of the speakers on the tape?

2. Do grammar and vocabulary practices move from input to output and follow the suggestions we listed in Chapters 5 and 6? Is mechanical drilling avoided, so that learners are always working with mapping form and meaning or form and function? Are learners invited to "try out" some of the things they will need to do in class (by making sentences about themselves)? Are learners engaged affectively with the materials (for example, comparing their own lives and interests with those of others, making opinions, inferences, and so on)?

3. Do the outside materials themselves contain goals and subgoals defined as tasks? Is there a listening task toward which students work by completing a set of activities? Is there a form-focused structured output task that requires that learners have completed previous activities?

4. Are the materials as engaging and as varied as in-class activities? Do they contain surveys, polls, "quizzes," visual materials, short readings, or culturally authentic ads to work with? Do learners check boxes, agree-disagree, fill in names, write out questions, prepare statements, listen for main ideas, or scan for specific information?

In terms of what learners do outside of class, instructors have various opinions and preferences. "Students should complete grammar activities before coming to class so that we don't have to spend time on that." "Students should practice and practice in the lab so that we can spend time on communication in class." "Students should read, read, read outside of class." It seems that many instructors want learners to do things outside of class that they (the instructors) think is a waste of class time. This position is partly due to the fact that instructors have not been able to envision grammar and vocabulary tasks that are meaning based—that is, the kinds of activities that we have examined in this and previous chapters.

Our position is that homework should be an *extension of the class*, not necessarily something different or unenjoyable. Outside assignments should be consistent not only with the lesson objectives but also with the general philosophy of communicative classrooms presented in this book. As one example, recall that comprehension of a short narrative about someone's daily routine could be the basis of the particular classhour goal for Day 1 of our lesson plan. What kinds of activities might extend this kind of practice outside of class? Homework could be a series of activities that reinforce comprehension related to daily routines. And just as in the classroom, these activities could help learners move from comprehending statements to comprehending a short narrative or dialogue. Following are three activities that would be natural extensions of Day 1 in our lesson on daily routines.

Activity 1. [*Learner has a set of black and white drawings depicting the daily routines of two distinct people, Genevieve and Josephine.*] Looking at the drawings that depict typical days for Genevieve and Josephine, listen to the speaker on the tape make a statement. Tell whether the statement describes Genevieve's day or Josephine's day.

EXAMPLE: [speaker] *She gets up late.*
           [you say] *That's Josephine.*

If you really want to challenge your memory, study the drawings for about five minutes and then listen to the statements. How many can you get right without looking at the drawings?

Activity 2. Listen to the speaker on the tape make a series of statements about a typical day in the life of a dog. After you hear each one, indicate whether or not you do the same thing by selecting one of the alternative responses below. How much do you and the pooch have in common?

Me, too.
Not me.

[Learner hears eight statements such as "He sleeps most of the day" and "He eats two meals."]

Activity 3. Listen to the speaker describe the schedules of two people, Mary Ziebart and John Hausserman. You might wish to take notes as you listen. Afterwards, indicate to whom each statement refers. In some cases, the statement could refer to both people.

1. This person works at the science lab.
2. This person reads the newspaper every day.
3. This person studies in the library almost every day.
4. This person has a class in the morning.
5. This person doesn't eat lunch.

Now see if you can fill in the missing information without listening again.

6. Mary runs _____ miles every day.
7. John drinks _____ when he reads the newspaper.
8. Mary has _____ classes in the afternoon.
9. John teaches _____ classes in the afternoon.

[*Tapescript:* Mary Ziebart is a student at South Central College. Every morning she gets up early, runs three miles, then eats breakfast. She goes to class at 10:00. At noon she goes to the library and studies. She has two afternoon classes and then goes to the science laboratory where she works twenty hours per week.

John Hausserman is a professor at South Central College. Every morning he gets up, drinks coffee, and reads the newspaper. He never eats breakfast. He goes to his office and reads or prepares his classes. At noon, he eats lunch with a friend who is also a professor. John teaches two classes from 2:00 until 5:00. After class, he goes to the gym and exercises.]

---

*P*ause to consider . . .

which learning activities are better done outside of class rather than in. Consider also the converse: Which learning activities are better done in class rather than outside? Make a list of as many things that you can think of that a learner could do on his or her own. Does your list reveal a pattern?

In our experience, there are some things that learners can do on their own to help move an instructor's "communicative agenda" forward more quickly than if the same things were done in class. The first is work on extended listening comprehension. Listening to narratives, extended conversations, and other discourse-level texts is certainly something that learners can do in a laboratory or even at home, given the popularity of tape players of all kinds. By working alone, learners can move through these activities at their own individual paces. In simple terms, some learners are faster listeners than others and a teacher-led listening comprehension activity does not allow for individual differences. Two requirements of outside listening, though, are that learners be able to perform the task on their own regardless of level (that is, the task should not be too difficult for them) and that they bring questions and comments to class to ask about what they listened to ("I couldn't quite get the word after the guy said _____" or "Gee! Where was that woman from who spoke on the tape? She spoke so fast!").

Another thing that learners can do on their own is work through structured input (and some types of structured output) activities that focus on vocabulary or grammar. Some instructors think that grammar must be explained in class because it is too difficult for students to understand without help. "They can't possibly understand the complexity of the subjunctive if they read all that stuff on their own." Such observations might be correct if one is working with a traditional give-it-all-to-them grammar focus. However, a recent study suggests that learners can indeed work through many traditional grammar explanations and practices on their own. Scott and Randall (1992) demonstrate that learners of French in a first-semester university course can easily learn meaning-related grammar points and syntax outside of class (in this case, negation formation with *ne... personne/personne... ne* and comparatives *plus... que, moins que..., aussi... que)*. Non-meaning-related grammar points seemed to be harder for their subjects to learn on their own (in this case, the relative pronouns *que* and *qui*). In their study, Scott and Randall found that learners could work on their own and come to class "ready to go" with the meaning-related grammar points but that the non-meaning-related grammar points caused them some difficulty. They conclude that "since proficiency-oriented instruction is based primarily on devoting class time to meaningful and communicative activities, teachers can designate the linguistic structures which can be learned outside of class so that class time is not wasted on needless explicit grammar rule presentation" (p. 361).

In another study, Doughty (1991) found that learners of English as a second language *could* learn the nonmeaningful elements on their own. In her study, subjects worked with computer-based materials in a laboratory. After the treatment period, Doughty found that the subjects had internalized rules for the use of relative clauses. Unlike the instruction in the Scott and Randall study, however, the grammar instruction in Doughty's computer-based materials was input- and meaning-oriented; learners did not practice output and did not work with drills or fill-in-the-blank exercises.

The significance of our reference at the start of this section to traditional grammar explanations and practices is now clearer. If we envision grammar learning as structured input and structured output, then the "problem" of working through traditional materials on one's own is obviated. Recall that structured input always keeps meaning in focus and that activities work on one thing at a time. Working with smaller bits of a verb paradigm or list of rules allows learners to "get the grammar" more easily. The problem with many current textbook presentations is that all of the grammar is presented up front, which might indeed *necessitate* instructor intervention since the materials themselves can induce cognitive overload. Thus, Scott and Randall's subjects might very well have been able to grasp and work with the relative pronouns *que* and *qui* if they had been given different kinds of materials and different kinds of practice.

Summarizing these comments on grammar, we see that explanation and initial work with grammar can indeed be done outside of class. There seems to be no learner-induced need to explain and practice grammar during class. Whether instructors will actually want to relegate grammar instruction to outside-of-class materials will depend on their teaching styles and the types of materials available to them (or their ability to create new materials themselves).

Pause to consider . . .

the possible practical problems of assigning obligatory grammar and vocabulary work outside of class. How realistic do you think it is to have learners do *all* the preparatory work *before* coming to class? What happens if your classhour becomes too dependent on learners "coming prepared" and then at least five people in class have not done the homework? What is the middle ground here?

A FINAL POINT

To be sure, not every waking minute of the class needs to be spent on activities that build toward the lesson goal. Classes would be boring if they were nothing but a plodding march toward "The Final Task." Like any human endeavor, classroom language learning needs its little detours, its roadstops that give the instructor and learners some breathing room. Brief cultural notes, an interesting advertisement or short blurb from a magazine, five minutes spent watching a commercial—these all can add spice to the routine. When such detours are topically related (a commercial for detergent if everyday events include doing the laundry), they make sense. And while not moving the learner toward the proficiency objective per se, they at least fit the flow of the lesson. In short, a lesson-final goal spelled out as some kind of task might imply a blueprint for organizing the pieces and parts of a lesson, but nowhere is it written that one cannot have fun getting to the end.

Pause to consider . . .

where readings fit into lessons that have clearly defined communicative goals (as tasks). What purposes do readings serve in such lessons? Where can they be placed during the sequencing of the lesson?

SUMMARY

In this chapter, we explored the concept of using an information-exchange task as a communicative lesson goal. We suggested that an actual task gives instructors and learners a concrete objective, and we have shown how a concrete objective can help instructors determine what linguistic tools need to be developed to be successful with the task at the end of the lesson. We then examined how the lesson-final task suggests subgoals for the lesson and how these subgoals can be represented by smaller tasks. In addition, we explored how subgoals might or might not be used as classhour objectives. We saw how at times one subgoal could take two days to reach; in other cases, subgoals might be small enough so that two can be reached in a single classhour.

It should be clear, however, that stating a communicative goal as a particular task does not necessarily mean that at the end of a lesson a learner can talk about (or write, or comprehend) a topic in all of its situations or contexts. Given what a language classroom is, instructors and learners cannot possibly cover all the linguistic ground needed to perform in all possible contexts or in all possible situations. As such, the task as lesson goal is an instructional device to help instructors and learners manage their time together. Like much of classroom language learning, it is a small piece of a complex and dynamic endeavor.

KEYS TERMS, CONCEPTS, AND ISSUES

communicative goal as statement
linguistic tools and traditional goals
communicative goal versus grammatical
   goal
communicative goal as task
task as blueprint
   subgoals
   classhour goals
out-of-class work
   homework as an extension of class
   listening
   grammar

EXPLORING THE TOPICS FURTHER

Tasks and lesson formation. See Nunan (1989) (Chapter 6). For a different perspective on lesson planning, see Omaggio Hadley (1993) (Chapter 10).

Epilogue

We chose the title *Making Communicative Language Teaching Happen* quite purposefully. It is our hope that our readers, especially those who are unsure about whether or not communicative language teaching is possible, have found it rewarding in terms of practical ideas for developing classrooms focused on the development of communicative abilities. We also hope that readers have become better informed about some of the theoretical tenets and research that underlie communicative language teaching, especially as concerns developing the skills of listening, reading, writing, and speaking. And we hope that we have provided those who are concerned about the "proper role of grammar" in the communicative classroom with an approach to grammar instruction that clearly shows how grammar can be presented and used in the service of communicating ideas. What follows is a summary of the major points that have been made in this text. We hope that, long after reading the book, when you may not even remember its title, you will remember the following:

1. For communicative classrooms to work, both instructors and learners must take on roles and responsibilities that they may not have adopted before (Chapter 1). Instructors must learn how to be facilitators and communicators in the classroom, and learners must learn how to be responsible for their share of the work in classroom language acquisition.
2. Second language acquisition research has revealed certain insights about the acquisition of grammar and communication that are important for instructors to remember (Chapter 2). On the one hand, many aspects of grammar acquisition cannot be altered by traditional instructional approaches. On the other hand, teaching for communication does not necessarily result in a loss of underlying grammatical competence. It may be useful to recall *Desiderata*: Grant me the courage to change the things I can, to accept the things that I cannot, and the wisdom to know the difference.

3. Instructors should strive to provide as much comprehensible input in class as possible (Chapter 3). Teaching vocabulary via comprehensible input is one way to approach this. But instructors should remember the difference between talking *at* passive learners and talking *with* active learners. In the latter situation, learners are actively listening and responding to what they hear. They draw, write, make selections, act out, shout out, demonstrating their active attention in a variety of ways.

4. Helping students learn to listen for informational purposes is an important part of communicative language teaching (Chapter 4). Learners should have the chance to participate in collaborative and non-collaborative listening tasks that mirror some of the listening situations occurring outside the classroom (e.g., watching a commercial on TV, listening to weather reports, talking on the phone, listening to a lecture). This is different from comprehensible input, which is concerned with the acquisition of vocabulary, grammar, and other features of language; here we are concerned with learners developing listening as a skill.

5. Grammar instruction does not necessarily mean explanation + drill + other kinds of output practice, as generally happens in traditional language classes (Chapter 5). As we saw, grammar instruction should be congruent with the newer emphasis on communication, meaning, and input-rich classroom environments. To this end, we proposed grammar instruction as structured input, an approach that recognized the important role of input in developing grammatical competence. This approach takes into consideration the fact that learners may not process input in optimal ways and sets up opportunities for learners to make better form-meaning connections in the input than they would if left to their own devices.

6. We have also seen that output practice may be necessary for developing accuracy and fluency in production (Chapter 6). It is one thing to develop grammatical competence, and another to have opportunities to access one's developing system to create messages. For this reason we outlined structured output activities in which learners combine meaningful, communicatively oriented output with a focus on grammar via certain types of information-based tasks. We also saw that grammar testing must be consistent with classroom practice (Chapter 7), and that both structured input and structured output activities could be adapted for testing purposes as the instructor considers economy, validity, and reliability in grammar testing.

7. In examining oral communication as psycho-social and cognitive-informational, we saw that language classrooms are ideally suited for developing the cognitive-informational uses of language (Chapter 8). In proposing and describing information-exchange tasks, we saw how interactive tasks need to have a clear informational goal or outcome. Thus, the point is not to practice language; the point is to use language to get information and then to do something with that information. In these kinds of activities, learners have a purpose for talking and that purpose lies in the informational outcome of the activity.

8. Oral tests of communicative language ability can be constructed depending on the particular goals of a program (Chapter 9). Although certain standard oral tests exist, instructors may want to adapt them to their own needs and to meet the features and goals they establish for their classes. We explored the adaptation of classroom information-exchange tasks for testing purposes and the greater benefits of componential evaluation over holistic evaluation. Componential evaluation offers the instructor and learner a more precise evaluation along with greater specificity regarding the learner's language. Last but not least, we should keep in mind the washback potential of oral testing; if learners know they are to be tested orally and if instructors keep this in mind, then it is likely that classrooms become places where oral communication takes place on a daily basis.

9. Reading should be a substantial component of any communicative classroom because it provides additional input and content (Chapter 10). However, this does not mean that reading should consist only of reading and answering questions, as in traditional approaches. As we saw, these approaches ignore the processes responsible for reading comprehension and encourage learners to read word for word or to simply look for the answers to the comprehension questions at the end of the reading. The communicative classroom uses insights from second language reading research to forge process-oriented reading lessons. In our approach, we advocate pre-reading activities for the purposes of establishing a common base of background knowledge. We also advocate reading a text in stages, with the learner getting different kinds of information from the text at different times. This stands in direct contrast to more traditional approaches in which learners struggle through a passage word by word. We follow up reading with a synthesis stage in which learners pull together the information that they have gathered from the text. And, because communicative classrooms are learner-centered, we also advocate a phase in which learners address the content of the reading in some personal way.

10. Writing should not be a neglected fourth skill in the communicative classroom, and instructors should distinguish between writing activities and composition development (Chapter 11). Instructors should understand what it means to communicate through writing and to keep in mind that composition development is not equivalent to transcription, however appropriate these may be for certain parts of a lesson. Composition involves a number of processes including thinking, organizing, reflecting, adjusting, and later, editing. There is no reason why the development of composition ability should wait until advanced stages of language learning. Indeed, it should be present at all levels of instruction, including basic language.

11. The testing of reading and the evaluation of composition require that instructors make certain decisions in the communicative classroom (Chapter 12). Recalling the rule-of-thumb to "test what and how you teach," we saw how reading can be tested as content learned from a previous reading or as skills development. Each has its place and instructors can make use

of both in the evaluation of learners' performance. For composition, we saw that evaluation can be either componential or holistic, as in oral testing, and we again favored componential evaluation for the specificity of the information that it provides both learners and instructors.

12. On every communicative classroom's agenda should be the goal of building toward proficiency or communication, but instructors may not always have materials that accomplish this (Chapter 13). We saw that many communicative goals in commercial materials are merely window dressing for grammatical goals. Communicative classrooms should put language-oriented activities at the service of communication. To do this, we suggest the use of information-exchange tasks as lesson goals. If instructors have a particular and concrete task as an end point for a lesson, then lesson planning is facilitated; the task suggests the agenda for the lesson by suggesting smaller sub-tasks that build toward the lesson-final task. Sub-tasks in turn may suggest class hour goals. The result is that an instructor thinks about where a lesson is headed and how the individual activities build toward something. This is different from thinking about how many pages need to be covered this week or that the subjunctive has to be introduced.

The preceding list comprises, we think, the essential building-blocks for making communicative language teaching happen from the earliest stages of classroom language learning. Each reader will no doubt develop personal approaches for the classroom using these ideas. This is to be expected, since communicative language teaching involves the personal investment of instructors in the process and the application of principles, not simply a rote technique.

Before closing we must address two important points. The first is about the limits of the language classroom. The second concerns culture in the classroom. No classroom can be or do everything for the second language learner. The classroom setting, however communicative, limits the breadth of interactions in which a learner can participate. Communication is the expression, interpretation, and negotiation of meaning in a given context. Underlying this ability are a number of competencies: grammatical, discourse, strategic, and sociolinguistic. We must recognize, as does Breen (1985), that classrooms will fall short of developing the sociolinguistic competence in learners that can be developed in an environment in which learners have constant contact with a variety of native speakers. No classroom in French, Spanish, or any other language can provide the opportunities for learners to develop the competence that regulates the use of *tu/vous* or *tú/usted,* for example. No class can provide learners with all the opportunities for learning sociolinguistically appropriate greetings, leave takings, and other linguistic markers of social custom. That happens primarily in the real world.

For this reason, we have focused in this book on the informational and cognitive purposes of communicative language use; this purpose of communication seems to be where classrooms excel in developing communicative language ability. And although the development of sociolinguistic competence will be minimal in communicative classrooms, the possibilities for the development of other components should not be underestimated. With time, opportunities to express, negotiate, and interpret meaning within the context of the classroom can have tremendous payoffs outside the classroom. If you see the classroom as a springboard to and not a substitute for the non-class-room world, then you and your learners will be able to achieve a manageable goal, and you will accomplish a great deal.

Our second point is about culture. We have not addressed the teaching of culture in this book, be it culture defined as the artistic, literary, and historical achievements of a group or groups of people, culture as the description of daily life (what people eat, what kind of money they have), or culture in its socio-anthropological sense (the values and belief systems of a people). We do not mean to signal that cultural content is not important. We have learned over the years, however, that the teaching of culture is very individual for most instructors. Instructors choose to teach different things about culture: songs, cooking lessons, geography lessons, the reading of literary texts. Instructors bring in slides, films, TV commercials, magazines, posters, stamps, money, and other objects into the classroom. Some instructors emphasize art; others emphasize the belief systems of a people; others, the daily habits of a culture. And some instructors stress the differences between cultures whereas others stress the similarities. We have seen just about everything when it comes to the teaching of culture. Much of what is taught depends on the instructors' own contacts with speakers of the languages they teach. It is inter-esting to observe how differently culture is taught by a native-speaking Spaniard, by a North American who lived in Argentina between the ages of 10 and 20, and by a North American who has had only minimal contact with the native-speaking culture(s).

For those interested in the teaching of culture, we can suggest a number of readings, some theoretical and philosophically oriented, others more practi-cal, and still others that link theory and practice. We list those at the end of this epilogue. No matter what position you eventually take on what to teach when it comes to culture, we invite you to pause and consider the teaching of culture within the framework we have advocated for reading. Because culture is a kind of "text," very often seen through actual written and visual texts, instructors may want to consider the pre-reading, reading, and post-reading phases of a lesson as a possible framework for developing cultural knowl-edge. As learners explore values and beliefs different from their own, they may need to build up background knowledge and explore their own values first. Instructors may need to lead them through stages of understanding the new cultural content, just as they lead them through successive stages of uncovering information from a written text. In the end, learners should be able to synthesize what they have learned and know what is similar to or dif-ferent from their own culture. In addition to adapting the reading framework for culture, the information-exchange task is well suited to helping learners explore their own culture(s). What we are suggesting, then, is that lessons on culture and cultural information do not necessarily need a pedagogy different from that we have been outlining in the present book. What every instructor needs to decide is what cultural content to teach.

We conclude with the following quotation from a language learner, hoping that it will serve as a source of inspiration for making communicative language teaching happen. It expresses, we think, what this book is about.

> I wasn't sure when I went to Paris whether I would be able to handle all the aspects of communication that I would have to deal with. I mean, would I be able to understand the natives? Would they understand me? I guess I must have had good training since after the initial cultural shock I was getting along fine. I wasn't perfect, but I managed. As I think back, I remember how most of my teachers insisted on using French all the time in the class. We seem to have had a lot of activities in class for practicing speaking with each other. And since we had to listen to a lot of French from them and from tapes they brought in, I guess our abilities just developed. I was grateful in Paris, too, for all the reading we had to do. I learned a lot about how to tackle a difficult reading and it sure came in handy when I first tried *Le Monde*. I felt kind of bad for some of the other people who arrived with me. They had studied French for three years like me and couldn't speak a word. I felt confident compared to them and don't think that my three years of French classes were wasted at all . . .
>
> A student of French after returning from a two-month summer program in France

Exploring the Teaching of Culture

We recommend the following three readings as initial forays into the learning and teaching of culture and cultural competence.

1. Kramsch (1991). This is a challenging and provocative essay on cultural competence, discourse, and language teaching.
2. Byrnes (1991). This essay complements Kramsch's, albeit from a different perspective.
3. Seelye (1993). This book is a classic in the area of language teaching. Both philosophical and practical in nature, it provides the reader with numerous pedagogical suggestions for developing cultural competence in language learners.

Bibliography

American Council on the Teaching of Foreign Languages. (1986). *ACTFL Proficiency Guidelines.* Hastings-on-Hudson, NY: American Council on the Teaching of Foreign Languages.

American heritage dictionary of the English language (1993). New York: American Heritage Publishers and Houghton Mifflin.

Anderson, R. C., Pichert, J., Goetz, E., Schallert, D. L., Stevens, K. & Trollip, S. (1976). Instantiation of general terms. *Journal of Verbal Learning and Verbal Behavior, 15,* 667–679.

Anderson, R. C. & Pearson, P. D. (1984). A schema-theoretic view of basic processes in reading comprehension. In P. D. Pearson (Ed.), *Handbook of reading research* (pp. 255–292). New York: Longman.

Bachman, L. F. (1990). *Fundamental considerations in language testing.* Oxford: Oxford University Press.

Bachman, L. F. & Palmer, A. S. (1983). *Oral interview test of communicative proficiency in English.* Urbana, IL: Photo-offset.

Barnett, M. A. (1989). *More than meets the eye: Foreign language reading theory and practice.* Englewood Cliffs, NJ: Prentice-Hall.

Bernhardt, E. B. (1986). Reading in the foreign language. In B. H. Wing (Ed.), *Listening, reading and writing: Analysis and application* (pp. 93–115). Middlebury, VT: The Northeast Conference on the Teaching of Languages.

Bernhardt, E. B. (1991). *Reading development in a second language.* Norwood, NJ: Ablex.

Binkowski, D. D. (1992). *The effects of attentional focus, presentation mode and language experience on second language learners' sentence processing.* Unpublished doctoral dissertation, University of Illinois, Urbana-Champaign.

Block, E. (1986). The comprehension strategies of second language readers. TESOL Quarterly, 20(3), 463–494.

Brandsdorfer, R. L. (1991). *Communicative value and linguistic knowledge in second language oral input processing.* Unpublished doctoral dissertation, University of Illinois, Urbana-Champaign.

Bransford, J. D. (1979). *Human cognition: Learning, understanding and remembering.* Belmont, CA: Wadsworth.

Bransford, J. D. & Johnson, M. K. (1972). Contextual prerequisites for understanding: Some investigations of comprehension and recall. *Journal of Verbal Learning and Verbal Behavior, 11,* 717–726.

Breen, M. (1985). The social context for language learning—a neglected situation? *Studies in Second Language Acquisition, 7,* 135–158.

Bretz, M. L., Dvorak, T., & Kirschner, C. (1983) *Pasajes: Actividades.* New York: Random House.

Brooks, F. B. (1993). Some problems and caveats in "communicative" discourse: Toward a conceptualization of the foreign language classroom. *Foreign Language Annals, 26* (2), 233–242.

Brooks, F. B. (1990). Foreign language learning: A social interaction perspective. In B. VanPatten & J. F. Lee (Eds.), *Second language acquisition—foreign language learning:* Clevedon, UK: Multilingual Matters.

Brooks, N. (1964). *Language and language learning: Theory and practice* (2nd ed.). New York: Harcourt Brace & World.

Brown, R. (1977). "Introduction". In C. Snow and C. Ferguson (Eds.), *Talking to children* (pp. 1–27). New York: Cambridge University Press.

Bybee, J. L. (1991). Natural morphology: The organization of paradigms and language acquisition. In T. Huebner & C. Ferguson (Eds.), *Crosscurrents in SLA and linguistic theories* (pp. 67–92). Amsterdam: John Benjamins.

Byrnes, H. (1991). Reflections on the development of cross-cultural communicative competence in the foreign language classroom. In B. F. Freed (Ed.), *Foreign language acquisition and the classroom* (pp. 205–218). Lexington, MA: D. C. Heath.

Cadierno-López, T. (1992). *Explicit instruction in grammar: A comparison of input-based and output-based instruction in second language acquisition.* Unpublished doctoral dissertation, University of Illinois, Urbana-Champaign.

Canale, M. & Swain, M. (1980). Theoretical bases of communicative approaches to second language teaching and testing. *Applied Linguistics, 1,* 1–47.

Carrell, P. L. (1983). Three components of background knowledge in reading comprehension. *Language Learning, 33,* pp. 183–207.

Carrell, P. L. (1984). Evidence of a formal schema in second language comprehension. *Language Learning, 34,* 87–112.

Carroll, J. B. (1980). *Testing communicative performance.* London: Pergamon.

Chastain, K. (1970). A methodological study comparing the audiolingual habit theory and the cognitive code-learning theory—A continuation. *Modern Language Journal, 54,* 257–266.

Cohen, A. D. (1984). On taking tests: What the students report. *Language Testing, 1* (1), 70–81.

Colomb, G., Kinahan, F., McEnerney, L., & Williams, J. (1991). *Little red schoolhouse.* Urbana, IL: Programs in Professional Writing.

Corder, S. P. (1981). *Error analysis and interlanguage.* Oxford: Oxford University Press.

Crookes, G. & Gass, S. M. (1993a). *Tasks and language learning: Integrating theory and practice.* Clevedon, UK: Multilingual Matters.

Crookes, G. & Gass, S. M. (1993b). *Tasks in a pedagogical context: Integrating theory and practice.* Clevedon, UK: Multilingual Matters.

Doughty, C. (1991). Second language instruction does make a difference: Evidence from an empirical study of SL relativization. *Studies in Second Language Acquisition, 13,* 431–470.

Doughty, C. & Pica, T. (1986). "Information gap" tasks: Do they facilitate second language acquisition? *TESOL Quarterly, 20,* 305–325.

Dubin, F., Esky, D. E., & Grabe, W. (Eds.). (1986). *Teaching second language reading for academic purposes.* Reading, MA: Addison-Wesley.

Dvorak, T. R. (1986). Writing in a foreign language. In B. H. Wing (Ed.), *Listening, reading and writing: Analysis and application* (pp. 145–163). Middlebury, VT: Northeast Conference on the Teaching of Foreign Languages.

Ellis, R. (1984). *Classroom second language development.* London: Pergamon.

Ellis, R. (1986). *Understanding second language acquisition.* Oxford: Oxford University Press.

Ellis, R. (1989). Are classroom and naturalistic acquisition the same? A study of the classroom acquisition of German word order rules. *Studies in Second Language Acquisition, 11*, 305–328.

Finkel, D. & Monk, G. S. (1983). Teachers and learning groups: Dissolution of the Atlas complex. In C. Bouton & R. Y. Garth (Eds.), *Learning in groups* (pp. 83–97). San Francisco: Jossey-Bass.

Flick, W. C. & Anderson, J. I. (1980). Rhetorical difficulty in scientific English: A study in reading comprehension. *TESOL Quarterly, 14*, 345–351.

Flower, L. & Hayes, J. R. (1981). A cognitive process theory of writing. *College Composition and Communication, 32*, 365–387.

Freed, B. F. (Ed.). (1991). *Foreign language acquisition research and the classroom.* Lexington, MA: D.C. Heath.

Garrett, N. (1986). The problem with grammar: What kind can the language learner use? *Modern Language Journal, 70*, 133–148.

Glass, W. R. and Cadierno, T. (1990). *The effects of temporal adverbs on comprehending the past tense.* Paper presented at the annual meeting of the American Association of Teachers of Spanish and Portuguese, Miami, FL.

Grellet, F. (1981). *Developing reading skills. A practical guide to reading comprehension exercises.* Cambridge: Cambridge University Press.

Hatch, E. M. (1978a). Discourse analysis and second language acquisition. In E. Hatch (Ed.), *Second language acquisition: A book of readings* (pp. 402–435). Rowley, MA: Newbury House.

Hatch, E. M. (Ed.). (1978b). *Second language acquisition: A book of readings.* Rowley, MA: Newbury House.

Hatch, E. M. (1983). Simplified input and second language acquisition. In R. W. Andersen (Ed.), *Pidginization and creolization as language acquisition* (pp. 64–86). Cambridge, MA: Newbury House.

Hedge, T. (1988). *Writing.* Oxford: Oxford University Press.

Hendrickson, J. M. (1978). Error correction in foreign language teaching: Recent theory, research, and practice. *Modern Language Journal 62*, 387–398.

Henning G. (1987). *A guide to language testing: Development, evaluation, research.* Cambridge, MA: Newbury House.

Hock, S. T. & PO, C. L. (1979). The performance of a group of Malay-Medium students in an English reading comprehension test. *RELC Journal, 10*, 81–89.

Hosenfeld, C. (1977). A preliminary investigation of the strategies of successful and non-successful readers. *System 5*, 110–123.

Hosenfeld, C. (1984). Case studies of ninth-grade readers. In J. C. Alderson & A. H. Urquhart (Eds.), *Reading in a foreign language* (pp. 231–244). London: Longman.

Hudson, T. (1982). The effects of induced schemata on the "short circuit" in L2 reading: Nondecoding factors in L2 reading performance. *Language Learning, 32* (1), 1–29.

Jacobs, H. J., Zingraf, S. A., Wormuth, D. R., Hartfiel, V. F., & Hughey, J. B. (1981). *Testing ESL composition: A practical approach.* Rowley, MA: Newbury House.

Johns, J. (1978). Do comprehension items really test reading? Sometimes! *Journal of Reading, 21*, 615–619.

Johnson, P. (1981). Effects on reading comprehension of language complexity and cultural background. *TESOL Quarterly, 15*, 169–181.

Kaplan, M. A. (1987). Developmental patterns of past-tense acquisition among foreign language learners of French. In B. VanPatten, T. R. Dvorak, & J. F. Lee (Eds.), *Foreign language learning: A research perspective* (pp. 52–60). Cambridge, MA: Newbury House.

Kinginger, C. (1990). *Task variation and classroom learner discourse.* Unpublished doctoral dissertation, University of Illinois, Urbana-Champaign.

Knorre, M., Dorwick, T., VanPatten, B. & Villareal, H. (1989). *Puntos de partida: An invitation to Spanish.* New York: Random House.

Kramsch, C. J. (1991). The order of discourse in language teaching. In B. F. Freed (Ed.), *Foreign language acquisition and the classroom* (pp. 191–204). Lexington, MA: D. C. Heath.

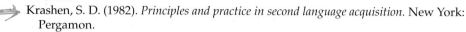Krashen, S. D. (1982). *Principles and practice in second language acquisition.* New York: Pergamon.

Krashen, S. D. (1984). *Writing: Research, theory and applications.* Oxford: Pergamon.

Krashen, S. D. (1993). *The power of reading.* Englewood, CO: Libraries Unlimited.

Krashen, S. D. & Terrell, T. D. (1983). *The natural approach.* New York: Pergamon.

Kroll, B. (Ed.). (1990). *Second language writing: Research insights for the classroom.* Cambridge: Cambridge University Press.

Lalande, J. F. (1982). Reducing composition errors: An experiment. *Modern Language Journal, 66,* 140–149.

Lamendella, J. (1977). General principles of neurofunctional organization and their manifestation in primary and secondary language acquisition. *Language Learning, 27,* 155–196.

Lado, R. (1957). *Linguistics across cultures.* Ann Arbor: University of Michigan Press.

Larsen-Freeman, D. (1985). State of the art on input in second language acquisition. In S. M. Gass & C. G. Madden (Eds.), *Input in second language acquisition* (pp. 433–444). Rowley, MA: Newbury House.

Larsen-Freeman, D. & Long, M. H. (1991). *An introduction to second language acquisition research.* New York: Longman.

Lee, J. F. (1986a). On the use of the recall task to measure L2 reading comprehension. *Studies in Second Language Acquisition, 8,* 201–211.

Lee, J. F. (1986b). Background knowledge and L2 reading. *Modern Language Journal, 70,* 350–354.

Lee, J. F. (1987a). Morphological factors influencing pronominal reference assignment by learners of Spanish. In T. Morgan, J. F. Lee, & B. VanPatten (Eds.), *Language and language use: Studies in Spanish* (pp. 221–232). Lanham, MD: University Press of America.

Lee, J. F. (1987b). The Spanish subjunctive: An information-processing perspective. *Modern Language Journal, 71,* 50–57.

Lee, J. F. (1989). Teaching and testing an expository text. In D. Koike & A. Simoes (Eds.), *Proceedings of the conference on Portuguese language: Teaching and testing* (pp. 92–107). Austin, TX: University of Texas at Austin.

Lee, J. F. (1990). Constructive processes evidenced by early stage non-native readers of Spanish in comprehending an expository text. *Hispanic Linguistics, 4* (1), 129–148.

Lee, J. F. & Paulson, D. L. (1992). Writing and compositions. In B. VanPatten (Ed.), *Instructor's manual and test bank for ¿Sabías que ...? Beginning Spanish* (pp. 30–34). New York: McGraw-Hill.

Lee, J. F. & Riley, G. L. (1990). The effect of prereading, rhetorically-oriented frameworks on the recall of two structurally different expository texts. *Studies in Second Language Acquisition, 12,* 25–41.

Leemann Guthrie, E. (1984). Intake, communication, and second language teaching. In S. J. Savignon & M. S. Berns (Eds.), *Initiatives in communicative language teaching* (pp. 35–54). Reading, MA: Addison-Wesley.

Lightbown, P. (1983). Exploring relationships between developmental and instructional sequences in L2 acquisition. In H. Seliger & M. Long (Eds.), *Classroom-oriented research in second language acquisition* (pp. 217–243). Rowley, MA: Newbury House.

Lightbown, P. & Spada, N. (1993). *How languages are learned.* Oxford: Oxford University Press.

Liskin-Gasparro, J. E. (1982). *ETS Oral proficiency testing manual.* Princeton, NJ: Educational Testing Service.

LoCoco, V. L. (1975). An analysis of Spanish and German learners' errors. *Working Papers on Bilingualism, 7,* 96–124.

LoCoco, V. L. (1987). Learner comprehension of oral and written sentences in German and Spanish: The importance of word order. In B. VanPatten, T. Dvorak & J. F. Lee (Eds.), *Foreign language learning: A research perspective* (pp. 119–131). Cambridge, MA: Newbury House.

Long, M. H. (1983). Does second language instruction make a difference? A review of research. *TESOL Quarterly, 17* (3), 359–382.

Long, M. H. (1990). The least a second language acquisition theory needs to explain. *TESOL Quarterly, 24* (4), 649–665.

Lowe, P., Jr. (1982). *Manual for LS oral interview workshop.* Washington, DC: DLI/FS Joint Oral Interview Transfer Project.

Lowe, P., Jr. (1988). The unassimilated history. In P. Lowe & C. W. Stansfield (Eds.), *Second language proficiency assessment: Current issues* (pp. 11–51). Englewood Cliffs, NJ: Prentice-Hall.

Madsen, H. S. (1983). *Techniques in testing.* Oxford: Oxford University Press.

Mangubhai, F. (1991). The processing behaviors of adult second language learners and their relationship to second language proficiency. *Applied Linguistics, 12* (3), 268–298.

McNeil, J. D. (1984). *Reading comprehension: New directions for classroom practice.* Glenview, IL: Scott Foresman.

Mohammed, M. A. H. & Swales, J. M. (1984). Factors affecting the successful reading of technical instructions. *Reading in a foreign language, 2,* 206–217.

Musumeci, D. (1990). *Il carciofo: Strategie di lettura e proposte di attività.* New York: McGraw-Hill.

Muyskens, J. A., Omaggio, A. C. & Convert-Chalmers, C. (1990). *Rendez-vous: An invitation to French.* New York: McGraw-Hill.

Newsweek. August 2, 1993. Volume CXIII (p. 4). New York: Newsweek, Inc.

Nunan, D. (1989). *Designing tasks for the communicative classroom.* Cambridge: Cambridge University Press.

Omaggio, A. C. (1986). *Language teaching in context: Proficiency-oriented instruction.* Boston, MA: Heinle & Heinle.

Omaggio Hadley, A. (1993). *Language teaching in context.* Boston, MA: Heinle & Heinle.

Paulson, D. L. (1993). *The effects of task focus and L2 grammatical knowledge on writing in Spanish as a second language.* Unpublished doctoral dissertation, University of Illinois, Urbana-Champaign.

Paulston, C. B. (1972). Structural pattern drills: A classification. In H. Allen & R. Campell (Eds.), *Teaching English as a second language* (pp. 129–138). New York: McGraw-Hill.

Perkins, K. L. (1983). Semantic constructivity in ESL reading comprehension. *TESOL Quarterly, 17* (1), 19–27.

Perkins, K. L. & Jones, B. (1985). Measuring passage contribution in ESL reading comprehension. *TESOL Quarterly, 19,* 137–153.

Peters, A. M. (1985). Language segmentation: Operating principles for the perception and analysis of language. In D.I. Slobin (Ed.), *The cross-linguistic study of language acquisition* (Vol. 2, pp. 1029–1067). Hillsdale, NJ: Lawrence Erlbaum.

Philips, J. K. (1984). Practical implications of recent research in reading. *Foreign Language Annals, 17* (4), 285–296.

Pica, T. (1983). Adult acquisition of English as a second language under different conditions of exposure. *Language Learning, 33* (4), 465–497.

Pichert, J. W &. Anderson, R. C. (1977). Taking different perspectives on a story. *Journal of Education Psychology, 69,* 309–15.

Politzer, R. L. (1965). *Foreign language learning: A linguistic introduction.* Englewood Cliffs, NJ: Prentice-Hall.

Porter, P. (1986). How learners talk to each other: Input and interaction in task-centered discussions. In R. Day (Ed.), *Talking to learn* (pp. 200–224). Rowley, MA: Newbury House.

Prince, E. (1990). *Write soon! A beginning text for ESL writers.* New York: Maxwell Macmillan.

Raimes, A. (1983). *Techniques in teaching writing.* Oxford: Oxford University Press.

Reves, T. (1982). *What makes a good language learner?* Unpublished Ph.D. dissertation, Hebrew University, Jerusalem.

Richards, J. C. (1983). Listening comprehension: Approach, design, procedure. *TESOL Quarterly, 17* (2), 219–240.

Richards, J. C. & Rodgers, T. S. (1986). *Approaches and methods in language teaching.* Cambridge: Cambridge University Press.

Riley, G. L. (1990). *Effects of story grammar on reading comprehension of L2 readers of French.* Unpublished doctoral dissertation, University of Illinois, Urbana-Champaign.

Rivers, W. M. (1983). *Communicating naturally in a second language: Theory and practice in language teaching.* Cambridge: Cambridge University Press.

Robb, T., Ross, S. & Shortreed, I. (1986). Salience of feedback on error and its effect on EFL writing quality. *TESOL Quarterly, 20,* 83–95.

Rooks, G. (1981). *Nonstop discussion book.* Cambridge, MA: Newbury House.

Rooks, G., K. Scholberg, D. & Scholberg, K. (1982). *Conversar sin parar.* Cambridge, MA: Newbury House.

Rost, M. (1990). *Listening in language learning.* New York: Longman.

Rulon, K. & McCreary, J. (1986). Negotiation of content: Teacher fronted and small-group interactions. In R. Day (Ed.), *Talking to learn* (pp. 182–199). Cambridge, MA: Newbury House.

Rumelhart, D. (1977). Toward an interactive model of reading. In S. Dornic (Ed.), *Attention and Performance,* 4 (573–603). New York: Academic Press.

Rumelhart, D. (1980). Schemata: The building blocks of cognition. In R. Spiro, B. Bruce & W. Brewer (Eds.), *Theoretical issues in reading comprehension* (pp. 33–35). Hillsdale, NJ: Lawrence Erlbaum.

Sato, C. (1986). Conversation and interlanguage development: Rethinking the connection. In R. Day (Ed.), *"Talking to learn": Conversation in second language acquisition* (pp. 23–45). Cambridge, MA: Newbury House.

Savignon, S. J. (1972). *Communicative competence: An experiment in foreign language teaching.* Philadelphia, PA: Center for Curriculum Development.

Savignon, S. J. (1983). *Communicative competence: Theory and classroom practice.* Reading, MA: Addison-Wesley.

Savignon, S. J. & Berns, M. S. (1984). *Initiatives in communicative language teaching.* Reading, MA: Addison-Wesley.

Savignon, S. J. & Berns, M. S. (1987). *Initiatives in communicative language teaching II.* Reading, MA: Addison-Wesley.

Schmidt, R. (1992). Psychological mechanisms underlying second language fluency. *Studies in Second Language Acquisition, 14* (4), 357–386.

Scott, V. & Randall, S. (1992). Can students apply grammar rules faster by reading textbook explanations? *Foreign Language Annals, 25* (4), 357–367.

Seelye, H. N. (1993). *Teaching culture: Strategies for intercultural communication.* Lincolnwood, IL: National Textbook Company.

Semke, H. (1984). Effects of the red pen. *Foreign Language Annals, 17,* 195–202.

Sharwood Smith, M. (1993). Input enhancement in instructed SLA: Theoretical bases. *Studies in Second Language Acquisition, 15* (2), 165–179.

Shohamy, E. (1984). Does the testing method make a difference? The case of reading comprehension. *Language Testing, 1,* 147–170.

Shohamy, E. (1987). Reactions to Lyle Bachman's Paper "Problems in examining the validity of the ACTFL Oral Proficiency Interview." In A. Valdman (Ed.), *Proceedings of the symposium on the evaluation of foreign language proficiency* (pp. 51–54). Bloomington, IN: Indiana University.

Shohamy, E. (1993). The power of tests: The impact of language tests on teaching and learning. *NFLC occasional papers* (June).

Shohamy, E., Reves, T. & Bejerano, Y. (1986). Introducing a new comprehensive test of oral proficiency. *English Language Teaching Journal, 40,* 212–222.

Snow, C. (1978). Mothers' speech to children learning languages. In L. Bloom (Ed.), *Readings in language development* (pp. 489–506). New York: Wiley & Sons.

Stanovich, K. (1980). Toward an interactive-compensatory model of individual differences in the development of reading fluency. *Reading Research Quarterly, 16,* 32–71.

Steffensen, M., Joag-Dev, C. & Anderson, R. C. (1979). A cross-cultural perspective on reading comprehension. *Reading Research Quarterly, 15,* 10–29.

Strother, J. B. & Ulijn, J. M. (1987). Does syntactic rewriting affect English for science and technology text comprehension? In J. Devine, P. L. Carrell, & D. E. Eskey (Eds.), *Research in reading in English as a second language* (pp. 89–100). Washington, DC: TESOL.

Swaffar, J. & Wälterman, D. (1988). Pattern questions for student conceptual processing. *Die Unterrichtspraxis, 21,* 60–67.

Swaffar, J., Kern, R. & Young, D. J. (1989). Reading as a classroom activity: Theory and techniques. In D. Koike & A. Simoes (Eds.), *Proceedings of the conference on Portuguese language: Teaching and testing* (pp. 61–91). Austin, TX: University of Texas at Austin.

Swaffar, J., Arens, K. & Byrnes, H. (1991). *Reading for meaning: An integrated approach to language learning.* Englewood Cliffs, NJ: Prentice-Hall.

Swain, M. (1985). Communicative competence: Some roles of comprehensible input and comprehensible output in its development. In S. M. Gass & C. Madden (Eds.), *Input in second language acquisition* (pp. 235–253). Rowley, MA: Newbury House.

Tarone, E. (1984). Teaching strategic competence in the foreign language classroom. In S. J. Savignon & M. S. Berns (Eds.), *Initiatives in communicative language teaching* (pp. 127–136). Reading, MA: Addison-Wesley.

Terrell, T. D. (1986). Acquisition in the Natural Approach: The binding/access framework. *Modern Language Journal, 70,* 213–227.

Terrell, T. D. (1991). The role of grammar instruction in a communicative approach. *Modern Language Journal, 75,* 52–63.

Terrell, T. D., B. Baycroft & C. Perrone. (1987). The subjunctive in Spanish interlanguage: Accuracy and comprehensibility. In B. VanPatten, T. R. Dvorak, & J. F. Lee (Eds.), *Foreign language learning: A research perspective,* (pp. 19–32). Cambridge, MA: Newbury House.

Terrell, T. D., Andrade, M., Egasse, J., & Muñoz, E.M. (1990). *Dos mundos: A communicative approach.* New York: McGraw-Hill.

Terrell, T. D., Tschirner, E., Nikolai, B., & Genzmer, H. (1992). *Kontakte: A communicative approach.* New York: McGraw-Hill.

Terrell, T. D., Rogers, M. B., Barnes, B. K., & Wolff-Hessini, M. (1993). *Deux mondes: A communicative approach.* New York: McGraw-Hill.

Valdman, A. (1987). The problem of the target model in proficiency-oriented foreign language instruction. In A. Valdman (Ed.), *Proceedings of the symposium on the evaluation of foreign language proficiency* (pp. 133–150). Bloomington, IN: Indiana University.

van Lier, L. (1988). *The classroom and the language learner: Ethnography and second language classroom research.* London: Longman.

VanPatten, B. (1984a). Morphemes and processing strategies. In F. Eckman, L. Bell, & D. Nelson (Eds.). *Universals of second language acquisition* (pp. 88–98). Rowley, MA: Newbury House.

VanPatten, B. (1984b). Learners' comprehension of clitic pronouns: More evidence for a word order strategy. *Hispanic Linguistics* (1) *1*, 88–98.

VanPatten, B. (1985a). The acquisition of *ser* and *estar* by adult classroom learners: A preliminary investigation of transitional stages of competence. *Hispania, 68*, 399–406.

VanPatten, B. (1985b). Communicative value and information processing in second language acquisition. In P. Larson, E. Judd, & D. S. Messerschmitt (Eds.), *On Tesol: A brave new world for TESOL,* (pp. 89–100). Washington, D.C.: TESOL.

VanPatten, B. (1986). Second language acquisition research and the learning/teaching of Spanish: Some research findings and implications. *Hispania, 69*, 202–216.

VanPatten, B. (1987). Classroom learners' acquisition of *ser* and *estar*: Accounting for developmental patterns. In B. VanPatten, T. R. Dvorak, & J. F. Lee (Eds.), *Foreign language learning: A research perspective* (pp. 61–75). Cambridge, MA: Newbury House.

VanPatten, B. (1988). How juries get hung: Problems with the evidence for a focus on form. *Language Learning, 38*, 243–260.

VanPatten, B. (1990). Attending to form and content in the input. *Studies in Second Language Acquisition, 12*, 287–301.

VanPatten, B. (1991). The foreign language classroom as a place to communicate. In B. F. Freed (Ed.), *Foreign language acquisition research and the classroom* (pp. 54–73). Boston, MA: D.C. Heath.

VanPatten, B. (1992a). Second language acquisition research and foreign language teaching: Part I. *ADFL Bulletin, 23*, 23–27.

VanPatten, B. (1992b). Second language acquisition research and foreign language teaching: Part II. *ADFL Bulletin, 23*, 52–56.

VanPatten, B. (1993). Grammar teaching for the acquisition-rich classroom. *Foreign language Annals, 26* (4), 435–450.

VanPatten, B. (1994). Cognitive aspects of input processing in second language acquisition. In P. Hashemipour, R. Maldonado, & M. van Naerssen (Eds.), *Festschrift in honor of Tracy D. Terrell* (pp. 170–183). New York: McGraw-Hill.

VanPatten, B. & Lee, J. F. (Eds.). (1990). *Second language acquisition—foreign language learning: Perspectives on research and practice.* Clevedon, UK: Multilingual Matters.

VanPatten, B., Lee, J. F., Ballman, T., & Dvorak, T. R. (1992). *¿Sabías que ...? Beginning Spanish.* New York: McGraw-Hill.

VanPatten, B. & Cadierno, T. (1993). Explicit instruction and input processing. *Studies in Second Language Acquisition, 15*, 225–244.

VanPatten, B. & Sanz, C. (In press). From input to output: Processing instruction and communicative tasks. In F. Eckman (Ed.), *Second language acquisition theory and pedagogy.* Hillsdale, NJ: Erlbaum.

Weiss, C. H. (1972). *Evaluation research: Methods for assessing program effectiveness.* Englewood Cliffs, NJ: Prentice-Hall.

White, L. (1977). Error analysis and error correction in adult learners of English as a second language. *Working Papers in Bilingualism, 13*, 42–58.

Wildner-Bassett, M. E. (1990). Coexisting discourse worlds: The development of pragmatic competence inside and outside the classroom. In B. VanPatten & J. F. Lee (Eds.), *Second language acquisition—foreign language learning* (pp. 140–152). Clevedon, UK: Multilingual Matters.

Wing, B. H. (1987). The linguistic and communicative functions of foreign language teacher talk. In B. VanPatten, T. R. Dvorak, & J. F. Lee (Eds.), *Foreign language learning: A research perspective,* (pp. 158–173). Cambridge, MA: Newbury House.

Winitz, H. (Ed.). (1981). *The comprehension approach to foreign language instruction.* Rowley, MA: Newbury House.

Wolf, D. F. (1993a). Issues in reading comprehension assessment: Implications for the development of research instruments and classroom tests. *Foreign Language Annals, 26* (3), 322–331.

Wolf, D. F. (1993b). A comparison of assessment tasks used to measure foreign language reading comprehension. *Modern Language Journal, 77* (4), 473–488.

Wolvin, A. D. & Coakley, C. G. (1985). *Listening,* 2nd ed. Dubuque, IA: William C. Brown Publishers.

Zamel, V. (1985). Responding to student writing. *TESOL Quarterly, 19,* 79–101.

Index

acceptability, in testing, 134, 135
access, 117–118
accuracy, and access, 118
acquired system, 31
acquisition orders, 23–24, 29–30
ACTFL. *See* American Council
  on the Teaching of Foreign
  Languages
active skills, 59, 114
adjective agreement, 101–102
affective activities, 109
affective function, 126–127
ALM (Audiolingual
  Methodology), 7–8, 11–12,
  22, 33
alternative-selecting activities,
  111–112
American Council on the
  Teaching of Foreign
  Languages (ACTFL), 79,
  80–82, 170
  Oral Proficiency Interview
  (OPI) of, 170–172, 184
  Proficiency Guidelines of, 238,
  245
analytical scoring, 238–240
Anderson, J. I., 197–198
Anderson, R. C., 192–194
anticipation of content, 76
approximation, 162–163
architect, instructor as, 14–16
Arens, K., 198, 213
Asher, James, 52
assessment, language of, 79, 228
assimilation, 207–209, 231–232

Atlas Complex, 5–6, 8–9, 12
Audiolingual Methodology
  (ALM), 7–8, 11–12, 22, 33
aural stimuli, 60–62
aural-visual modality, 63, 65
authoritative transmitter of
  knowledge role, 4–12

Bachman, L. F., 144, 169, 176,
  177, 179, 184, 185, 227, 242
Barnett, M. A., 213
Baycroft, B., 31
behaviorism, 7, 90
Bejerano, Y., 173, 174, 185
Bernhardt, E. B., 213
Berns, M. S., 20, 36
bias, in testing, 172
binary option activities, 110
binding, in vocabulary
  acquisition, 49–51
binding/access framework, 117
Binkowski, D. D., 98
blueprint metaphor for texts,
  192
brain, and input, 28–29
brainstorming, 75, 200–201,
  234–235
Bransdorfer, R. L., 115
Bransford, J. D., 194, 197, 213
Breen, M., 168
Bretz, M. L., 163
Brooks, F. B., 120, 152, 154, 156,
  221
Brooks, N., 20
Brown, R., 45–46

Bybee, J. L., 125, 126
Byrnes, H., 198, 213

Cadierno, T., 98, 102, 103, 115
Canale, M., 168
Carrell, P. L., 197, 199
Carroll, J. B., 134, 137, 138, 139,
  146, 172, 227
Chastain, K., 20
children
  expansions in adult
  interactions with, 40
  input with, 38–40
  nonlinguistic means of
  communicating with, 44–45
chunks, of formulaic speech, 26
circumlocution, 163
clarification checks, 165
classhour goals, 257–263
classroom
  dynamic of, 3–6
  input and, 44–48
  listening in, 66–69
  social dimensions of, 16–18
  superiority of learning in,
  31–33
  vocabulary acquisition and, 51
  work outside of, 263–267
classroom activities, and output,
  139–143
classroom discourse. *See*
  discourse
CLT (communicative language
  teaching), 8–12
Coakley, C. G., 60

cognitive-process theory of writing, 215–219
Cohen, A. D., 228
collaborative listening, 63, 65, 66, 67
College Entrance Examination Board (CEEB) tests, 33–34
Colomb, G., 237
communication, 147–168
  breakdowns in, 148–150
  contexts of, 148
  defined, 14, 147, 215
  as information exchange, 156–162
  learning, 33–35
  listening as, 63–66
  meaning and, 148
  multilayered communicative event, 15–16
  nonlinguistic means of, 44–45
  purposes of, 150–151
communicative burden, 179–180
communicative competence, 149, 177, 178–179
communicative drills
  discourse and, 151–154
  in grammar, 92–93, 119, 120–121
communicative function of reading, 210, 232–234
communicative goals, 246–257
communicative language ability, 29, 33–35, 148–150
communicative language teaching (CLT), 8–12
communicative value, 97–98
comparability, in testing, 135
compensation, negative connotations of, 196
compensation function of schemata, 194–195
competence
  communicative, 149, 177, 178–179
  discourse, 149, 177, 178–179
  grammatical, 149, 177, 178
  pragmatic, 178–179
  sociolinguistic, 149, 177, 179
  strategic, 149, 150, 162–167
componential rating scales, 177–179
composition, 214, 222–224, 240. See also writing

comprehensible input, 29, 37–57
comprehension
  defined, 96, 191–192, 229
  listening, 76–79
  See also reading comprehension
comprehension checks, 205–207
content
  anticipation of, 76
  in evaluating writing, 236–237, 240
  of listening test, 77
  personalizing, 209–211
  tests focusing on, 229–234
conversation. See discourse
Corder, S. P., 22–23, 24, 36
corrective feedback, 235–236
criteria
  in evaluation of compositions, 240
  in evaluation of spoken language, 175–176, 184
  for tests, 134–135
Crookes, G., 168

definition
  explicit, 197
  implicit, 198
developmental stages, 24–25, 30
diagnostic feedback, 177
dialogue-level listening practice, 70
direct objects, 89, 91–93, 98
disambiguating function of schemata, 193
discourse, 66–69
  classroom vs. nonclassroom, 10–11
  communicative drills, 151–154
  connected, 106–107, 122–123
  free-form vs. structured, 167
  listener's role in, 65
  maintaining, 65
  paired interactions, 10, 153, 154–156
  planned, 32
  question-and-answer model of, 9
  teacher-fronted, 153, 154–156

discourse competence, 149, 177, 178–179
Doughty, C., 168, 266
drafts, evaluating, 237–238
drills
  communicative, 92–93, 119, 120–121, 151–154
  meaningful, 91–92, 119, 120
  mechanical, 91, 119–121
  substitution, 7
  transformation, 7
Dubin, F., 213
Dvorak, T. R., 163, 214, 219, 226

economy, in testing, 134
Educational Testing Service, 170
elaborative function of schemata, 193–194
elicitation phases, 170–172
elicitation procedures, 170–174
Ellis, R., 24, 30, 58, 115
entrance tests, 227
errors
  feedback on, 166
  in language acquisition, 21, 22–23, 27
  in writing, 235–236
Esky, D. E., 213
evaluation
  defined, 169
  in writing, 218
  of writing, 235–240
  See also spoken language evaluation; tests
evaluation criteria
  for compositions, 240
  in spoken language evaluation, 175–176, 184
exercise sequencing, 91–93
expansions, in adult-child interactions, 40
explicit definition, 197
explicit instruction in grammar, 29–33

feature analysis, 191, 192
feedback
  corrective, 235–236
  diagnostic, 177
  on output errors, 166
filtering function of schemata, 194

Finkel, D., 6, 12
Flick, W. C., 197–198
Flower, L., 215–218, 219, 221, 222–224
fluency, and access, 118
form, in writing, 235–236
formulaic speech, 26–27
Freed, B. F., 36
functors, 23

gambits, listening, 68–69
games, 54, 73
Garrett, N., 115
Gass, S. M., 168
global listening proficiency, 79–84
global query, 65
goal, 245. *See also* proficiency goals
goal setting, in writing, 217
Grabe, W., 213
grammar
    explicit instruction in, 29–33
    in information-exchange tasks, 161, 249, 254–257
grammar acquisition
    developmental stages and, 24–25, 30
    errors in, 21, 22–23, 27
    formulaic speech and, 26–27
    orders of acquisition and, 23–24, 29–30
    outside of class, 263, 264, 266–267
    research on, 21–29
grammar instruction, 89–114
    in adjective agreement, 101–102
    binary option activities in, 110
    communicative drills in, 92–93, 119, 120–121
    connected discourse in, 106–107, 122–123
    in direct objects, 89, 91–93, 98
    exercise sequencing in, 91–93
    focusing on learner in, 108–109
    focusing on meaning in, 104–105, 122
    input and, 93–99
    learner's processing strategies and, 96–102, 108–109

grammar instruction, *continued*
    matching activities in, 100, 110
    meaningful drills in, 91–92, 119, 120
    mechanical drills in, 91, 119–121
    oral and written input in, 107, 123
    as structured input, 99–114
    surveys in, 112–113
    traditional, 90–95
    in verb morphology, 99–101, 105
grammar testing, 31, 133–144
grammatical competence, 149, 177, 178
grammatical goals, 247–248, 254–257
Grellet, F., 209, 213
group decision activities, 165–166
group discussion tests, 174
guided interaction, 204–207, 230–231

habits
    formation of, 7–8
    negative transfer of, 21, 27–28
Hatch, E. M., 34, 41, 42, 43, 44, 58
Hayes, J. R., 215–218, 219, 221, 222, 223, 224
headings, and reading comprehension, 201
Hedge, T., 226
Hendrickson, J. M., 168
Henning, G., 185
historical inertia, 90
Hock, S. T., 228
holistic scores, 176, 177, 238–239
homework, 264–267
Hosenfeld, C., 213
Hudson, T., 199

idea generation, 217
illocutionary meaning, 61–62
illustrations, and reading comprehension, 202
implicit definition, 198
inertia, historical, 90

inference, 62–63
informational-cognitive purpose of communication, 150
information-exchange tasks, 156–162
    adapting as oral tests or quizzes, 179–184
    grammar in, 161, 249, 254–257
    identifying topic of, 157–158
    information sources of, 159–161
    language demands in, 161–162
    as lesson objective, 249–257
    purpose of, 158–159
    structured output vs., 166–167
    vocabulary in, 251–254, 259–260, 261
information-gap tasks, 164–165
information gatherer, learner as, 16–18
information sources, identifying, 159–161
information-supplying activities, 110–111
INOPT (Israeli National Oral Proficiency Test), 170, 172–174, 184
input, 37–57
    brain and, 28–29
    with children, 38–40
    classroom and, 44–48
    comprehensible, 29, 37–57
    defined, 28
    intake vs., 94–95
    language acquisition and, 28–29, 40–42
    meaning-bearing, 38, 96
    oral and written, 107, 123
    simplified, 39–42
    structured, 32, 99–114
    Total Physical Response and, 52–54
    traditional grammar instruction and, 93–95
    useful characteristics of, 38
    vocabulary and, 41, 48–56
input enhancement, 32
Input Hypothesis, 29
input processing, 96–99
insight, 21. *See also* research
instruction, explicit, 29–33

instructional orders, vs. acquisition orders, 29–30
instructor
  as architect, 14–16
  as authoritative transmitter of knowledge, 4–12
  as resource person, 12–14
  responsibility for learning and, 4–12
intake, 42, 94–95
interaction, 42
  expansions in adult-child, 40
  guided, 204–207, 230–231
  negotiation and, 42–44
  structured vs. free-form, 167
interactive model
  of reading, 190–192
  stage models vs., 216
interference errors, 21, 22, 27
interrater reliability, 172, 239
intrarater reliability, 239
Israeli National Oral Proficiency Test (INOPT), 170, 172–174, 184
issue, defined, 227
item construction, in testing, 228–229

Jacobs, H. J., 242
Joag-Dev, C., 194
Johns, J., 228
Johnson, M. K., 197, 213
Johnson, P., 196
Jones, B., 228

Kaplan, M. A., 30
Kern, R., 242
Kinginger, C., 120, 221
Kirschner, C., 163
knowledge
  lexical, 191
  reading comprehension and, 199–204
  review of, 74–75
  semantic, 191
  sources of, 190–191
  syntactic, 191
  transmission of, 4–12
  world, 202–203
  in writer's long-term memory, 217

Krashen, S. D., 20, 29, 31, 46, 49, 51, 58, 115, 132, 134, 140, 144, 226, 229–230
Kroll, B., 226, 242

Lado, R., 20
Lalande, J. F., 235–236
Lamendella, J., 119
language
  of assessment, 79, 228
  as evaluation criterion for compositions, 240
language acquisition
  developmental stages and, 24–25, 30
  errors in, 21, 22–23, 27
  formulaic speech and, 26–27
  input and, 28–29, 40–42
  instruction and, 93–95
  negative transfer of habits in, 21, 27–28
  orders of acquisition and, 23–24, 29–30
  role in second language acquisition, 27–29
  See also second language acquisition
language classroom, social dimensions of, 16–18
language laboratory, 33, 70–74
Larsen-Freeman, D., 36, 40–41, 58, 115, 168
learners
  acceptability of testing and, 135
  as builders or coworkers, 16
  defined, 17
  as information gatherers, 16–18
  as negotiators, 16–18, 34, 42–44
  processing strategies of, 96–102, 108–109
  as receptive vessels, 4–6
  responsibility for learning and, 16–18, 139–143
  role of, 4–6, 16–18
  self-selection of, 32
  students vs., 17
  vocabulary acquisition and, 51
Lee, J. F., 20, 79, 98, 195, 196, 197, 213, 228, 239, 240, 242

Leemann Guthrie, E., 9–10, 15, 18, 20, 149, 151–152, 154
lesson goals, 246–257
lesson mapping, 257–261
letter analysis, 191
letter cluster analysis, 191, 192
lexical knowledge, 191
Lightbown, P., 29–30
linguistic breakdown, 171
linguistic characteristics, 41–42
linguistic tasks, 77–78
Liskin-Gasparro, J. E., 185
listener performance, 64–65
listening, 59–85
  collaborative, 63, 65, 66, 67
  as communication, 63–66
  defined, 59
  in language laboratory, 70–74
  as means to an end, 72
  noncollaborative, 63, 65, 69, 70–71
  outside of class, 263
  prelistening activities and, 74–76
  processes in, 60
  as psycholinguistic process, 59–63
  in second language classroom, 66–69
listening activity, 13
listening comprehension, testing, 76–79
listening gambits, 68–69
listening proficiency, testing, 79–84
local query, 65
LoCoco, V. L., 27, 98
Long, M. H., 29, 36, 58, 115, 168
long-term memory, of writer, 217
look-back-and-lift-off approach to reading, 189, 221
look-back strategy, 189
Lowe, P., Jr., 173, 176

Madsen, H. S., 185
management strategies, 205–207
Mangubhai, F., 115
matching activities, 55, 100, 110
McCreary, J., 154, 155
McNeil, J. D., 192

meaning
  assigning to aural stimuli, 60–62
  communication and, 148
  focusing on, 104–105, 122
  illocutionary, 61–62
  negotiation of, 237
meaning-bearing input, 38, 96
meaningful drills, 91–92, 119, 120
mechanical drills, 91, 119–121
memory, long-term, 217
mime, 162
modality, 63, 65
mohammed, M. A. H., 198–199
monitor, 31, 218
monitoring, 117, 218
Monk, G. S., 6, 12
monologue-type listening practice, 70
morphemes, 23
multilayered communicative event, 15–16
Musumeci, D., 58

natural stages of development, 30
negative transfer of habits, 21, 27–28
negotiation
  interaction and, 42–44
  of meaning, 237
negotiation devices, 165
negotiator, learner as, 16–18, 34, 42–44
noncollaborative listening, 63, 65, 69, 70–71
nonlinguistic means of communication, 44–45
nonlinguistic tasks, 77–78
Non-Stop Discussion Book (Rooks), 165
null subjects, 99
Nunan, D., 268

objects, direct, 89, 91–93, 98
Omaggio, A. C., 168
Omaggio Hadley, A., 146, 170–172, 175–176, 185, 226, 242, 268
opaque words, 197
open-ended questions, 11, 15

oral proficiency. See spoken language evaluation
oral questions, 76–77
orders of acquisition, 23–24, 29–30
organization
  of discourse and reading comprehension , 197–198
  in writing, 217, 240
output
  classroom activities and, 139–143
  defined, 116
  form-focused, 118–121
  structured, 121–131, 166–167
  traditional approaches to, 118–121
  vocabulary and, 128–130
overgeneralizations, 30
overlearning, 29–30

paired interaction, 10, 153, 154–156
Palmer, A. S., 177, 179
paradigms, 125–128
paraphrasing, 162–165, 229
passive skills, 59–60, 114
pattern practices, 7
Paulson, D. L., 226, 239, 240
Paulston, C. B., 91, 119, 132, 151
Pearson, P. D., 192
perception of aural stimuli, 60
Perkins, K. L., 193, 228
Perrone, C., 31
Philips, J. K., 213
photographs, and reading comprehension, 202
Pica, T., 30, 168
Pichert, J. W., 194
picture file, 53
placement tests, 227
planned discourse, 32
planning, in writing, 217
Poh, C. L., 228
Politzer, R. L., 20
Porter, P., 154, 155
posttest, 202
pragmatic competence, 178–179
prelistening activities, 74–76
pretest, 203
Prince, E., 226
probes, 171, 173

processes, and testing, 229
processing strategies, 96–102
  adjective agreement and, 101–102
  structured input activities and, 108–109
  verb morphology and, 99–101
production strategies, 117
productive skills, 59, 114
proficiency goals, 245–268
  ACTFL guidelines for, 238, 245
  classhour goals, 257–263
  communicative goals, 246–257
  grammatical goals, 247–248, 254–257
  lesson goals, 246–257
  subgoals, 252–254, 256–263
  work outside of class and, 263–267
Proficiency Guidelines, 238, 245
proficiency tests, 79–84
psycholinguistic processes, 59–63
psycho-social purpose of communication, 150

queries, types of, 65
question(s)
  open-ended, 11, 15
  oral, 76–77
question-and-answer model of conversation, 9
quizzes, vs. tests, 180, 184

Raimes, A., 226
Randall, S., 266
rating scales, componential, 177–179
reader
  background knowledge of, 199–204
  contribution to comprehension, 193–196, 198–199
reading
  communicative function of, 210, 232–234
  interactive model of, 190–192
  look-back-and-lift-off approach to, 189, 221
  as private and social act, 204
  surface, 229

reading comprehension, 189–213
  assimilation and, 207–209,
    231–232
  brainstorming and, 200–201
  comprehension checks for,
    205–207
  defined, 191–192
  guided interaction and,
    204–207, 230–231
  headings and, 201
  illustrations and, 202
  instructional framework for,
    199–209
  look-back-and-lift-off
    approach to, 189, 221
  management strategies for,
    205–207
  organization of discourse and,
    197–198
  photographs and, 202
  readers' background
    knowledge and, 199–204
  readers' contribution to,
    193–196, 198–199
  scanning for specific
    information and, 203–204
  tests of, 203, 227–235
  text features and, 191, 192,
    196–199
  titles and, 201
  translational approach to,
    189–190
  vocabulary and, 196–197
  world knowledge and,
    202–203
receptive role, 4–6
receptive skills, 59–60, 114
referentially oriented activities,
  109
reflexive verbs, 247–249,
  254–256
reliability
  interrater, 172, 239
  intrarater, 239
reporting test, 174
research, 21–35
  on communicative language
    ability, 29, 33–35
  on grammar acquisition,
    21–29
  on limited effects of explicit
    instruction, 29–33

research, continued
  on structured input activities,
    102–103
resource, instructor as, 12–14
response, strategic, 64–65
responsibility for learning, 14
  instructor and, 4–12
  learner and, 16–18, 141–145
restructuring, 126
Reves, T., 173, 174, 185
review
  of existing knowledge, 74–75
  in writing, 218
revising, in writing, 218
rhetorical problem, 216, 221–222
Richards, J. C., 20, 61, 86
Riley, G. L., 193–194, 197
Rivers, W. M., 134
Robb, T., 235, 236
Rogers, T. S., 20
role(s)
  authoritative, 4–12
  changing, 14–16
  defined, 3
  of instructor, 4–16
  of learner, 4–6, 16–18
  of listener, 65
  receptive, 4–6
  secondary, 4
  tasks and, 4, 12–16
role play, in oral proficiency
    tests, 173–174
Rooks, G., 165
Rost, M., 64, 65, 66, 83, 86
routines, formulaic, 26–27
Rulon, K., 154, 155
Rumelhart, D., 190

sampling, in testing, 134
Sanz, C., 103
Sato, C., 35
Savignon, S. J., 20, 33–34, 36, 148,
    149, 162, 168, 176
scanning, 203–204
schemata
  activating appropriate,
    199–204
  functions of, 193–196
schema theory, 190
Schmidt, R., 119–120
Scholberg, K., 165
Scholberg, N., 165

scoring
  analytical, 238–240
  holistic, 176, 177, 238–239
Scott, V., 266
scripts, 61
secondary roles, 4
second language acquisition
  input and, 40–42
  interference errors and, 21, 22,
    27
  listening in, 66–69
  negative transfer of habits
    and, 21, 27–28
  role of first language in, 27–29
  written language
    comprehension and,
    199–209
self-selection, 32
semantic knowledge, 191
semantic map, 208–209
Semke, H., 235, 236, 242
Sentence-level listening practice,
  70
Sharwood Smith, M., 32
Shohamy, E., 146, 170, 172–173,
    174, 176, 177, 185, 228
Shortreed, I., 235, 236
signature searches, 113
"Significance of Learners' Errors,
    The" (Corder), 22–23
simplified input, 39–42
single-format test, 172
single holistic scores, 176, 177
skills application, tests focusing
  on, 234–235
Snow, C., 39
social dimensions, of language
  classroom, 16–18
sociolinguistic competence, 149,
  177, 179
specificity, in listening test, 77
speech, formulaic, 26–27
speech styles and functions, 172
spoken language evaluation,
  169–184
  adapting information-
    exchange tasks as oral tests
    or quizzes in, 179–184
  componential rating scales in,
    177–179
  evaluation criteria for,
    175–176, 184

spoken language evaluation, *continued*
tests for, 170–177
stage, developmental, 24–25, 30
stage models, vs. interactive models, 216
Stanovich, K., 196
Steffensen, M., 194
strategic competence, 149, 150
description of, 162
developing, 162–167
group decision activities for, 165–166
paraphrase activities for, 162–165
strategic responses, 64–65
Strother, J. B., 196–197
structured input, 32, 99–114
adjective agreement and, 101–102
verb morphology and, 99–101, 105
structured input activities
developing, 104–109
research on, 102–103
types of, 109–114
structured input formats for tests, 135–137
structured interaction, vs. free-form conversation, 167
structured output, 121–131
structured output activities
characteristics of, 121
developing, 121–124
information-based communication tasks vs., 166–167
structured output formats for tests, 139–141
student, vs. learner, 17. *See also* learners
study skills, 207–208
subgoals, 252–254, 256–263
substitution drill, 7
subtitles, and reading comprehension, 201
surface reading, 227
surveys, in grammar instruction, 112–113
Swaffar, J., 198, 213, 229, 242
Swain, M., 34, 132, 168
Swales, J. M., 198–199

syntactic knowledge, 191
syntax, simplified, 41, 42
synthesis, 72–73

Tarone, E., 162
task(s)
linguistic vs. nonlinguistic, 77–78
roles and, 4, 12–16
See also information-exchange tasks
task environment, 216–217
task type, in testing, 228
teacher. *See* instructor
teacher-fronted discourse, 153, 154–156
tense, verb, 99–101, 105
Terrell, T. D., 20, 31, 49–51, 58, 115, 117, 118, 128, 132, 134, 140, 144, 229–230
tests, 227–241
acceptability of, 134, 135
adapting information-exchange tasks as, 179–184
analytical scoring of, 238–240
assimilation activities and, 231–232
bias in, 172
classroom activities and, 139–143
College Entrance Examination Board (CEEB), 33–34
comparability of, 135
criteria for, 134–135
defined, 133
diagnostic uses of, 177
economy in, 134
entrance, 227
evaluation criteria for, 175–176, 184, 240
focus on content in, 229–234
focus on skills application in, 234–235
of global listening proficiency, 79–84
of grammar, 31, 133–144
group discussion, 174
guided interaction activities and, 230–231
holistic scoring of, 176, 177, 238–239

tests, *continued*
interrater reliability in, 172, 239
intrarater reliability in, 239
Israeli National Oral Proficiency Test (INOPT), 170, 172–174, 184
item construction in, 228–229
language of assessment in, 228
of listening comprehension, 76–79
placement, 227
posttest, 203
pretest, 203
processes and, 229
proficiency, 79–84
purpose of, 227
quizzes vs., 180, 184
of reading comprehension, 203, 227–235
relevance of, 134
reporting, 174
role play in, 173–174
single-format, 172
of spoken language, 170–177
structured input formats for, 135–137
structured output formats for, 137–139
task type in, 228
TOEFL Test of Written English, 238
washback effect of, 134, 139–140, 180, 184, 230
texts
blueprint metaphor for, 192
communicative function of, 210, 232–234
headings in, 201
illustrations in, 202
as information sources, 161
organization of, 197–198
personalizing content of, 209–211
photographs in, 202
reading comprehension and, 191, 192, 196–199
selection of, 198
titles in, 201
titles, and reading comprehension, 201

TOEFL Test of Written English, 238

topic, in information exchange, 157–158

Total Physical Response (TPR), 52–54

transcription-oriented writing practices, 214, 219–222

transfer, negative, 21, 27–28

transformation drill, 7

transitional query, 65

translating, 7, 218, 219

translation approach to comprehension, 189–190

transparent words, 197

Ulijn, J. M., 196–197

unitary scores, 176, 177

Valdman, A., 185

van Lier, L., 20

VanPatten, B., 24–25, 27, 28, 30, 36, 47, 58, 96, 97, 98, 101, 102, 103, 104, 115

verb, reflexive, 247–249, 254–256

verb morphology, 99–101, 105

verb paradigms, 125

visual(s), and vocabulary, 49–51, 53

visualization activities, 54–55

vocabulary
  binding in acquisition of, 49–51
  classroom acquisition of, 51
  as evaluation criterion for compositions, 240
  familiar situations and, 46–48

vocabulary, *continued*
  in information-exchange tasks, 251–254, 259–260, 261
  input and, 41, 48–56
  lists of, 48–49
  output and, 128–130
  reading comprehension and, 196–197
  Total Physical Response and, 52–54
  visuals and, 49–51, 53
  work outside of class and, 263, 264, 267

vocabulary activities, 54–56

vocabulary preparation, 74

Wälterman, D., 229

washback effect, 134, 139–140, 180, 184, 230

Weiss, C. H., 169

White, L., 27

Wildner-Bassett, M., 20

Wing, B. H., 44

Winitz, H., 58

Wolf, D. F., 79, 228, 242

Wolvin, A. D., 60

word(s), transparent vs. opaque, 197

word coinage, 163

word-order processing strategy, 98–99

world knowledge, 202–203

writer, long-term memory of, 217

writing, 214–226
  cognitive-process theory of, 215–219

writing, *continued*
  composing-oriented, 214, 222–224, 240
  defined, 214, 215, 218
  errors in, 235–236
  evaluating, 235–240
  goal setting in, 217
  holistic vs. analytical scoring of, 238–240
  language in, 240
  organization in, 217, 240
  responding to content of, 236–237, 240
  responding to drafts of, 237–238
  responding to form in, 235–236
  rhetorical problem in, 216, 221–222
  task environment in, 216–217
  transcription-oriented, 214, 219–222
  vocabulary in, 240
  writer's long-term memory and, 217

writing processes, 217–219
  monitoring, 218
  planning, 217
  reviewing, 218
  translating, 218, 219

written language comprehension. *See* reading comprehension

Young, D. J., 242

Zamel, V., 237